Multilateral
Negotiation
and Mediation

Multilateral Negotiation and Mediation

Instruments and Methods

Edited by Arthur S. Lall
Published for the International Peace Academy

PERGAMON PRESS
New York   Oxford   Toronto   Sydney   Paris   Frankfurt

Pergamon Press Offices:

U.S.A.   Pergamon Press Inc., Maxwell House, Fairview Park,
                    Elmsford, New York 10523, U.S.A.

U.K.   Pergamon Press Ltd., Headington Hill Hall,
                    Oxford OX3 0BW, England

CANADA   Pergamon Press Canada Ltd., Suite 104, 150 Consumers Road,
                    Willowdale, Ontario M2J 1P9, Canada

AUSTRALIA   Pergamon Press (Aust.) Pty. Ltd., P.O. Box 544,
                    Potts Point, NSW 2011, Australia

FRANCE   Pergamon Press SARL, 24 rue des Ecoles,
                    75240 Paris, Cedex 05, France

FEDERAL REPUBLIC Pergamon Press GmbH, Hammerweg 6,
OF GERMANY   D-6242 Kronberg-Taunus, Federal Republic of Germany

Library of Congress Cataloging in Publication Data
Main entry under title:

Multilateral negotiation and mediation.

    Includes index.
    1. Mediation, International--Addresses, essays,
lectures. 2. Negotiation--Addresses, essays, lectures.
3. United Nations--Addresses, essays, lectures.
I. Lall, Arthur S. (Arthur Samuel), 1911-
II. International Peace Academy.
JX4475.M85   1985   341.5′2   84-19062
ISBN 0-08-031957-2

Printed in the United States of America

Contents

PART 5: DISARMAMENT NEGOTIATIONS

PART 6: NORTH-SOUTH NEGOTIATIONS

PART 7: INTERNATIONAL LAW AND NEGOTIATION

About the Contributors

Lord Caradon is the former Permanent Representative of the United Kingdom to the United Nations and former consultant to the UN Special Fund. From 1957 to 1960 he was governor and Commander in Chief in Cyprus. He is author of *A Start in Freedom* (1964).

Muchkund Dubey, Ambassador of India to the United Nations Conference on Disarmament, was former high commissioner for India in Bangladesh and earlier served with the UN Development Programme.

Abba Eban was the Minister of Foreign Affairs of Israel, following a diplomatic career as Ambassador of Israel to the United States (1950–59) and Permanent Representative of Israel to the United Nations (1949–59). He is author of *My Country* (1972), *Autobiography* (1977) and *The New Diplomacy* (1983).

Adrian S. Fisher, a specialist in international law and trade, was appointed by President Kennedy as deputy director to the newly created U.S. Arms Control and Disarmament Agency in 1961, where he was involved in the negotiation of two important security agreements of the 1960s — the Limited Test Ban Treaty and the Nuclear Nonproliferation Treaty. From 1969–1975 he was dean of the Law Center, Georgetown University, and in 1977 President Carter appointed Mr. Fisher U.S. ambassador to the Conference on Disarmament in Geneva.

Johan Kaufmann is professor of law at the University of Leiden. He has served as ambassador of the Netherlands to Mexico, the United States and the United Nations. He is co-author of *How UN Decisions are Made* (1962) and author of *United Nations Decision Making* (1980).

Manfred Lachs is a member of the International Court of Justice, the Hague, serving on the Court since 1967. He has been ambassador of Poland to the United Nations and chairman of the Legal Committee of the UN General Assembly. He is author of *Multilateral Treaties* (1958) and *The Law of Outer Space: An Experience in Law Making* (1972).

Arthur Lall has represented India at many United Nations conferences and was Permanent Representative of India to the United Nations. He later was adjunct professor at the School of International Affairs, Columbia University, during which time he was author of *Modern International Negotiation: Principles and Practice* (1966), *The United Nations and the Middle East Crisis* (1968) and *How Communist China Negotiates* (1968).

Clovis Maksoud is the Permanent Observer of the League of Arab States to the United Nations and Chief Representative of the League of Arab States to the United States. Prior to this Dr. Maksoud served as Arab League Ambassador to India and Southeast Asia, from 1961–1966, and was its special ambassador in the United States 1974/75. He was senior editor of *Al-Ahram* in Cairo, 1967–1971, and is the author of several publications on the Middle East, including: *The Meaning of Non-Alignment, The Crisis of the Arab Left* and *The Arab Image*.

Mircea Malitza is ambassador of the Socialist Republic of Romania to the United States. He has served as representative of Romania to the UN Office in Geneva, as chief of the Romanian delegation to the Disarmament Committee and as ambassador of Romania to Switzerland. He is author of *Theory of Practice of Negotiations* (1972) and *Automatic Approaches to International Relations* (1978).

Arnold Smith was Secretary-General of the Commonwealth from 1965 to 1975 and chairman of the board of the International Peace Academy from 1976 to 1982. Prior to that post he had a distinguished and varied international career in university teaching, journalism and diplomacy, including twenty-two years' service in the Department of External Affairs of Canada. He is the author of *Stitches in Time: The Commonwealth in World Politics* (1981).

Inga Thorsson is former Under Secretary of State, Ministry of Foreign Affairs, of Sweden and was a member of the Swedish Parliament. She served as ambassador of Sweden to Israel and director of the Social Development Division of the United Nations.

Jorge Luis Zelaya Coronado, a Guatemalan diplomat and attorney at law, is the former assistant secretary general of the Organization of American States (OAS). Prior to this appointment he was chief of the Special Advisory Staff of the Department of Legal Affairs of the General Secretariat and Secretary of the Administrative Tribunal of the OAS.

Foreword

Arthur Lall

The International Peace Academy is fortunate in being able to present to the reader — whether practitioner, scholar, or member of the general public — this unique compilation on international mediation and negotiation. It is unique because the pieces brought together represent over thirty years of activity in this field by persons of distinction and authority, drawn from a variety of countries and backgrounds. In these pages, they both conceptualize about mediation and negotiation as well as unravel the operational intricacies of these highly important aspects of international life.

The writers remind us of what often tends to be overlooked, namely, that the United Nations system is in itself an institutionalizing among nations of the processes of mediation for the settlement or adjustment of international disputes and situations — whether political, economic, or social. In joining the United Nations, member states have in fact subscribed to the utilization of the large array of the United Nations forums as mediatory agencies, even though the charter does not, except in regard to decisions by the Security Council, oblige parties to disputes or situations to abide by the findings and resolutions of such agencies. Discussions in United Nations' forums serve to remind states of their obligations and duties as responsible members of the world community; they set the broad parameters for actions by states and they remind states of the corrective possibilities enshrined in the United Nations system. These are some of the fundamentals of international life today, and they are made vivid in this handbook written by persons who, personally, have had long experience in upholding them. There is another side of this coin. What happens when the carefully constructed international system does not work or partially works? At worst war results. But even when it does, attempts to return to peaceful norms continue, either regionally or through such organizations as the Commonwealth or through ad hoc meetings of groups of states, sometimes at the summit or through the U.N. Security Council. This side of the coin also emerges in these chapters, sometimes with startling lucidity.

PART 1

SECURITY COUNCIL NEGOTIATIONS

Chapter 1

The Security Council as an Instrument for Peace

Hugh Caradon

THE TASK

The Security Council of the United Nations met for the first time in London on January 17, 1946.

Before the end of that month, the council was already faced with urgent and controversial international problems, and since then, it has had to try to tackle nearly every danger of conflict in the world, as required by the United Nations Charter, in exercise of its "primary responsibility for the maintenance of international peace and security."

With the old confrontations between East and West and the new divergencies between North and South, the council can claim few clear-cut successes. (When there were successful conclusions, they were usually soon forgotten.) The issues in which the council has so far failed — in the Middle East and southern Africa for instance — remain as the menacing and mounting dangers of the world.

How has the council set about its task? What procedures and changes in procedure have been adopted? What confidence can there be that the methods employed by the council will enable it to become an increasingly effective instrument for peace? How can the council be expected in the future to exercise its primary responsibility for maintenance of international peace and security?

ASSETS: SIZE AND SPEED

The council has two unique advantages, first in size and then in speed. When the Security Council was created in 1945, the provision was for only eleven members: five permanent and six elected by the General Assembly. In 1965 the total number was increased from eleven to fifteen, the number of non-permanent members being increased from six to ten. So the council now has five permanent members and ten elected by the General Assembly for two-year periods on the basis of regional representation.

In recent years, there have been proposals for again increasing the membership, perhaps, to a total of twenty-one (or more), but even if a limited increase in membership takes place, the important feature of the Security Council is, and will remain, its small membership compared with a General Assembly of over 150 members and, indeed, with the membership of nearly all other international organizations.

It may well be that the principal achievement of the United Nations Charter was the creation of a small council representing the whole world with responsibility and power in the vital area of international peace and security. If the smallness of membership is the council's main asset, its next principal advantage is its consequent capacity for speed in action.

Article 28 of the charter requires that "The Security Council shall be so organized as to be able to function continuously. Each member of the Security Council shall for this purpose be represented at all times at the seat of the Organization."

There have been many occasions when the council has been called to meet at a few hours notice, by day or night. The council's responsibility is indeed nonstop, and when there are current international disputes or conflicts, the members of the council, either in formal session or in contributing consultations, must be constantly on duty and in times of crisis sometimes supported by the foreign ministers of the nations directly concerned. The council, with its manageable membership and permanent preparedness, thus, constitutes a most valuable innovation in international relations. The existence of a small council with worldwide responsibilities and representation, wielding effective powers and able to meet at a few hours notice, is surely one of the most hopeful developments of modern times.

PROCEDURE

With these assets of size and speed, how have successive councils dealt with the unprecedented questions of method and procedure?

The charter, in Article 30, laid down that "the Security Council shall adopt its own rules of procedure." There were those who early on advocated the preparation of a complete set of detailed and explicit rules, but the council, the jealous master of its own procedure, was anxious not to restrict freedom of action in the proceedings of the council, and the need for freedom to change and to advance the procedure has been widely accepted. Indeed, it is a strange fact that the basic procedures under which the council acts today are still "provisional."

Article 27 of the charter deals with voting, the veto, and abstentions as follows:

> Decisions of the Security Council on procedural matters shall be made by an affirmative vote of seven [since the enlargement of the Council in 1965, nine] members.
> Decisions of the Security Council in all other matters shall be made by an affirmative vote of seven [since 1965, nine] members including the concurring votes of the permanent members; provided that, in decisions [on the pacific settlement of disputes], a party to a dispute shall abstain from voting.

These provisions, which sound simple and sensible enough, could have led to all kinds of difficulties and even deadlocks had they been exactly followed, particularly from the requirement of the concurring votes of all five permanent members. But, in fact, the practical interpretations placed upon these rules have shown the extent that all members have been prepared to go to avoid procedural impasse. Decisions on whether a question is procedural or not usually have been avoided, the abstention of a permanent member has not been regarded as a veto, and the idea that a state should not be a judge in its own cause has been largely forgotten or avoided. These working decisions are open to some doubt or disagreement but they illustrate the determination, particularly of the permanent members, not to be held up by procedural obstacles.

Still more important has been the steady advance, in recent years, away from formal council debate, in favor of private negotiation in search of consensus. There was a time when most of the work of the council was done in public debate. Adlai Stevenson claimed that "the startling candor and vigor of the debates in the Security Council was wholesome." Certainly, the council debates were often lively and even exciting, particularly when Adlai Stevenson participated. Some of us remember the old days when public debates in the council (with full, live public television) led to confrontations and sometimes to decisions but seldom to agreements. The council speeches were often directed to home audiences rather than the search for compromise, but now there is recognition and acceptance that negotiation in confidence is to be sought rather than confrontation in public. There has been a growing determination to insure that however deep disagreements may at first appear, there must be an overriding endeavor to preserve and use the council as an instrument for settlement and peace.

And recently the move toward informal consultations has developed still further. Now there is what amounts to a Security Council in private, where all the members, together with the president of the council and the secretary-general, meet in a separate, and specially provided, room with full interpretation facilities, the only difference from the open Security Council being that in the private meetings there is no record and no report and no audience. Now a council meeting will seldom, if ever, take place without a preliminary round of informal consultations in the private council. The method of full consultation in confidence has almost completely won the day. Open debate in the chamber of the council has become little more than a ritual, the result not the means of reaching agreement, and has lost its dramatic appeal. Clearly, the system of closed discussion facilitates frank exchanges of view and helps the search for common ground. Although the new methods of private search for consensus are now so well accepted and practiced, some misgivings remain. It has been suggested that consensus reflects only the lowest common denominator. Ambassador Kosciusko-Morizet of France gave the following assessment (quoted in F. Y. Chai's admirable Unitar Study entitled *Consulta tion and Consensus in the Security Council*):

> The reasons for this development (consensus), though not very clear, are rather disturbing. A consensus indeed indicates the absence of major objections but it also shows lack of enthusiasm. Its excessive use reflects an increasing reluctance to take a clear stand through a vote and must thus be ascribed to a conception rather remote from that of public diplomacy as envisaged by the authors of the Charter; at the same time it shows a growing disinclination for any firm commitment, i.e., for shouldering the responsibilities that are encumbent upon the members of the Council.
> On the more positive side, this practice also reveals a development in the relations among the Great Powers, which now prefer to avoid confrontations, wherever possible. To a certain extent, the unanimity achieved by consensus is indeed artificial, but it indicates a more conciliatory attitude, which shows how far we are from the era of the cold war.

Stronger views in favor of the search for consensus rather than public debate have been expressed by other United Nations representatives. Some members have contended that:

> The method of consensus, based on a spirit of mutual cooperation, was not only the most appropriate method, but in fact the only one. . . . A text adopted by consensus, however imperfect, would be more likely to be faithfully respected and observed by all States in their relations with each other.[1]

The arguments for and against obsession with consensus are now largely academic. The present system, based on the council doing most of its work in private, is here to stay (for the present, at least), though it would be unwise to exclude the possibility that in the future there will be some swing back to public debate and open voting.

One development, partly due to the new method of consultation in the private session of the council, is the geographical grouping of members. There is now a clearly defined nonaligned group of six or seven members of the council that usually acts together as a group and takes a leading part in preparing draft resolutions and new proposals. (Another new development arising from the greater involvement of the nonaligned group is the increase in the number of non–Security Council participants in debates.)

All this represents a major change in Security Council procedure, practice, and purpose. The council has become not so much an open forum for statements of national policies as a private pursuit of the highest level of international agreement. This is a development of the greatest importance. It has yet to be seen whether peace is better pursued in public or in private, but either way, the Security Council must take the lead.

PROPOSALS FOR CHANGE

Reference has already been made to the enlargement of the council in 1965 from eleven to fifteen members. This led to a better representation of the wider membership of the United Nations and a somewhat greater influence of Third World nations. But this reform, though now well recognized as being welcome and salutary, has not stopped a strong movement in favor of further changes. Opinion seems to be fairly evenly divided on an Indian proposal for an increase in the total membership of the Security Council from fifteen to twenty-one. There is, on the other hand, considerable support for the view that the total membership should be left unchanged. But in any event, a change to twenty-one from fifteen might well be recognized as a change in structure, giving a greater influence to the general membership of the United Nations, rather than a fundamental change in the function and capacity of the council.

A far more important and controversial proposal for change concerns the power of the veto now exercised only by the five permanent members. From the earliest days of the United Nations and, indeed, even at the San Francisco Conference, the issue was raised and what might be called the vendetta against the veto began. On June 8, 1945, the four sponsoring powers at the San Francisco Conference, with France agreeing, stated that the veto should apply when the Security Council had to make decisions involving

> its taking direct measures in connection with settlement of disputes, adjustment of situations likely to lead to disputes, determination of threats to the peace, removal of threats to the peace, and suppression of breaches of the peace.[2]

The assumption was that other decisions on such matters as rules of procedure, selecting the council's president, organizing the council's work, and the participation of nonmembers in the council's discussions would not be subject to a veto.

At the first session of the General Assembly in 1946, Resolution 40 was passed, with the United States and the United Kingdom voting in favor, France and China abstaining, and the Soviet Union voting against:

[The Soviet Union] earnestly requests the permanent members to make every effort, in consultation with one another and with fellow members of the Security Council, to ensure that the use of the special voting privilege of its permanent members does not impede the Security Council in reaching decisions promptly

The anti-veto tide has continued to flow ever since, culminating in a recent Libyan resolution in the Sixth Committee proposing that the Special Committee on the Charter should draft an alternative to replace the rule requiring unanimity of the permanent members of the Security Council for the adoption of decisions on all nonprocedural matters. No decision was taken on the Libyan resolution, but the Nonaligned Summit in September 1979 had passed a resolution:

Nonaligned countries should continue to participate actively in the efforts to amend the Charter of the United Nations particularly its provisions relating to the right of veto exercised by the permanent members of the Security Council so as to attain their aspirations and give effect to the principle of equality among states members of international organizations.

The issue is still alive — a continuing difference of purpose as between the permanent members of the council and most others — but it is difficult to see how any essential change can be made. All the permanent members will resist any total abolition of the veto, but they are divided. China (since representatives of the Peoples Republic took the China seat in 1971) has taken a line of its own, generally in favor of change; but the United States and the United Kingdom are not prepared to go further than to agree to a limited list of issues that should not be subject to the veto, and France and the Soviet Union throughout have been opposed to any change at all.

The basic fact is that, in spite of agitation from the general membership, there is no likelihood that the permanent members of the council will permit questions of international importance, particularly when they affect their own interests and security, to be decided by a council of fifteen members in which they have only one vote and no veto.

NEGOTIATIONS AND PERFORMANCE

While procedures have improved and methods have changed, the basic divisions between East and West and between North and South persist. Cold war attitudes, particularly between the Soviet Union and the United States, continue and recently were intensified. Differences and suspicions grow between the developed nations of the North and the nonaligned nations of the South. These basic rivalries between opposing interests seriously limit the capacity of the Security Council to act promptly and decisively. Indeed, only once has it been possible for the council to take unanimous action on an important issue under Chapter VII in the charter. Under Article 41 of that chapter of the charter, the council is empowered to take measures, including "complete or partial interruption of economic relations and of rail, sea, air, postal, telegraphic, radio and other means of communication, and the severance of diplomatic relations," and under Article 42 the council may take "such action by air, sea, or land forces as may be necessary to maintain or restore international peace and security. Such action may include demonstrations, blockade, and other operations by air, sea, or land forces of Members of the United Nations."

But the differences and divisions on such questions as the Middle East, Namibia, and Afghanistan have so far prevented the council from agreeing or taking measures to make use of these full and drastic powers even when there has been defiance by one nation against the decision of the whole. And it is sad to record that in the one main case in which the powers of Article 41 were invoked to impose sanctions against the illegal regime in Southern Rhodesia, the full effect of the council's unanimous decision in May 1968 was frustrated by deceitful evasions.

Nevertheless, with all the limitations and restrictions and disagreements, it is well to remember the many occasions when an independent international initiative in the council has shown the way forward, with both sides to a dispute eventually accepting what neither could have originally proposed.

This is not the place to list such endeavors—that would require a separate book—but I give one example with which I am familiar, an example that shows the complications of Security Council negotiation and also shows that even in the most intractable situations the members of the council can all contribute to an agreement.

I was recently asked, when I was at Georgetown University, to record what took place in 1967 in the Security Council's endeavor to settle the principles of a Middle East peace, and I repeat the story now. It illustrates better than any generalizations how the members of the council can sometimes work together effectively.

Let me go back to the day when Resolution 242 was adopted unanimously in the Security Council on November 22, 1967. It was a dramatic and unforgettable moment when a cheer went up from the crowded gallery and I turned to my right to see, much to my surprise and delight, Deputy Foreign Minister Kuznetsov of the Soviet Union with his finger raised, voting for the British resolution and thus making it unanimous.

All the previous summer in the United Nations General Assembly there had been a long, fruitless, and frustrating debate with no indication and apparently no possibility of agreement. Various resolutions had been proposed in the Assembly, but it never appeared that there would be agreement. In the end the Soviet resolution was voted down clause by clause until there was nothing left to vote on, and the United States had no hope of putting forward a resolution which had any prospect of the two-thirds majority required in the Assembly.

So, at the end of the hot, hopeless summer of 1967, we left the Assembly with nothing achieved. Worse still, we had shown up the gulf that existed not only between the Arab governments and the government of Israel but also between the two superpowers. It seemed that the Middle East was doomed to continue as the center of a bitter and deep-seated, irreconcilable dispute that would divide the world and in the end lead to another conflict on a far wider scale. We, the members of the United Nations, had not only failed to resolve the international dispute, we had intensified and prolonged it. What hope could there be that by returning to the Security Council with its fifteen members we could make progress on an issue in which the members of the Assembly had utterly failed?

But the danger was that to do nothing would certainly lead to ultimate disaster, with another war becoming inevitable. Israel, with the military confidence of its sweeping successes in the June war, was in no mood for compromise, still less for concession; and equally certain, the Arab world could never tolerate or accept the Israeli occupation of East Jerusalem, the West Bank, Gaza, the Golan, and the whole of the Sinai. Nothing else in our worldwide preoccupations at the United Nations seemed nearly so urgent or nearly so dangerous as the apparently insoluble Middle East confrontation.

So we set to work at the end of the summer to search for some way out of the impasse. Was there no area of possible accord, no hope that a way forward could be found that would prevent another war from which all concerned would dreadfully suffer?

The great advantage of United Nations negotiations is that representatives of all concerned are immediately available in New York. Discussion can take place all day long and often part of the night, without the formalities or the delays or the publicity in the exchange of diplomatic visits to the capitals of the countries involved. During the persistent and prolonged negotiations with the members of the council, I could meet with any one of them or with groups of them at any time at very short notice and without the intervention of the press. No communiques need follow such meetings. And when the participating governments were fearful or furious, there was no reason why the personal relations between the representatives in New York need be strained or stopped. I had frequent meetings with Abba Eban of Israel and Mahmoud Riad of Egypt and the ambassadors of all the countries concerned, many of them friends with whom I could speak in confidence at any time.

So, slowly from these personal and private discussions, some ideas emerged that seemed to show that it might be possible to escape from complete deadlock. In going back to review what had been said in the Assembly debate and in studying the statements already made in the council and even more in private exchange, it did appear that there might be some hope of a positive outcome. Not agreement — that often seemed beyond the prospect of attainment — but some positive plan to prevent another conflict.

I had the advantage of a respectful understanding with the United States ambassador, Arthur Goldberg, who could speak with the authority of his government. And I had closely worked for several years with Ambassador Fedorenko of the Soviet Union. And in view of the extreme importance of the issue at stake, the Soviet Union sent Deputy Foreign Minister Kuznetsov to speak for the Soviet government in the Council. As we were to discover later, he had the unusual but outstanding qualification of carrying full weight with his own government.

By November 1967, we were ready to attempt a British draft resolution. With other Europeans and with Africans, Asians, and Latin Americans, we seemed to be making some progress.

When I introduced our British resolution to the Security Council on November 15, 1967, I said:

> The Arab countries insist that we must direct our special attention to the recovery of their territories. The Israelis tell us that withdrawal must never be to the old precarious peace but to secure boundaries. Both are right. The aims of the two sides do not conflict. To imagine that one can be secured without the other is a delusion. They are of equal validity and equal necessity. We want not a victory in New York but a success in the Middle East.

And then after such long endeavor, our hopes of finding a genuinely acceptable initiative were suddenly dashed.

Only a few days before the final vote was to take place in the council, late at night I received a message from members of my mission. At this last moment, the Soviet Union had put down a rival and extreme resolution. Quickly, I calculated who would vote for the Russian resolution, who would stay with the British resolution, who would take refuge in abstention. But anyhow the prospect of agreement seemed gone. All our painstaking work seemed wasted as the telegrams went out all over the world reporting the new situation: the rival resolution, the persisting disagreement.

We went down to the council on a Monday evening for the vote. There were several members who wished to see me before the meeting.

Then Deputy Foreign Minister Kuznetsov asked to see me. Could he see me alone? Of course. We went into a room near the council. He said at once, "I want you to give me two days." I hesitated. What would my government say? They might assume that the Russians wanted the time to gather more support for their lately presented resolution. But then, Kuznetsov said something strange. He said, "I am not sure that you fully understand what I am saying to you. I am personally asking you for two days."

I knew Kuznetsov very well. I had worked with him on other difficult issues. I greatly respected him. When he said, "I am personally asking you for two days," I knew that he could not work against me. I thought that he might even be thinking of abstaining on the British resolution. I knew I could trust him, as he trusted me. I went back into the council and said that a last-minute request had been made for a postponement of this all-important vote. I asked for a postponement until the following Wednesday evening.

So on Wednesday, the council met again. There could be no more post-ponement now. This was the culmination of all our efforts. We listened to a long speech from the representative of Syria, and then, unexpectedly, we were called to vote, when I had imagined that this final debate would go on all night.

The president of the council called for a vote first on the British resolution, which had been down first. I raised my hand to vote for it. And then there was a cheer from the galleries. I looked to my right to see Kuznetsov's finger raised, voting for our resolution and withdrawing his own, thus, making the vote for the British Resolution 242 unanimous.

He had made good use of the two days. He had come to the conclusion that a unanimous vote and full agreement were essential. He had gone back to his government and, I have no doubt, to the Arab governments, too, and he had persuaded them.

When I was in London a few days later on other business, satisfaction was expressed about a unanimous vote in the United Nations on such a difficult and dangerous issue. I wrote to the London *Times* to say that the main credit for the unanimous resolution must go to Deputy Foreign Minister Kuznetsov.

We have maintained our friendship. At times of subsequent crisis in the Middle East he has sometimes sent me a personal message: "Our resolution is still doing well." After the unanimous vote in the council that day, I said:

> The Resolution which we have prepared is not a British text: it is the result of close and prolonged consultation with both sides and with all Members of the Council. As I have respectfully said every Member of the Council has made a contribution in the search for common ground on which we can go forward.

I tell the story again because the overriding importance of resolution 242 is, of course, that it was adopted unanimously; and no country involved in the unanimous vote has gone back on it. It still provides the only agreed basis for a lasting settlement to bring freedom to the Palestinians and security for Israel, one dependent on the other, and peace at last.

The story illustrates many of the characteristics of negotiations in the Security Council. The need never to give up when other efforts have failed; the effectiveness of an independent initiative; the dominant position of the two superpowers; the importance of the personal qualities of the main actors, such as Kuznetsov and Goldberg and Mahmoud Riad and Abba Eban; the requirement for consultation with all the regional groups; the availability of the council to meet at any time; the importance of the capacity of the delegates to the council to influence their own governments; personal confidence and trust between the members; and a belief that even in circumstances of the utmost difficulty, not all the luck need be on the wrong side.

NOTES

1. UN Doc. G. A. 6955 of 1967, Report of the Sixth Committee on the item entitled "Report on the Special Committee on Principles of International Law Concerning Friendly Relations and Cooperation Among States."

2. UNCIO Doc. 852, III/1/37(1), 11 UNCIO Documents, pp. 699–709, of June 7, 1945.

Editor's Comments on Security Council Negotiations

The Security Council is both a negotiating and a mediatory body. Its members negotiate among themselves in an effort to arrive at agreed positions. They also constitute a highly prestigious force that attempts to mediate between the parties to a conflict.

For several reasons, the Security Council is at the apex of the international system for dispute resolution: it can function continuously, it contains the big powers, in the background are its enforcement powers, and its membership is drawn from all the major regions of the world.

The following contributions to the processes of negotiation and mediation emerge from the work of the council, as set out in Section A:

1. The substantive work on negotiation and mediation is done in off-the-record, private sessions among the members, or among groups of members. Increasingly, the council's public meetings announce the decisions taken in these private sessions.
2. Especially in highly contentious issues, the degree of effectiveness of the council is directly proportional to the degree of closeness of the main representatives to the decision makers in their governments. Thus, in the case of the Council's meetings leading to the adoption of Resolution 242, the fact that both Arthur Goldberg and Vassily Kuznetsov carried full weight with their governments greatly assisted the council's search for common ground.
3. Unanimity or consensus is necessary if the council's work is to succeed, even in a measure.
4. Determination and perseverance in carrying negotiations through to a conclusion are necessary for success.

PART 2

REGIONAL NEGOTIATIONS

Chapter 2

OAS Negotiations

Jorge L. Zelaya Coronado[†]

TERMS OF REFERENCE

This chapter is a review of the more basic of the many contributions the Organization of American States (OAS) has made, through negotiation and mediation, in preserving and maintaining peace, so that differences between states are settled peaceably, with a minimum of suffering by the people in the American hemisphere who often are unaware of the real causes of the conflicts, but who are always mindful of their consequences, since it is the people who inevitably bear the brunt.

I shall deal with the various treaties containing provisions that in one way or another are related to negotiation and mediation in the inter-American system, including the American Treaty on Pacific Settlement, referred to as the Pact of Bogotá, and the Inter-American Treaty of Reciprocal Assistance, referred to as the Rio Treaty.

INTRODUCTION

In the broad field covered by inter-American treaties and conventions aimed at the preservation of peace and the peaceful settlement of disputes, it is necessary to explain the nature of each problem in order to identify the procedures applicable. To put these procedures in their proper categories, under their right headings, I shall sketch briefly the procedures and the juridical instruments that embody them until I reach the methods known as negotiation and mediation in the regional framework of the OAS.

The first large classification consists of the procedures aimed at the observance and maintenance of peace that envisage collective action. Mention

---

[†]The personal views of the author do not necessarily represent the opinions of the general secretariat of the Organization of American States.

must also be made, in this connection, of the procedures for the peaceful settlement of disputes in which, strictly speaking, there is no threat to the peace
and, consequently, there is no need to apply provisions that, although legitimate, may be coercive.

In the first category, we can distinguish the operations for the observance
of peace and those for the maintenance of peace. Some aim at enlightening
the political bodies called upon to take decisions, and the others aim at fulfillment of those decisions.

Under the inter-American system, the maintenance of peace falls within
the competence of "The Meeting of Consultation of Ministers of Foreign Affairs" (Chapter XII of the OAS Charter). This organ of the OAS may be convoked to consider problems that are urgent, and of common interest, to the
American states or to serve as an organ of consultation, when there is the
possibility of applying collective action. This can be done only under the Rio
Treaty, adopted by the Inter-American Conference for the Maintenance of
Continental Peace and Security, held in Rio de Janeiro in 1947.

We can make an initial subdivision within the procedures for the peaceful
settlement of disputes. First, there are peaceful means that do not involve the
delegation of decision-making authority or capacity; in this instance, the parties involved reserve that authority. A second category of procedures for the
peaceful settlement of disputes consists of those means that indeed provide
for a delegation of authority with decision-making capacity to make judg-
ments or awards, as the case may be.

As an example of the former, we may mention good offices, mediation,
investigation, and conciliation, including the advisory opinions of jurisdictional bodies. Such is the case envisioned in Chapter VII of the Pact of
Bogotá, whose Article LI stipulates the following:

> The parties concerned in the solution of a controversy may, by agreement, peti-
> tion the General Assembly or the Security Council of the United Nations to re-
> quest an advisory opinion of the International Court of Justice on any juridical
> question. The petition shall be made through the Council (now called Permanent
> Council) of the Organization of the American States.

The second category would include the judicial and arbitrational procedures.

The experience of the inter-American system has shown, over the years,
the successful application of both means of peaceful settlement of disputes
and the frequent mutual relationship existing between these means and others
that theoretically belong to a different category. It is indispensable to distinguish, as part of this experience, the different methods followed by the OAS
in applying its instruments and, above all, to stress the fact that the highly
flexible manner in which the organization has always acted has contributed
much to the fact that many potential conflicts have been settled without even

convoking the competent organs of the system and by taking only preventive measures.

It is advisable, first, to sketch the institutional framework at the highest governing level and, then, to analyze what the Pact of Bogotá is, what the Inter-American Peace Committee was, and what the Inter-American Committee on Peaceful Settlement is, under the terms of the OAS Charter. Thereafter, reference will be made to the Meeting of Consultation of Ministers of Foreign Affairs and, in particular, to the Rio Treaty, which on many occasions and for reasons I will explain later has turned into a useful instrument for negotiation and mediation.

INSTITUTIONAL FRAMEWORK

The United Nations Charter and the OAS Charter

Both the UN Charter and the OAS Charter reflect the belief that emerged in the immediate postwar period for the constant need to preserve peace in the world and, more particularly, in the case of the OAS Charter, in the American hemisphere.

Against the background of the League of Nations and the lengthy experience of the inter-American system, both the Charter of San Francisco and the Charter of Bogotá took as their essential principle the structuring of a new world order based on ethical principles that, of course, prohibit war and the use of force in the search for solutions to existing or potential conflicts. Thus, Article 1 of the UN Charter stipulates the following:

The purposes of the United Nations are:

1. To maintain international peace and security, and to that end: to take effective collective measures for the prevention and removal of threats to the peace, and for the suppression of acts of aggression or other breaches of the peace, and to bring about by peaceful means, and in conformity with the principles of justice and international law, adjustment or settlement of international disputes or situations which might lead to a breach of the peace. . . .

Like the Charter of San Francisco, the charter adopted by the American states three years later in Bogotá stipulated in Article 2:

The Organization of American States, in order to put into practice the principles on which it is founded and to fulfill its regional obligations under the Charter of the United Nations, proclaims the following essential purposes:

a) To strengthen the peace and security of the continent;
b) To prevent possible causes of difficulties and to ensure the pacific settlement of disputes that may arise among the Member States;
c) To provide for common action on the part of those States in the event of aggressions;

d) To seek the solution of political, juridical, and economic problems that may arise among them; and

e) To promote, by cooperative action, their economic, social, and cultural development.

Pact of Bogotá

Prior to 1948, despite the long standing of the inter-American system, it had not been possible to codify American international law in the field of the peaceful settlement of disputes. There were various treaties in effect, some bilateral, and others multinational, in nature. It must be recalled that there was no legal institutional framework for the eight inter-American conferences held before 1948; this did not come into being until the adoption of the Bogotá Charter in that year. Previously, the following instruments had been adopted: the Treaty on Compulsory Arbitration, signed on January 29, 1902, at the Second International Conference of American States, held in Mexico; the Treaty to Avoid or Prevent Conflicts Between the American States, known as the Gondra Treaty, signed on May 3, 1923, at the Fifth International Conference of American States, in Santiago, Chile; the General Convention of Inter-American Conciliation, signed in Washington on January 5, 1929, during the Conference on Conciliation and Arbitration, in accordance with the resolution adopted a year earlier, February 18, 1928, at the Sixth International Conference of American States, in Havana, Cuba; the General Treaty of Inter-American Arbitration and the Protocol of Progressive Arbitration, both signed on January 5, 1929, at the aforementioned 1929 conference; the Anti-war Treaty of Nonaggression and Conciliation signed in Rio de Janeiro, on October 10, 1933, and popularly referred to as the Saavedra Lamas Pact (Carlos Saavedra Lamas was the minister of foreign affairs and worship of Argentina at the time the conference was held); the Additional Protocol to the General Convention of Inter-American Conciliation, signed in Montevideo on December 26, 1933, during the Seventh International Conference of American States; the Convention for the Maintenance, Preservation, and Reestablishment of Peace, signed in Buenos Aires on December 23, 1936, during the Conference on the Maintenance, Preservation, and Reestablishment of Peace (at this conference the procedure of consultation was first established, a principle that was later refined at the Lima Conference of 1938 and gave rise to the Meeting of Consultation of Ministers of Foreign Affairs, which was included as a principal organ of the OAS in the Bogotá Charter of 1948); the Additional Protocol relative to Nonintervention of December 23, 1936, signed in Buenos Aires at the previously mentioned peace conference; and the Treaty on the Prevention of Controversies, signed at the same Buenos Aires Conference of 1936, as were the Inter-American Treaty on Good Offices and Mediation and the Convention to Coordinate, Extend, and Assure the Fulfillment of the Existing Treaties between the American States. Finally the Pact of Bogotá, which compiled and codified all the aforementioned treaties and conventions, was adopted and signed on April 30, 1948.

The Pact of Bogotá opens with a solemn reaffirmation by high contracting parties of the commitments made by them in earlier international conventions and declarations as well as in the Charter of the United Nations. The contracting states agree to refrain from the threat or use of force, or from any other means of coercion for the settlement of their controversies, and to have recourse at all times to peaceful procedures.

This solemn commitment, established in Article II, includes the obligation to settle international controversies by regional peaceful procedures before referring them to the Security Council of the United Nations.

Special reference is made to direct negotiations through usual diplomatic channels, and the Pact takes in all the principles of international law, particularly those contained in the aforementioned conventions and protocols. It is made clear, of course, that the procedures set forth may not be applied to matters that by their nature fall within the domestic jurisdiction of the state. This represents an affirmation of the principle that matters of domestic public order come exclusively within the competence of the states, and that public international law governing the settlement of disputes can be applied only in those situations that affect international order.

FRAME OF REFERENCE

Negotiation

This method of peaceful settlement of disputes is, by its nature, customarily applied bilaterally rather than multilaterally. Negotiation is regarded as the most direct method. In negotiation, there is the assumption that the parties are willing to deal with each other face to face to settle their differences.

Unlike mediation, in which three parties are concerned—that is, the two parties in dispute and the mediator—negotiation involves only the parties in dispute. This being said, the logical conclusion would be that the procedure of negotiation is never applied in the international sphere. Such a conclusion is untrue, however, as we shall now see.

Peaceful settlement of disputes is not of concern solely to the parties directly involved; in an era of interrelations, it is safe to say that the concern is shared by the international community. Hence, when any of the mechanisms for the peaceful settlement of dispute is activated, the interest aroused transcends that of the parties, and it is then that the inter-American community enters into negotiations with them. This is seen very clearly when the Rio Treaty is invoked, for example. Once the crisis jeopardizing international public order has been overcome, the organ of consultation or a committee created by it enters into open negotiations. The Salvador-Honduras case of 1969 clearly illustrates this point. For years the Special Committee of the Thirteenth Meeting of Consultation of Ministers of Foreign Affairs negotiated with the parties until they accepted the mediation of the former president of Peru, Dr. José Luis Bustamante y Rivero, which ended the dispute and made possible the signing of the peace treaty.

The Pact of Bogotá refers to "direct negotiations" (Article II), only to indicate that "in the event that a controversy arises between two or more signatory states which, in the opinion of the parties, cannot be settled by direct negotiations through the usual diplomatic channels, the parties bind themselves to use the procedures established in the present treaty, in the manner and under the conditions provided for in the following articles, or, alternatively, such special procedures as, in their opinion, will permit them to arrive at a solution."

Mediation

The Pact of Bogotá provides an appropriate definition for mediation in Chapter II, Article XI, which reads:

> Article XI. The procedure of mediation consists in the submission of the controversy to one or more American Governments not parties to the controversy, or to one or more eminent citizens of any American State not a party to the controversy. In either case the mediator or mediators shall be chosen by mutual agreement between the parties.

The procedure of mediation is set forth more fully in Articles XII, XIII, and XIV of the pact, which also establishes its method of operation. For further clarification, these articles are quoted here:

> Article XII. The functions of the mediator or mediators shall be to assist the parties in the settlement of controversies in the simplest and most direct manner, avoiding formalities and seeking an acceptable solution. No report shall be made by the mediator and, so far as he is concerned, the proceedings shall be wholly confidential.
>
> Article XIII. In the event that the High Contracting Parties have agreed to the procedure of mediation but are unable to reach an agreement within two months on the selection of the mediator or mediators, or no solution to the controversy has been reached within five months after mediation has begun, the other parties shall have recourse without delay to any one of the other procedures of peaceful settlement established in the present Treaty.
>
> Article XIV. The High Contracting Parties may offer their mediation, either individually or jointly, but they agree not to do so while the controversy is in process of settlement by any of the other procedures established in the present Treaty.

The procedure of investigation and conciliation, judicial procedure, procedure of arbitration, fulfillment of decisions, advisory opinions, and final provisions are covered in Chapters III through VIII of the pact. These chapters, however, are beyond the scope of this study.

The final provisions are those common to all treaties: ratifications, entry into force and continued validity, reservations, and the possibility of denunciation.

Unfortunately, little use has been made of the Pact of Bogotá within the inter-American system, chiefly because many reservations touching on fundamental aspects have made it virtually inoperable. Nevertheless, the pact has served as an auxiliary instrument when other treaties have been invoked to settle problems of broader context; that is, without activating the mechanisms established in the pact, its procedures have been used on many occasions, even within the application of the Rio Treaty.

APPLICABLE MECHANISMS

Inter-American Peace Committee

Although the establishment of this committee was not a matter of the same hierarchical level as adherence to a treaty or international convention, it is useful to recall the origins of the organ that now performs its functions within the structure of the OAS. I refer to the Inter-American Committee on Peaceful Settlement, whose establishment was provided for in Articles 82–90 of the charter of the organization.

During the middle of 1940, the foreign ministers of the American republics, assembled at the Second Meeting of Ministers in Havana, adopted Resolution XIV to the effect that since "in behalf of the closest possible unity of the Continent, it is imperative that differences existing between some of the American nations be settled," it was necessary "to recommend to the Governing Board of the Pan American Union (the predecessor of the present Permanent Council of the OAS) that it organize, in the American capital deemed most suitable for the purpose, a committee composed of representatives of five countries, which shall have the duty of keeping constant vigilance to insure that states between which any dispute exists or may arise, of any nature whatsoever, may solve it as quickly as possible, and of suggesting, without detriment to the methods adopted by the parties or to the procedures which they may agree upon, the measures and steps which may be conducive to a settlement." Note, for the moment, the broad scope of the committee's competence in the matter, since the resolution made reference to *any dispute of any nature whatsoever*. Moreover, the committee was to report to each meeting of ministers of foreign affairs and to each international conference of American states on the status of such conflicts and on any steps taken to bring about a solution.

On December 4, 1940, the governing board of the Pan American Union decided that the headquarters of the committee would be in Washington,

D.C., and it chose as its members two countries from the North (the United States and Mexico), two from the South (Argentina and Brazil), and one from Central America and the West Indies (Cuba). Starting in 1956, other countries were appointed in a system of partial rotation in which one of the members was replaced each year.

The committee was inactive for a number of years, and it was only at the insistence of the Dominican Republic, which at that time was encountering difficulties with Cuba, that the committee was installed at the end of July 1948. The committee began its work a few days later, also, at the request of the Dominican Republic.

The committee adopted its statutes on May 24, 1950, and transmitted them to the governments of the member states of the Union of American Republics. Earlier, the committee had been governed by provisional rules of procedure, which it called "Basis for Action," and until July 6, 1949, it had operated under the name of "Inter-American Committee on Methods for the Peaceful Solution of Conflicts."

The 1950 statutes formally gave the committee the name of Inter-American Peace Committee; it stated that the term of the chairman would be one year, and that the post would be held on a rotating basis. More importantly, it clearly set forth the committee's jurisdiction and procedures. The Tenth Inter-American Conference, held in Caracas in March 1954, took up the Committee's report on its work, and adopted two resolutions: Resolution CI, in which it applauded the "fruitful work in the interest of the peace of the Continent, carried out in a timely and effective manner and in a lofty American spirit by the Committee;" and Resolution CII, in which it expressed its confidence in the committee, decided to maintain it in existence, and instructed the council to draft new statutes for it. Those statutes were adopted by the council on May 9, 1956. Thereafter, a certain decline is to be noted in the committee's importance and usefulness as a simple, flexible instrument for dealing with serious, politically tense situations among countries, without any need to resort to the stricter and more complicated procedures called for in the Rio Treaty and the Pact of Bogotá, with the greater publicity they involved.

There was, in fact, a decline in the committee's importance due to a change in the 1956 statutes that radically limited its jurisdiction. Under the 1948 "Bases for Action" and the 1950 statutes, the committee had been able to act at the request of any of the parties directly interested in the conflict, without requirement for the consent of the other party. By contrast, under the 1956 statutes, the committee could act only with the consent of all interested parties. Furthermore, the 1950 statutes had provided that any American state, even though it is not a directly interested party or a member of the committee, could at any time call the committee's attention to any inter-American conflict that, in its opinion, warranted consideration by the committee.

We may conclude from what has been said, and from the committee's field of jurisdiction as described earlier, that before 1956 it was really very broad. However, it should be explained that the committee's essential mission was not to pass judgment on events, conflicts, or situations, but rather, in the words of the resolution that created it, to seek to have states solve their conflicts as soon as possible and, to that end, to suggest methods and steps conducive to a settlement.

The committee itself noted the decline in its activities after the adoption of the 1956 statutes when, in its report to the Fifth Meeting of Consultation in Santiago, Chile, in August 1959, it stated:

> The Committee wishes to state that since May 9, 1956, the date on which the new Statute entered into force, no case has been submitted to it for consideration, which leads to the deduction that the governments have preferred to utilize other procedures of the inter-American system to settle problems or resolve situations that have arisen between them. The Committee considers that this lact may be due to changes introduced into (its) Statute . . .

The same meeting of consultation, which was discussing the complicated situation that had arisen in the entire Caribbean area shortly after the triumph of the Cuban revolution, assigned the committee additional functions and gave it back the authority to act at the request of any government or on its own initiative but only on matters that had brought about the convocation of the meeting, that is, primarily the "consideration of the situation of international tension in the Caribbean area in its general and several aspects, in light of the principles and standards that govern the inter-American system, and of means to assure the observance by states of the principles of nonintervention and nonaggression." It should be said that the nature of the additional functions given to the committee, at that time, were substantially different from those it had traditionally had; but since it also retained those traditional functions, it was subsequently able to act in a similar manner in a number of important cases such as the border dispute between Honduras and Nicaragua in 1961 and the dispute between Panama and the United States over the events in Panama in January 1964. In those cases, the committee played a decisive role in solving the conflicts through the missions that it sent to the scene of the action. It should be pointed out that in both cases, the committee acted with the consent of the interested parties, as required under the 1956 statutes.

It is interesting to note some of the outstanding features of the committee's history, which may be pertinent.

1. The committee was a body that met almost informally and without any publicity.
2. Its procedures were simple, and its deliberations were generally secret. The parties could be present or not, appearing either one after the other or at the same time, and the secretariat staff was kept to what was strictly neces-

sary. However, the reserved nature of its deliberations resulted in there being very few records of its actions, particularly of initial meetings.

3. Its prime function, as indicated earlier, was not to pass judgment on events, situations, or disputes. It did not look for the guilty party. It tried to bring the parties together and suggested to them methods or procedures for solving their disputes, but it could not oblige them to accept them.

4. Its action, both at headquarters and in the field — whether in full committee or through missions of part of its membership — was not subject to rigid mandates, nor did the committee give rigid instructions to its missions; it acted in a very flexible way and adjusted itself to the circumstances of the case. Missions could be either for observation or fact finding. The purpose, above all, was for the committee to lend its good offices or to serve as a conciliation or mediation mechanism, even though, formally speaking, it was neither the one nor the other. It suggested measures and procedures, but if by their action alone the parties were able to come to a final solution, so much the better.

5. The cases it took up were generally less serious than those presented to the organ of consultation under the Rio Treaty; however, it is important to note that the intervention of the committee prevented a number of those cases from becoming more serious and requiring invocation of the Rio Treaty with all its consequences.

Inter-American Committee on Peaceful Settlement

The Third Special Inter-American Conference held in Buenos Aires in February 1967, which adopted the Protocol of Amendment to the Charter of the OAS, provided that the old Inter-American Peace Committee be included within the organization's institutional framework as a subsidiary organ of the Permanent Council, under the name of Inter-American Committee on Peaceful Settlement (Article 83). Both the council and the committee require the consent of the parties to a dispute before using their good offices to assist them in a solution. They may then recommend to the parties the procedures they believe would be appropriate for solving the problem. It is important to note that if one of the parties prevents the committee from intervening by withholding its consent, the committee must not only so inform the Permanent Council but it may also negotiate for a resumption of relations between the parties, if they had been broken, or for the reestablishment of harmony between them. If that party persists in its refusal of the committee's good offices, the council in turn must report that fact to the General Assembly, which, in accordance with the powers vested in it under the terms of Article 52 of the OAS Charter, particularly the power to "consider any matter relating to friendly relations among the American States," could perhaps adopt some recommendation with respect to the peaceful settlement of the dispute.

The functions that had been entrusted to the Inter-American Peace Committee were included in the Charter of the OAS under the chapter on the Permanent Council of the Organization. In other words, good offices and mediation are now within the competence of the Permanent Council of the OAS, which is assisted by the Inter-American Committee on Peaceful Settlement, described in Article 83 of the charter as a subsidiary organ of the council. There is still the limitation that I referred to when discussing the statutes of the Inter-American Peace Committee. As a consequence, under the terms of Article 87 of the Charter of the OAS, should one of the parties refuse the offer of good offices, the committee will limit itself to informing the Permanent Council, without prejudice to its taking steps to restore relations between the parties if they have been interrupted or to reestablishing harmony between them.

As a recent example of the use of the Permanent Council's power under the terms of Articles 82–92 of the OAS Charter, one need only cite the situation that developed between Nicaragua and Costa Rica in 1978 and 1979. The Permanent Council of the OAS acted immediately and directly. It sent observers to the area and made a positive contribution, so that what was a complicated case that could have taken on international dimensions was resolved without further consequences and without altering international public order.

Meeting of Consultation of Ministers of Foreign Affairs

The Meeting of Consultation of Ministers of Foreign Affairs referred to in Article 59 of the Charter of the OAS serves two entirely different juridical purposes, which must be distinguished. The first part of the article states that "the Meeting of Consultation of Ministers of Foreign Affairs shall be held in order to consider problems of an urgent nature and of common interest to the American States," while the second part of the article adds the phrase "and to serve as the Organ of Consultation." It is only this second part of the article that concerns application of the Rio Treaty. The Treaty does not come into play for the first part.

In view of the foregoing and in spite of what has been said, it is essential to make specific reference to the Meeting of Consultation of Ministers of Foreign Affairs as it functions under the terms of the first part of the article in question. In effect, when this organ of the system has met, leaving aside the Rio Treaty entirely, it has also acted as a negotiator. The most recent example is the Nicaraguan-Costa Rican case in which, after great difficulty, it resolved the following in September 1978:

WHEREAS:

At its meeting on September 15, 1978, the Permanent Council decided to form an Ad Hoc Committee of Observers to verify the events brought to its attention by the governments of Costa Rica and Nicaragua;

At its meeting on September 18, 1978, the Permanent Council resolved to convoke, in accordance with the first part of Article 59 of the Charter of the Organization, a Meeting of Consultation of Ministers of Foreign Affairs to consider the serious events in the Central American region;

Those events included regrettable incidents in that region, among them incursions by armed forces of one country into the territory of another, which create a serious risk of international conflict;

The human suffering in Nicaragua as well as in the border areas of neighboring countries appears to be of such magnitude that urgent humanitarian relief efforts are necessary to mitigate it;

The Inter-American Commission on Human Rights has accepted the invitation of the Government of Nicaragua to visit that country on October 5; and

Peaceful settlement of international disputes, nonintervention in the internal or external affairs of States, and respect for the fundamental rights of the individual are basic principles of this Organization, THE SEVENTEENTH MEETING OF CONSULTATION OF MINISTERS OF FOREIGN AFFAIRS RESOLVES:

1. To urge the governments directly concerned to refrain from taking any action that might aggravate the present situation.

2. To request the General Secretariat of the Organization, to consult with the governments of the region affected, with the International Committee of the Red Cross, with United Nations organs, and with other inter-governmental humanitarian organizations which are known to be working in the area, to determine what humanitarian assistance is needed to relieve the suffering in that region, and to urge the Member states to give urgent and generous support to efforts that will provide such assistance.

3. To request the Permanent Council to submit to this Meeting for examination the report that the Ad Hoc Committee established by Resolution CP/RES. 249 (341/78) must make to that body, and to keep that Committee in existence as long as this Meeting of Consultation remains in session, so that it may fulfill any other mission the latter may entrust to it.

4. To take note that, having accepted the invitation of the Government of Nicaragua, the Inter-American Commission on Human Rights will visit that country, and to express the hope that the Commission may, in agreement with the government concerned, expedite its visit to Nicaragua if possible.

5. To take note that, without prejudice to full observance of the principle of nonintervention, the Government of Nicaragua has stated that it is willing in principle to accept the friendly cooperation and conciliatory efforts that several Member states of the Organization may offer toward establishing the conditions necessary for a peaceful settlement of the situation without delay.

6. To keep the Seventeenth Meeting of Consultation of Ministers of Foreign Affairs in session as long as the present situation continues.

7. To request the Secretary-General of the Organization to keep the Security Council of the United Nations informed of the decisions that the Meeting of Consultation takes.

In June 1979, that same Meeting of Consultation resolved the following:

WHEREAS:

The people of Nicaragua are suffering the horrors of a fierce armed conflict that is causing grave hardships and loss of life, and has thrown the country into a serious political, social, and economic upheaval;

The inhumane conduct of the dictatorial regime governing the country, as evidenced by the report of the Inter-American Commission on Human Rights, is the fundamental cause of the dramatic situation faced by the Nicaraguan people; and

The spirit of solidarity that guides Hemisphere relations places an unavoidable obligation on the American countries to exert every effort within their power, to put an end to the bloodshed and to avoid the prolongation of this conflict which is disrupting the peace of the Hemisphere, THE SEVENTEENTH MEETING OF CONSULTATION OF MINISTERS OF FOREIGN AFFAIRS DECLARES:

That the solution of the serious problem is exclusively within the jurisdiction of the people of Nicaragua.

That in the view of the Seventeenth Meeting of Consultation of Ministers of Foreign Affairs this solution should be arrived at on the basis of the following:

1. Immediate and definitive replacement of the Somoza regime.

2. Installation in Nicaraguan territory of a democratic government, the composition of which should include the principal representative groups which oppose the Somoza regime and which reflects the free will of the people of Nicaragua.

3. Guarantee of the respect for human rights of all Nicaraguans without exception.

4. The holding of free elections as soon as possible, that will lead to the establishment of a truly democratic government that guarantees peace, freedom, and justice.

RESOLVES:

1. To urge the Member states to take steps that are within their reach to facilitate an enduring and peaceful solution of the Nicaraguan problem on the bases set forth above, scrupulously respecting the principle of nonintervention and abstaining from any action that might be in conflict with the above bases or be incompatible with a peaceful and enduring solution to the problem.

2. To commit their efforts to promote humanitarian assistance to the people of Nicaragua and to contribute to the social and economic recovery of the country.

3. To keep the Seventeenth Meeting of Consultation of Ministers of Foreign Affairs open while the present situation continues.

There is also the Ecuador-Peru case, which ended with a resolution whose importance warrants its being transcribed below since it was the outcome of enormous efforts in the field of multilateral negotiation. The resolution in question reads as follows:

THE NINETEENTH MEETING OF CONSULTATION OF MINISTERS OF FOREIGN AFFAIRS,

HAVING SEEN the agenda of this Meeting, entitled "Cessation of the military operations in the Peruvian-Ecuadorian border area in the El Condor mountain range, which were the reasons for convening the Nineteenth Meeting of Consultation of Ministers of Foreign Affairs, and maintenance of peace";

CONSIDERING:

That at the request of Ecuador, the Permanent Council convoked the Nineteenth Meeting of Consultation with the urgency required, in accordance with resolution CP/RES. 323 (450/81) of January 29, 1981;

That the basic purpose of the Organization of American States is to strengthen the peace and security of the hemisphere;

That in that same resolution, the Permanent Council expressed "its profound concern over the events that are disturbing the friendship and solidarity of two brother countries," and urged "the governments not to take any action that might aggravate the situation";

That the information from the governments of Argentina, Brazil, Chile, and the United States announcing the ceasefire achieved through their intervention with the governments of Ecuador and Peru was confirmed to this Meeting by the Ministers of Foreign Affairs of the two countries, with the clarifications they felt pertinent;

TAKING INTO ACCOUNT the statement by the Special Delegate of Brazil "on behalf of the governments of Argentina, Brazil, Chile, and the United States on the work they are doing with the consent of Ecuador and Peru," and

HAVING HEARD the statements by the Ministers of Foreign Affairs of Ecuador and Peru on the events that occurred in the Ecuadorian-Peruvian border area,

REAFFIRMS:

The principles and purposes set forth in the Charter of the Organization of American States to strengthen the peace and security of the hemisphere, and the need to maintain a permanent climate of understanding and friendship among the nations of the Americas;

STATES:

That the Organization of American States has the ineluctable obligation to watch over the preservation, maintenance, and consolidation of peace in the hemisphere, and

RESOLVES:

1. To note with regret that armed confrontations have taken place between Member states of the Organization, disrupting the peace and security of the hemisphere.

2. To receive with satisfaction the announcement by the two governments of the ceasefire in the zone of the conflict, as confirmed to this Meeting by their Foreign Ministers.

3. To urge both countries to demobilize and disperse their forces and dismantle, as soon as possible, the military operations conducted as a result of the confrontations, restricting themselves to maintaining normal border-patrol troops.

4. To express its satisfaction with the solemn commitment made by both countries to this Meeting of Consultation, as a genuine representation of the peoples and governments of the Americas, to reestablish and consolidate the peace and avoid any act that might endanger that peace, and to make every effort to overcome the present difficulties.

5. To take note that both countries have accepted the visit of a Committee composed of representatives of Argentina, Brazil, Chile, and the United States, which is now in operation, to monitor observance of the cease-fire, and to create conditions of peace between them; and to express its thanks for the work done by the countries.

6. To reiterate the vigilant presence of the Organization of American States for the maintenance and strengthening of peace, and to contribute to understanding between the two countries.

7. To instruct the Permanent Council to remain informed of the actions that both governments take in compliance with the high purposes indicated herein.

Rio Treaty

As said earlier, despite its characteristics of a law of international public order, in practice the Rio Treaty has come to fill the gap left by the Pact of Bogotá. In fact, the many uses made of the organ of consultation have not been limited to a plain and rigid interpretation of the articles of the Treaty. To the contrary, even when situations have seemed to be highly tense and dangerous, the parties have nevertheless been induced, after the crisis endangering the peace has been overcome, to approach each other, to negotiate, and in fact, to accept the mediation of the organ of consultation.

I would like to say once again that, perhaps due to the coercive force of the Rio Treaty when it is invoked, the parties are in some degree forced to accept the presence of the inter-American system and its contribution to the settlement of their problems.

Opinions criticizing the Rio Treaty as an instrument of intervention are often heard. In this regard, it suffices to say that whenever intervention has occurred, it has been without application of the Rio Treaty and it is necessary to distinguish between intervention as an abusive and illegal act and *collective action*, which is the result of a prior agreement with the force of an international treaty that guarantees American international public order.

In conclusion, I would like to repeat that one of the outstanding positive features of the inter-American system is the fact that there are no barriers to negotiation and mediation in application of the instruments in force each time a conflict arises.

Chapter 3

Arab League Negotiations

Clovis Maksoud

FORMATION OF THE ARAB LEAGUE SYSTEM

The Arab League came into existence, formally, on March 22, 1945, as the first regional organization in the post–World War II era.

The initial founders of the Arab League were Egypt, Iraq, Lebanon, Saudi Arabia, Syria, Transjordan and Yemen. However, the league now encompasses twenty-two Arab states.[1]

The initial founders established a regional political organization primarily to strengthen and consolidate the ties that bind the Arab world. The Arab League system was formed with the understanding that it would be an initial step toward establishing Arab unity. Its purposes were defined in the Arab League Pact as follows:

1. safeguarding the independence and sovereignty of Arab states;
2. strengthening relations between member states;
3. coordinating their policies in order to further close cooperation between member states, specifically in economic and financial affairs, commercial relations, customs, currency, agriculture and industry, communications and cultural affairs; and
4. establishing a general concern for the affairs and interests of Arab countries.

The organs established under the Arab League Pact consist of the League Council, the permanent specialized committees, and the permanent secretariat.

The League Council

The League Council is the supreme organ. Its task is to achieve the realization of the objectives of the league, and to supervise the execution of agreements between member states. It is composed of representatives from member states, with each state having one vote. This council meets in ordinary session twice a year but may be convened in extraordinary session at the request of two member states.

The voting procedure for the council makes unanimity the general rule. Decisions taken unanimously are binding upon all member states, while majority decisions only bind those states that have accepted them. In cases of the aggression of one member state against another member state, decisions are taken by unanimous vote, except that the vote of the aggressor is not counted. This rule also applies in the case of a decision to suspend a member state from the league.

On the other hand, decisions of the council relating to arbitration or mediation and decisions on administration and procedural matters require only a majority vote. The amendment of the pact and the appointment of the secretary-general require a two-thirds majority.

The Permanent Specialized Committees

These committees are set up for each of the functional areas mentioned in Article II of the pact and are to assist the council. They are charged with the tasks of laying down the principles and extent of cooperation in their specialized fields. These committees are:

1. the Political Committee
2. the Cultural Committee
3. the Economic Committee
4. the Communications Committee
5. the Social Committee
6. the Legal Committee
7. the Information Committee
8. the Petroleum Exports Committee
9. the Health Committee
10. the Financial and Administration Committee

The Political Committee, created in 1946, generally meets at the foreign ministers' level. It adopts, in most cases, recommendations on political matters which are submitted to the League Council for adoption as resolutions.[2]

The Permanent Secretariat

This organ consists of a secretary-general, whose appointment requires a two-thirds majority vote of the League Council, and several assistant secretaries-general, and an appropriate number of officials.

In addition to the above three principal organs of the Arab League, a number of secondary organs and specialized agencies have been created over the years by the League Council such as the Centre for Industrial Development, the Arab Organization for Agricultural Development, and the Arab Organization for Education, Science, and Culture.

THE ARAB COLLECTIVE SECURITY TREATY
AND THE ARAB JOINT DEFENCE

The Arab Collective Security Treaty, officially known as the Joint Defence and Economic Co-Operation Treaty,[3] concluded in 1950, seems to have resulted from three main considerations.

The first is the necessity for establishing an effective collective security mechanism, in particular, because of the creation of the so-called state of Israel in Palestine in 1948.

The second consideration is the Arab League's desire to adapt the provisions of its system for peace and security to the system established under the United Nations Charter. This would be considered a regional arrangement. In fact, this treaty is based on Article 52 of the United Nations Charter.

The third consideration is the attempts and various efforts undertaken from within and outside the region to bring the Middle East into the Western collective defense arrangement, particularly after the establishment of the North Atlantic Treaty Organization (NATO).

In the face of these attempts, the Arab League's desire was to initiate an Arab policy of nonalignment.

The preamble of this treaty defines its aims to be, primarily, "to cooperate for the realization of mutual defence and the maintenance of security and peace." *A basic notion in this treaty is that an aggression against any of the parties, that is, member states of the league, is an aggression against all.*

This treaty has established the following principal organs:

1. a joint defence council that comprises foreign ministers, and ministers of defense and whose decisions require a two-thirds majority vote and are binding on all parties;
2. a permanent military commission that is composed of representatives of the general staff of the parties, charged with drawing up the plans for a joint defense and the means for their implementation;
3. a consultative military council that is composed of the chiefs of staff of the contracting states; and
4. a military annex to the 1950 treaty that provides for the appointment of a joint Arab commander in chief, in the event of war.

This 1950 treaty includes the following features:

1. It was concluded for an indefinite period of time.
2. The treaty reaffirmed the intention of contracting parties to settle their international disputes by peaceful means.
3. The contracting parties, under this treaty, cannot conclude agreement that may be contrary to the provisions of the treaty, or to act in their international relations, in a way, contrary to the treaty purposes.

4. The system created by this treaty, is considered subordinate and complementary to the Arab collective security system adopted under the pact.

THE OPERATION OF THE ARAB LEAGUE SYSTEM IN REGIONAL NEGOTIATIONS

Under the provisions of the pact, the Arab League Council has been endowed with the primary competence with respect to regional disputes. In fact, Article 5 specifically refers to the council's function as an organ of arbitration and mediation, while Article 6 deals with its role in the case of aggression against a member state.

In practice, the League Council had actually exercised such competence almost exclusively. Bear in mind that the League Council can operate through various organs (i.e., a political committee or a meeting of permanent representatives, heads of states, and foreign ministers) and through various procedures and techniques, as well.

Procedures Developed by the Council

Conciliation, Mediation, and Good Offices. The emphasis of the council has been based upon conciliation between disputant parties rather than adjudication of their claims. Many regional disputes have occurred in which the Council resorted to conciliation. In the dispute between Syria and the United Arab Republic (UAR) in 1961, the council abstained from pronouncing upon the claims put forward by the parties after the secession. Instead, it attempted to conciliate between them with a view to settling the problems that had arisen out of the union. The League Council was successful in achieving this objective.

A similar conciliatory approach was used in the Lebanese complaint of indirect aggression by the United Arab Republic in 1958. However, this approach was rejected by Lebanon in favor of resort to the United Nations to solve the conflict.

There have been occasions when the League Council departed from its conciliating approach and envisaged the adoption of effective measures: in the dispute of Kuwait and Iraq in 1961. The council rejected the Iraqi territorial claim upon Kuwait and adopted effective measures for the preservation of Kuwait's independence.

The council's approach to intermember disputes favoring conciliation rather than other measures is mainly due to two reasons: 1. the league's fundamental policy of seeking to preserve solidarity and unity among its member states, and 2. the special relationship existing between the Arab states, as states belonging to one Arab nation.

In disputes that are not intermember disputes, such as the Arab-Israeli conflict, or the Tunisian-French dispute of 1961, the League Council has always acted in support of its member states rather than attempting to settle the question between the disputant parties. Such a course of action is more a regional response to an external threat, rather than a regional procedure for the settlement of disputes.

Fact-Finding. The Arab League Pact did not provide any particular procedure of investigation in a dispute, nor did it mention that the League Council was empowered to establish a fact-finding body.

In the absence of specific provisions under the pact, the League Council seems to have assumed that the power of fact-finding was implied in its broad function of mediation (Article 5), as well as in the measures within its competence to counter an aggression (Article 6).

The league fact-finding missions, established in connection with the Lebanon crisis in 1958, the Yemen situation of 1962 and the Morocco-Algeria dispute in 1963, had dual functions covering both fact-finding and conciliation.

There are some cases where the fact-finding role is entrusted to the secretary-general himself, explicitly or implicitly.

Arbitration. In regard to arbitration, the council's jurisdiction under Article 5 of the pact is limited, both in substance and in form.

On the one hand the dispute must not concern a state's independence, sovereignty, or territorial integrity.

On the other hand, the parties to the dispute must agree to have recourse to the council. This agreement is a prerequisite for arbitration.

On only one occasion in the history of the league have member states ever had recourse to arbitration. This occurred in May 1949 in a Syria-Lebanon dispute over a minor territorial violation.

The two countries agreed, after the league's intervention, to entrust Egypt and Saudi Arabia with the settlement of the dispute by arbitration.

The reluctance of member states to have recourse to the League Council for arbitration may be explained by the fact that most if not all their disputes are of a political nature.

Use of the Secretary-General. The fourth procedure is the use of the secretary-general as provided under specific sections of the pact or under a special mandate or upon his own initiative. The pact has defined only the administrative and budgetary functions of the secretary-general. The other functions of the office have been defined in the internal regulations of the League Council.

In practice, however, the secretary-general's role has developed by virtue of the functions entrusted to him by the League Council and by virtue of his personal initiative. Article 12 of the internal regulations of the council (formerly Article 20) states that the secretary-general has the right to draw the attention of the council or member states to any question that might prejudice relations between member states or between them and other states. The power is similar to that of the United Nations' secretary-general under Article 99 of the charter. In the Algeria-Morocco dispute of 1963, the secretary-general requested the convening of the League Council on his personal initiative.

The secretary-general's power to bring disputes to the attention of the council would imply a further power to make investigations and inquiries on his own initiative so as to be able to fully inform the League Council about any matter that might be referred to it. Furthermore, Articles 12 and 13 have authorized the secretary-general to attend council meetings and to submit verbal reports or statements on any question under discussion. This participation in discussions implies participation in the drafting of resolutions, if not in proposing them.

The importance of the secretary-general's role appears to result from the following:

1. the absence in the league system of an established formal machinery with detailed procedures for the settlement of disputes, which has resulted in relying on the secretary-general in the settlement of disputes;
2. the limitations placed on the League Council in handling disputes related to independence, territorial integrity, or sovereignty of a member state has made the council rely on the secretary-general's intervention in dealing with such disputes; and
3. the office of the secretary-general is an impartial institutionalized agency that has proved its value in the settlement of disputes. This was shown in the case of the Syria-United Arab Republic dispute of 1961.

The Arab League and the United Nations

This relationship between the league and the United Nations involves three main interrelated matters:

1. the nature of disputes referred to the league;
2. the Security Council's responsibility for disputes involving potential or actual threat to peace and security; and
3. the question of the priority of the league procedures over those of the United Nations with respect to local disputes.

Some disputes brought before the league have been of a purely local character (e.g., the Syria-United Arab Republic dispute of 1961). Other disputes have been a potential threat to peace, either as a result of the possible outbreak of hostilities or the involvement of extraregional powers (e.g., the Lebanon crisis of 1958). Additional disputes have been an actual threat to international peace and security (e.g., the Arab-Israeli conflict).

In all these categories of disputes, the Security Council's intervention depended on the nature of the dispute. Basically, it did not intervene in disputes of a local nature. In the case of potential threat to international peace and security, the council kept a supervisory jurisdiction over the disputes. As for disputes involving actual threats to peace and security in the world, the council intervened as it is the primary responsibility of the council to deal with such matters.

The question of the priority for the league's procedures over those of the United Nations with respect to local disputes is explained in the provisions of Articles 33 and 52 of the United Nations Charter. Article 33 refers to the obligation of the parties to seek, first of all, a solution through regional arrangements. Article 52 provides that members of regional arrangements shall make every effort to settle local disputes through regional arrangements before referring them to the Security Council. Hence, priority of the league's procedures over those of the United Nations with respect to local disputes is not in question.

Finally, the collective security function of the Arab League operates on two levels: as a regional collective security system concerned with suppression of conflicts within its ranks, and as a regional collective self-defense system aimed at providing joint security against external threats.

The success achieved by the League in the field of peaceful settlement of disputes does not only derive from the adequate use made by the organization of its limited machinery but it also stems from the impact of its functional activities on the process of peaceful settlement. The functioning of the league with respect to regional disputes has both reflected, and been influenced by, the special relationships between its members. Solidarity and unity of feeling and purpose have been a main factor in the settlement of disputes, and this is why the conciliatory approach between member states remains the basic technique used in regional negotiations.

NOTES

1. The league is presently comprised of twenty-two member states whose ratification of, or accessions to, the pact occurred as follows: Transjordan, April 10, 1945; Egypt, April 12, 1945; Saudi Arabia, April 16, 1945; Iraq, April 25, 1945; Lebanon, May 16, 1945; Yemen Arab Republic, May 19, 1945; Syria, February 9, 1946; Libya, March 28, 1953; Sudan, January 19, 1956; Morocco, November 1, 1958; Tunisia, November 1, 1958; Kuwait, July 20, 1961; Algeria, August 16, 1962; People's Democratic Republic of Yemen, December 12, 1967; Bahrain, September 11, 1971; Qatar, September 11, 1971; Oman, September 29, 1971; United Arab Emirates, December 6, 1971; Mauritania, November 23, 1973; Somalia, February 14, 1974; Djibouti, September 4, 1977, and Palestine Liberation Organization, September 9, 1976.

2. For an insight into the creation and role of the Political Committee, the work of Arawa Taher Radwan, the Political Committee of the League of Arab States, and its role in joint political action, 1973.

3. Ratifications of, or accessions to, the Treaty occurred as follows: Syria, October 31, 1951; Egypt, November 22, 1951; Jordan, March 31, 1952; Iraq, August 7, 1952; Saudi Arabia, August 19, 1952; Lebanon, December 24, 1952; Yemen Arab Republic, October 11, 1953; Morocco, June 13, 1961; Kuwait, August 12, 1961; Tunisia, September 11, 1964; Algeria, September 11, 1964; Sudan, September 11, 1964; Libya, September 11, 1964; Bahrain, November 14, 1971; Qatar, November 14, 1971; and the People's Democratic Republic of Yemen, November 23, 1971.

Chapter 4

Multilateral Diplomacy in the Arab-Israeli Conflict

Abba Eban

THE RECORD

> The great things remaining to be done can only be done with the whole world
> as stage and in the light of the universal interests of mankind.

In these resounding words, Woodrow Wilson set out the principle of multilateralism as a device for the solution of conflicts. The word "stage" is significant. It draws attention to the dramatic and histrionic character of the multilateral process. Traditional diplomacy had been marked by reticence and
secrecy; henceforward, everything was to be in the open. But Wilson's emphasis was equal on the "universal interests of mankind." The tradition, according to which conflicts were the responsibility of those directly concerned,
was to yield to a new ideology of universal participation. Every dispute was
everybody's business.

It was not until the aftermath of World War II that this approach to
conflict-resolution became widely used. In the period between the world wars,
the role of the League of Nations had been more modest than the founders
of the international organization had dreamed or hoped for. The relatively
narrow composition of the league; the absence, at various times, of major
powers such as Germany, the Soviet Union, and above all, the United States;
and the preference of most world leaders for traditional diplomacy prevented
the league from implementing the idea of "the whole world as stage." Nothing
in previous history can compare with the vast proliferation of international
agencies and of multinational assemblies in the past three and a half decades.
Some governments send delegations to as many as seven thousand meetings
and conferences each year, most of which have a diplomatic character in that
they affect the relations between states.

The potentialities and limitations of the multilateral process can well be
studied in depth through the treatment of the Arab-Israeli conflict by inter-

national agencies. No other theme has come before so wide a range of tribunals, forums, and institutions. It may well be the only conflict that in one way or the other has found expression in every important international organ.

The story begins on February 14, 1947, with the decision of the United Kingdom to submit the "Palestine Question" to discussion by the UN General Assembly. This was a period in which Britain was divesting itself of responsibility for governing India and defending Greece and Turkey. Since the British position in Palestine was grounded in a League of Nations mandate, it was natural to use the successor organization as the arena for debate about the future course of Palestine.

The problem has not left that arena for a single day ever since February 14, 1947. In April 1947, the General Assembly appointed an eleven-member committee, formed by representatives of medium-sized states to recommend a policy for the mandatory power. This committee, the UN Special Committee on Palestine (UNSCOP), recommended partition in its majority report. In a memorable and tense session of the General Assembly in November 1947, a resolution was adopted calling for the partition of Palestine into a Jewish and an Arab state. This resolution was followed by the appointment of a five-power Partition Committee to oversee implementation. In April–May 1948, the General Assembly was debating a proposal by the United States to postpone partition in favor of a plan for international trusteeship. This proposal did not win approval, whereupon, the General Assembly nominated a mediator, Count Folke Bernadotte, who worked until his assassination in Jerusalem in September 1948. In December 1948, after the proposals of the late Count Bernadotte had failed to win acceptance, the General Assembly named the United States, France, and Turkey to form the Palestine Conciliation Commission (PCC) with a mandate to make proposals for the establishment of peace and a solution to the Arab refugee problem. In May 1949, the General Assembly endorsed a resolution of the Security Council, made two months previously, to admit Israel as a member of the United Nations.

In the meantime, the Security Council had played an active role against a background of war and intermittent violence. It called for cease-fires in May and June 1948, which were temporarily implemented. On July 15, 1948, the Security Council "ordered" a cease-fire in the terms of Chapter VII of the charter in a successful attempt to bring about Arab compliance with a cease-fire. In November 1948, the Security Council called for the development of the cease-fire into armistice agreements. Between January and August 1949, armistice agreements were successfully negotiated and concluded between Israel, Egypt, Jordan, Lebanon, and Syria. The Security Council was represented in these negotiations by Ralph J. Bunche, the acting mediator who succeeded Count Bernadotte. Shortly after the conclusion of the armistice between Israel and Egypt in January 1949, the Security Council approved Israel's application for UN membership. Under the armistice agreements, mixed armistice commissions (MACs) were established with UN chairmanship to consider complaints of violation.

The armistice agreements, the admission of Israel to UN membership, and the pursuit of the work of the PCC helped to create relative stability in the early fifties. General Assembly debates became perfunctory, with the exception of a reaffirmation in December 1949 of the plan for the internationalization of Jerusalem, which was ignored by Jordan and Israel. Yet there was never a period of uninterrupted tranquility, and the Security Council became the active arena for consideration of the Arab-Israeli relationship. In September 1951, it adopted a decision, destined to have strong effects, in support of Israel's appeal for an end to Egyptian blockade practices in the Suez Canal. At this time, however, the effectiveness of the Security Council was reduced by the habit of the Soviet Union to veto majority resolutions. This prevented the Security Council from proposing a compromise to enable the Jordan waters to be utilized by Israel, Syria, and Jordan. In what turned out to be a symptomatic indication of UN decline, this problem was passed on to the United States for unilateral mediation. Since then it has become a general rule that detailed and complex issues are fitted more for traditional diplomacy than for UN solutions.

But the United Nations did not give up easily. One of the features of the multilateralism is tenacity; a problem once inscribed on the agenda of a UN body seldom leaves that agenda. Annual discussions in the General Assembly took place with occasional Security Council debates on individual outbreaks of violence. The Arab states kept up their pressure on Israel through the infiltration of small groups of fedayeen who carried out attacks on civilian targets in Israel. Israel responded by retaliation or hot pursuit. In all cases, the previous border was restored, so that the paradoxical effect was to strengthen the image of the armistice lines as permanent frontiers. The lengthy debates seldom produced anything but the reiteration of previous resolutions — In December 1952, a resolution calling on Israel and the Arab states to "negotiate" peace agreements nearly won a two-thirds majority in the General Assembly but was thwarted by Soviet opposition. The UN role could be described fairly as a holding action designed to avoid explosion rather than to promote a settlement.

Events outside the UN brought about a dramatic change in 1956. Israel was driven to distraction by a sense of vulnerability as the Arab states, especially Egypt, increased their offensive power through the purchase of Soviet arms, while the western powers reinforced Jordan and Iraq. France and Britain were in conflict with Nasser's policy of Egyptian hegemony in the Arab and Muslim worlds. When the United States refused to finance the Aswân Dam, Nasser responded by nationalizing the Suez Canal, which Britain and France had a traditional power of control in. In October 1956, the armies of Britain, France, and Israel marched against Egypt. The Security Council was deadlocked, this time by a British and French veto of a call for withdrawal. The General Assembly came into special session under the Uniting for Peace Resolution. Simultaneously, a parallel UN debate was being held, with no visible result, on the subject of the Soviet action against Hungary. In the Middle East, there was a different story. As a result of pressures and discussions by the United States outside the UN, Britain and France were ready to negotiate a cease fire, and a few weeks later, Israel was satisfied with United States assurances of free navigation for Israel in the Straits of Tiran and of security from attack in the Gaza Strip. The result was the acceptance of the United Nations Emergency Force (UNEF), an international peace force, in the Sinai and Gaza. The speed with which Secretary-General Hammarskjöld improvised this force was regarded as a success for the United Nations. UNEF marked the first stage in the evolution of the UN's "peace-keeping" role.

For eleven years, from 1956 to 1967, the presence of UNEF symbolized the acceptance of a basic stability, disturbed but never destroyed by occasional outbursts across the armistice lines. The presence of UNEF was so vividly associated with the idea of stability that Egypt's demand for the removal of the force from the Sinai and Gaza, in May 1967, was bound to be regarded as an indication that war was imminent. Nor did President Nasser's rhetoric leave much doubt that this was his intention. The blockade of the Straits of Tiran, announced by Egypt on May 22, 1967, confirmed this prediction.

The reaction of the Security Council in May 1967 marked the lowest point in the UN record as a stabilizing factor in the Middle East. Indeed, most historians would agree that the UN itself has never recovered from the spectacle of impotence revealed in those tense days. Whatever the juridical compulsions were, the fact of UNEF's docile retirement was bound to weaken the credibility of the UN's peacekeeping function. The knowledge that war would follow the withdrawal did not prevent the withdrawal from taking place by a decision of Secretary-General Thant. The Security Council was not even capable of adopting a resolution calling for abstention from belligerency and for a blockade. It watched helplessly while the preparations for war went forward; indeed some members even expressed doubt whether the council should consider the matter at all. The mediation for ending the 1967 conflict went forward in communications between the Great Powers during the summer. The General Assembly concluded a dramatic session without a substantive resolution in early July. In November 1967, however, the Security Council recaptured some prestige for the UN by its unanimously adopted Resolution 242 setting out the principles for the establishment of peace and the withdrawal of Israeli forces to secure and recognized boundaries.

The Security Council's emissary, Ambassador Gunnar Jarring, had no success in promoting an agreed-upon interpretation of Resolution 242, and when the Yom Kippur war broke out in October 1973, no change had taken place either in the territorial configuration, or in the relations, between the Arab states and Israel. For several crucial days, the Security Council declined to negotiate a cease-fire for the simple but depressing reason that the continuation of the war was always in the military interest of whatever party was doing well on the battlefield. When the United States and the Soviet Union were ready to agree to a cease-fire at the positions reached by the armies, the text was brought for notarization to the Security Council. It would be naively inaccurate to say that the Security Council "initiated" or formulated the resolution. At the same time, the Security Council obediently ratified a text worked out in Moscow between the United States and the Soviet Union, calling for a negotiated peace. This resolution (338) became the juridical basis for the convening of a peace conference in Geneva, in which the secretary-general of the United Nations had a ceremonial and symbolic role. But once the conference had come into session, its work branched out into disengagement agreements, interim accords, and a treaty negotiation between Egypt and Israel. All these procedures were conducted outside the United Nations through the mediation of the United States, represented first by Secretary of State Henry A. Kissinger and, thereafter, by President Jimmy Carter.

Parallel with these interventions in the issues of security, the United Nations involved itself in new developments in the context of the Palestinian-Arab problem. In 1974 it admitted the Palestine Liberation Organization (PLO) leader, Yasir Arafat, to the General Assembly rostrum for a riotous and deferential welcome. Subsequently, in a new departure for international organizations, it treated the PLO as a member government and accepted its militant views at the expense of its previous UN support of Israel's statehood. General Assembly resolutions against Israel were marked by a virulence and rancor unparalleled in international literature; but perhaps for that very reason, these texts had little effect or resonance. The PLO, however, could feel that its ambition to be recognized in the Arab world as the authentic representative of Palestinian nationalism was powerfully advanced by its privileged status within the UN system.

THE RESULTS

Any attempt to summarize the record of multilateral agencies in the Arab-Israeli conflict must take account of the time factor. The UN was most active and effective in the dispute during its first five years when it was celebrating its ascendancy in other sectors of the international system, as well. For a time it seemed that the UN would be the central arena for the elucidation and solution of international disputes. From the early fifties onward, it lost this primacy under the impact of the Korean war which had been preceded by the establishment of NATO and the Warsaw Pact and other developments such as the Marshall Plan and the beginnings of the European unity movement, which stressed the marginal character of the UN compared with the growing weight and importance of extra–UN movements and tendencies. But during its years of maximal preoccupation, the multilateral system had left a deep impress on this problem. The UN could not always control events on the ground, but its determination of status, as in the admission of Israel and its attitude to the PLO, sketched the parameters within which the conflict had been enacted. Once Israel was admitted to membership, however, the principle of sovereignty worked in favor of processes that diminished the UN role. When the discussions in the General Assembly had begun in 1947, the UN enjoyed an unusual advantage: the territory under discussion was of undetermined status, and the history of the League of Nations system made it seem natural for the UN to exercise jurisdiction. Before the partition resolution of November 29, 1947, all parties accepted the UN as the qualified forum for the discussion of the Palestinian problem, and even after being disappointed by that resolution, the Arab states continued to have recourse to UN forums.

When it came to concrete and detailed diplomacy beond the general determination of principle, the multilateral method has been less effective. In general, Middle Eastern wars have taken their military course irrespective of the preventive or restraining efforts of the Security Council. It was only when the military situation made a cease-fire congenial to both or all parties that it was adopted. Thus, it would not be accurate to say that the Security Council "achieved" a cease-fire. It is also true, however, that even the mutual desire of the belligerents to have a formal cease-fire might not have come to effective expression without the machinery and recognized authority of the UN in these matters.

The same is true of the peacekeeping groups (UNTSO, UNEF, UNDOF, UNIFIL, etc.). These agencies could not compel any state to do what it did not want to do or prevent any of them from doing what it was determined to do, so that the concept of "force" expressed in these titles is misleading and pretentious. But it remains true that when the belligerents desired to formalize a measure of stability and mutual restraint, the availability of suitable UN symbols and myths helped them to create periods and areas of restraints in what would otherwise have been an uncontrolled conflict. On the opposite side of the coin, we must inscribe the tendency of UN forces to encourage inertia. When a conflict, even if unresolved, ceases to be explosive and intolerable, there is a diminished incentive to tackle the issues involved and to find a permanent solution. The international organizations thus become accomplices in the prolongation of temporary arrangements that, by the nature of things, become weakened with the passage of time. The UN is more effective as a restraining barrier than as a bridge to understanding. It is more equipped to separate adversaries than to bring them together in meaningful conciliation.

The same tendency to freeze situations amidst growing antagonism comes to light in the multilateral approach to political solutions. After the establishment of Israel, the UN became a spectator or commentator of the conflict rather than an active mediating agency. When consensus could be achieved by the national diplomacy of member states, such as the "arrangements, hopes and expectations" that ended the Suez-Sinai campaigns in 1956–57, or in the case of Security Council Resolution 242 (after the 1967 war) and Resolution 338 (after the 1973 war), it was possible to notarize and legitimize the agreements in UN terms. But these achievements owed much more to private negotiation than to public UN debate; indeed, it could be proved that the acrimonies of the public exchanges often clouded and impeded the efforts to reach consensus. In the Arab-Israeli conflict, the cease-fires, armistices, and agreements on principles of negotiation were possible only when American-Soviet agreement converged with a measure of Arab-Israeli adjustment, usually inspired by a military stalemate or an incentive to suspend the military phase of the dispute. The entire history proves that multilateral debate is not a substitute for diplomacy.

Unfortunately, the indictment of the technique of public debate goes even further. By its very nature, it tempts the parties to commit themselves to rigid positions designed to win domestic applause. Seated on a stage, with the whole world as an audience, the parties in conflict speak not to each other but to the outside world, each seeking condemnation of its adversary's positions and character. The atmosphere is polemical, not conciliatory. Compromise becomes difficult when it entails the frank abandonment of positions that were defended as immutable only a short while before. In his final report, the late Dag Hammarskjöld warned against the recourse to public debate with the resultant tendency to integrate the appeal to public opinion into the negotiating process. His words went unheeded. In the ensuing years the atmosphere has become even worse. The tone and style of UN debates, especially on the Middle Eastern conflict, represent a profound degradation of the diplomatic tradition. Invectives and insults are exchanged in a way quite unknown in traditional diplomacy, even amongst implacable opponents. It is conventional wisdom to assert that speech is better than war, yet much of the speech in UN forums comes not as an alternative to making war but as an alternative to making peace. States whose representatives have been describing each other in demonological terms in public debates are more easily persuaded to have recourse to arms than are states whose tone and level of discourse obey the norms of civility and human solidarity.

The consciousness that every public debate constitutes a step backward from the prospect of peace afflicts multilateral diplomacy with an air of paradox. In this particular context, the paradox found unbearably sharp expression in the debate on the Egyptian-Israeli peace treaty. There have been few similar victories in our generation for the principle of international conciliation. Two nations bearing ancient historic names, whose encounters in history have been memorable for mankind, suddenly came together on terms totally different from anything that they had known in the past. Decades of hostility, violence, rancor, and contempt were transcended in an effort to lay the foundation of a new regional harmony. The fact that this peace settlement was not comprehensive does not alter the fact that a large sector of conflict was neutralized from the prospect of imminent war and that the ideology of irreconcilable antagonism was reversed for the first time. The response of the General Assembly was to "condemn" the peace treaty. Franz Kafka and George Orwell in the moments of their gloomiest imagination could not have described a peace organization condemning a peace treaty ending thirty years of war between sovereign states. This episode draws attention to the danger of intellectual and emotional inertia. A multilateral organization can become so accustomed to a conflict that it subconsciously regrets having to part with it.

In this case, the deformation of a peace forum was aided by the disproportionate preoccupation of the UN with a conflict that, despite its undoubted virulence, is not by any means the greatest source of threat to international stability. The fact that the UN was silent on the death of tens of thousands in Vietnam and Cambodia, in the Iraqi-Iranian war, in the repression of nationalist revolts in Czechoslovakia and Hungary, and in the massacre of thousands of Africans by brutal regimes in Uganda and the Central African Republic, lent an unreal air to solemn debates on individual incidents affecting very few people in the Israeli-Palestinian context. When moralization becomes selective, it loses its essential moral quality. The failure of multilateral diplomacy to contribute even to the solution of problems with a diplomatic and humanitarian character, such as the capture and massacre of Israeli athletes at the Olympic Games and the torment of American diplomats held in captivity in Tehran, has also lessened public respect for UN processes. Even in the Middle East, multilateralism has had few successes in the past quarter of a century, and its preoccupation has not embraced all the factors of turbulence in the region as a whole.

The devotees of international organization have traditionally praised two conflict-resolution principles: publicity ("open covenants openly arrived at") and universal participation ("since war is everybody's tragedy, peace is everybody's business"). We have seen that publicity is more likely to impede than to promote the compromises and concessions necessary for international agreements. The notion of universal participation also emerges as a fallacy. The idea that more than 150 states have an equal interest in the solution of a dispute is not well-founded. States that have no real interest or emotional commitment in a dispute and whose welfare and destiny are totally unaffected by what is decided or proposed can band together to outvote those whose very survival is at stake. There is a great deal to be said for compact negotiation between directly interested parties, that is to say, those who would gain from successful conciliation and suffer if something went wrong.

Another defect of universalism is the tendency toward irrelevance. In a parliamentary environment there is always a temptation to fix positions in one dispute by reference to another. If Turkey, Greece, and Cyprus are involved in a UN debate on the Cypriot problem, they will be tempted to seek votes in the Arab bloc by committing themselves to a certain position in the Arab-Israeli dispute. If there is an African controversy, the African states will fix their positions in non-African conflicts by considerations of their voting prospects in other blocs. If a statesman aspires to election as president of the General Assembly, his delegation will show restraint and solicitude in speech and voting without any specific relevance to the matter at issue. Universal participation involves a dispersion of intellectual effort instead of concentration on one specific element of a dispute.

Thus, the treatment of the Arab-Israeli dispute in multilateral forums illustrates many of the predicaments that afflict multilateralism in general. The United Nations has never made a firm decision about its central guiding principle. The choice is between the diplomatic and the parliamentary principle. The diplomatic principle tells me that I need my adversary's agreement. The parliamentary principle tells me that I do not need his agreement: I can seek to humiliate and vanquish him by mobilizing a majority against him. The tone and atmosphere are quite different in the two cases. It is consensual in the one and adversarial in the other. It is almost possible to assert them both. In the test of action, multilateralist bodies have opted for the parliamentary principle. They have thus inherited the worst of both worlds; they have obtained the contentiousness of parliaments without their power of legislative decision. The result is disquieting: The UN is not so much an instrument for solving conflicts as an arena for waging them.

There is nothing inherently irremediable in these conditions. The Charter of the UN does not ordain exclusive reliance on techniques of public debate culminating in division between majorities and minorities. Emphasis on compact mediating techniques is theoretically available. But a recognition of past weaknesses is the first condition of future reform. Before it addresses itself to other issues, the UN should take a closer look at itself.

Editor's Comments on Regional Negotiations

A region raises the presumption of special closeness among the states concerned, a presumption of neighborliness. To some extent this is true and explains the emergence of regional organizations such as the OAS, ASEAN, the OAU and the Arab League. However, the presumption does not always correspond with the facts. Within some regions, sharp rivalries have existed, and in the Middle East region there is the major Arab-Israeli dispute. Nevertheless, negotiations within the Organization of American States and within the Arab League, which are the subjects of two of the chapters in this section, reflect the factor of special closeness. The following points related to the processes of mediation and negotiation emerge from the chapters on regional negotiations:

1. Even more so than in the case of the UN Security Council, the activities and procedures of the OAS and the Arab League stress conciliation, good offices, mediation, and arbitration. But to some extent, the difference is superficial rather than substantive. In the UN system, these methods of dispute settlement are to be utilized before states come to the Security Council (Article 33 of the UN Charter). In substance, the dispute settlement activities of the regional organizations are not very different from the Security Council's activities under Chapter VI of the UN Charter.
2. As in the case of the Security Council, the effective work of the regional organizations is performed at a high level of participation signifying closeness to the power centers of the member states.
3. When a state in a region is excluded from participation in the regional organization of that region, then disputes involving that state and others in the region have to find other forums of settlement. This is why the Arab-Israeli dispute has gone into other channels of consideration, primarily the UN but also Camp David and the (projected) Geneva conferences.
4. The chapter on the Arab-Israeli conflict points out that open, multilateral debate in the UN has failed to bring the parties together in meaningful conciliation and has, on the other hand, become a vehicle for invectives and a war of words totally unconducive to peaceful settlement. Hence, the need has arisen for non–UN channels of settlement.

PART 3

INTER-REGIONAL NEGOTIATIONS

Chapter 5

Commonwealth Cross Sections: Prenegotiation to Minimize Conflict and to Develop Cooperation

Arnold Smith

The Commonwealth of Nations has proved to be a remarkably useful instrument for developing understanding — and for working out practical multilateral understandings in a wide range of fields — among its member nations. Since these number about one quarter of the world's sovereign states, with about a quarter of the world's population, and since they transcend the differences of race, geographic region, and level of economic development that could become humanity's lines of political cleavage and alienation, it is an important instrument.

The value of the Commonwealth as a practical agency for international consultation, multilateral negotiations, and occasionally mediation, as well as for functional cooperation in various fields, derives above all from the unique nature of its membership and the relative informality and intimacy of its procedures.

Most international organizations — other than highly specialized bodies such as the Organization of Petroleum Exporting Countries (OPEC) — are in principle either universal in membership, such as the United Nations and its family of specialized agencies, or regional, such as the Organization of African Unity (OAU), the OAS, and the European Economic Community (EEC). While universal ones are essential, albeit formal and not very intimate, smaller bodies are often more effective.

For example, the problem of a minority racist regime in Southern Rhodesia was on the agenda of the UN, the OAU, and the Commonwealth from November 1965 (when Ian Smith obligingly made his government illegal internationally by his unilateral declaration of independence and thus facilitated international action against his regime) until it was replaced by Robert Mugabe's democratically elected government of independent Zimbabwe in 1980.

The role of the freedom fighters of the African nationalist parties was crucial in bringing about this transition, especially after 1976. Multilateral negotiations, and a good bit of mediation to help achieve agreements, were also essential at various stages: first, in obviating sell-out deals between Britain and Ian Smith that would have entailed some significant recognitions of the racist regime; and eventually, in getting acceptance by all the parties concerned to a cease-fire, to procedures for working out a new and democratic constitution, to a peaceful integration of the warring forces, and to democratic elections. It was the Commonwealth that provided the forum for these negotiations, most of the mediation, and the small but effective multinational teams of military observers for the cease-fire and of civilian observers for the elections.[1]

Most regional bodies have the advantages, but also the limitations, of relative homogeneity: a similarity racially and often in stages of economic development—most regions are rather rich, like the EEC, or not, like the OAU.

Heterogeneity, on the contrary, is one of the significant features of the Commonwealth of Nations. Its forty-seven members are spread throughout all continents—some are large countries such as India and Nigeria; some are small such as the Gambia, Barbados, or Tonga (in the Pacific, on the date line "where time begins"). There are rich countries such as Canada, Australia, and Britain; and many very poor ones: a prominent "NIC" (newly industrialized country) such as the city-state of Singapore; a prominent member of OPEC (Nigeria); and many oil importers. Members are of virtually every racial group and represent the world's major religions. There are no superpowers and no totalitarian regimes; but in other respects, the Commonwealth is a fairly representative cross section of mankind and of the traditions, interests, and problems of mankind.

This remarkable heterogeneity is balanced by a number of shared facilities, habits, working methods and traditions that, while they do not make understanding or agreement among nations easy, unquestionably do make them less difficult to achieve. Functional cooperation becomes more economical and more effective than would otherwise be possible on such an international scale.

One shared element is the ability of participants at Commonwealth meetings, governmental or nongovernmental, to feel at home with English as the common working language, though it is not the mother tongue of the great majority. Other common factors are widespread similarities in habits of administration, in the organization and ethics of most liberal professions, and in many of the principles and methods of education, especially at the university level. Though some parts of the Commonwealth (e.g., Scotland, Sri Lanka, Quebec) use civil law rather than the more widespread common law, the latter's implied respect for precedent and custom, and the tendency toward pragmatism and ad hoc decisions rather than the application of predetermined general rules, are typical of Commonwealth approaches to issues.

There are significant elements of a shared history or somewhat analogous aspects of individual history. And there are inherited networks of contacts and habits, developed in the Commonwealth, of frank informal consultation and cooperation.

The way in which the Commonwealth came into being and its procedures differ from those of most international bodies. Unlike the United Nations, with its specialized agencies, and most regional organizations, the Commonwealth was not created by a multilateral treaty. It has no written constitution – though its heads of government, in 1964, unanimously adopted a Declaration of Racial Equality, which I had drafted, and in 1971, a Declaration of Commonwealth Principles based on a draft proposed by President Kaunda. The Commonwealth is a product not of social engineering but rather of what the philosopher Henri-Louis Bergson called creative evolution. Its creators have behaved more like gardeners trying to guide living forces than like architects. To explain how the Commonwealth works, it is necessary to give a brief outline of its history.

Most Commonwealth members were once British colonies or protectorates, but not all – Western Samoa was once a New Zealand mandate and trust territory, New Guinea a mandated territory of Australia. Namibia, which Commonwealth heads of government have declared that they will welcome into Commonwealth membership should the government of an independent, democratic Namibia so desire, was a mandated and now revoked trust territory of South Africa.

The British built up an empire during the seventeenth, eighteenth, and nineteenth centuries, partly by settlement and partly by conquest. Karl Marx claimed that no "class" ever voluntarily gives up power over others and the American Revolution might seem to illustrate this thesis. But the British gradually absorbed its lesson that it is not possible, nor even desirable, for a free people indefinitely to maintain control over another people determined to obtain independence. Canada pioneered a new road to national freedom after a bit of fighting (mainly in 1837), some imprisonments, but more demonstrating and pressing and negotiating, which led to independence by agreement with Britain in 1867. This road has since been followed by hundreds of millions of people in Asia, Africa, the Caribbean, the Mediterranean, and the Pacific.

Those who think, however, that the Commonwealth is a sort of ghost of the British Empire have not begun to grasp its nature. Many lands once ruled by Britain are not members of the Commonwealth, for example, Egypt, Palestine, Jordan, Iraq, the Sudan, Burma, and Aden. They did not apply. Ireland and more recently (West) Pakistan have withdrawn.

Those countries that joined the Commonwealth upon obtaining independence, did so because their leaders decided that there would be value in membership in the association, both in what they could get out of it in the way of trade, aid, and other opportunities for cooperation and contacts, and in what they could put into it, using it as one of the instruments to influence the thinking and actions of others and thus help shape the future of our planet.

Thus, the Commonwealth is largely the creation of leaders of successful liberation movements, who saw value in having it both ways, as it were. Having obtained freedom for their peoples, they wished to retain and develop an association, on the new basis of sovereign equality, both with the former administering power and with the other members of the group.

I occasionally point out that it was Canada that originally invented the Commonwealth. Our first prime minister, Sir John A. Macdonald, had good, hard-headed, forward-looking Canadian reasons for proposing it when we negotiated independence from Britain in 1867. Canadians wanted to make their own decisions just as their American neighbors did; but Macdonald and his colleagues did not wish to turn their backs on Europe as the Americans had done on George Washington's advice at the time of the revolution. In 1867, the Americans had just had a civil war; they had not demobilized entirely, and many of them talked of the "manifest destiny" to liberate the whole of North America to their particular version of freedom, a good version but not the only one and not ours. A current slogan among some Americans was "fifty-four-forty or fight," a reference to a parallel of latitude up toward the Arctic Circle. So having rid itself of the subservience to the Empire, Macdonald saw the value in retaining an association in a new form, based on sovereign equality, as a two-way channel of influence that might prove useful for trade and other purposes. An explicit defense agreement was not part of the Commonwealth concept even in those days, but there was an implied recognition of a community of interest and the Commonwealth link was a countervailing element for Canada as a North American country.

It was only after the end of World War II that Commonwealth membership expanded to include governments representing people of the various races of our planet. Until then, its member governments generally represented peoples who were white and relatively affluent. But already the consultations were wide ranging and served to broaden horizons remarkably.

Two examples will suffice. The first relates to the two world wars. (Commonwealth membership did not involve any automatic military commitments, and Ireland decided to remain neutral throughout World War II, which Canada entered by a decision of its parliament a week after Britain.) Canada recognized that a mortal threat to democracy in Western Europe implied also a vital threat to democracy in North America, and it therefore declared war in 1914 and 1939, fighting to defend its freedom with its allies and on territory well outside its own. If Canada's appreciation of a threat to North America was accurate, it obviously applied just as much to its American neighbors, yet it took them two and a half years on each occasion to come around to sharing the Canadian assessment of a common interest.

My second example relates to decolonization – a not less vital stage in world politics. Commonwealth experience helped teach the British the key lesson that friendly and constructive relationships with peoples who had been governed by British imperial power are possible on the basis of sovereign equality. Hence the peoples in what had been the British Empire in Asia, Africa, and elsewhere, in their struggles for independence, did not have to fight all-out wars, as the Vietnamese did against France until 1954 and the Algerians until 1962, or the people of Mozambique and Angola did against Portugal until the Portuguese revolution of 1974.

There were important negotiations as well as consultations in the pre-World War II "Old Commonwealth" which I have sometimes called the "rich man's white man's club." An example is the Ottawa meeting of Commonwealth leaders in 1932 that negotiated a system of Commonwealth and Imperial preferences, in part as a reaction to the move toward protectionism illustrated by the American Smoot-Hawley Tariff of 1930. This preference system played a significant role in world trade until the 1970s.

But the "Old Commonwealth" was, as such, peripheral to the gravest issues of the time in world politics, whereas the modern multiracial Commonwealth is central to them because both its range of membership and the major issues are very different. Until the early 1940s, the most dangerous problems on the world's political agenda were relations between the nation-states of Europe, which were so mishandled that they led to two world wars in our century. On both occasions the Commonwealth helped defend democracy by fighting to clear up the mess; but it was not central to the prewar policies that caused, and could have prevented, the mess. From 1945 until about 1962, the greatest danger was confrontation between the Soviet Union and Western democracies. This danger remains important.

But as technological advance makes our world ever more interdependent and increases men's capacity to help or harm each other, it seems clear that the range of problems summed up in the catch phrase "North-South relations," problems of development and equity of opportunity among peoples of the various races and regions of our planet, are the most difficult – and unless adequately handled could prove the most dangerous – problems of world politics. The Commonwealth today is central to those problems and has demonstrated that it can contribute significantly to understanding and tackling them.

If Canada played a pioneering role in the evolution of the "Old Commonwealth," Indian leadership played a key role in pioneering the development of the new multiracial Commonwealth. Jawaharlal Nehru emphasized the value of an association that brought together for frank discussion, but without binding commitments, leaders from various parts of the earth, providing, as he put it, "a touch of healing for a troubled world." And he remarked that Mahatma Gandhi "taught us a technique of action that was peaceful; yet it was effective and yielded results that led us not only to freedom but to friend ship with those with whom we were, till yesterday, in conflict." Shortly after achieving independence in 1947, India decided to become a republic; Nehru's desire that India remain a Commonwealth member precipitated a useful clari- fication of thought on the whole question of structure. The Statute of West- minster two decades before (which itself changed nothing but made explicit the preexisting quality of status of the members) and the neutrality of George VI as King of Ireland in World War II, had long since made it clear that the Commonwealth was not a bloc and that membership was not in any sense a derogation from sovereignty but an optional additional attribute of it — as a great New Zealander once put it, "not independence minus but independence plus." So a sensible way was found of meeting Nehru's request, and of course, it has proved to be not the beginning of disintegration but a condition of growth.

There are now over twenty-five republics among the membership, nearly twenty countries sharing Elizabeth II as head of state in her distinct capacity as queen of each of them, and four members headed by a separate hereditary or elected monarch. All recognize Queen Elizabeth II as the symbol of the free association of sovereign countries and, as such, head of the Common- wealth. Her role in making the Commonwealth links better appreciated and, through her extensive travels among countries and the media coverage they inevitably attract, in making its peoples better known to each other has been invaluable. And on occasion, such as her timely visits to some African coun- tries and then to Lusaka on the occasion of the 1979 heads of government meeting that dealt so successfully with the Rhodesian crisis, the relaxation of tensions and dissipation of suspicions between various parties that she did so much to bring about have been major political assets.

The entry into the Commonwealth of hundreds of millions of Asians, led by Nehru, Jinnah, and Senanayake of Ceylon, led naturally to a broadening and deepening of the scope of consultations and cooperative actions. Con- cern about development, and the establishment in 1950 of the Colombo Plan to mobilize and coordinate programs involving significant amounts of capital and technical assistance for Southeast Asia, was one example — which at the time involved far-reaching precedents. Another example was the beginning, that same year, of a series of annual meetings of Commonwealth ministers of finance; but more about these later. A third was a discussion among gov- ernments, and a fillip to increasing discussion and pressures among publics in British colonies in Africa, the Caribbean, the Mediterranean and elsewhere, about further decolonizations.

Independence for the peoples of the British Empire in Africa began with

Ghana, which sought and gained Commonwealth membership under Kwame Nkrumah in 1957. During the next seven years, seven more African states became free and all chose membership in the Commonwealth. So did Malta and Cyprus, and the West Indian islands that became independent – beginning with Jamaica, Trinidad and Tobago, and Barbados.

Meanwhile there was a further significant structural development. In 1961, when South Africa applied to remain a Commonwealth member as a republic, its withdrawal was forced by a solemn collective decision on the basic importance of racial equality and nondiscrimination. This decision involved, at the time, a conscious choice by the governments already members about their priorities in world politics and looked forward to the prospect, since realized, of a substantial growth in Commonwealth membership that would lead to a broad multiracial association.

Another essentially structural decision was that taken by heads of government of member countries at their meeting in 1964 to establish a secretariat of the Commonwealth. The suggestion, which took the older members by surprise, was put forward tentatively by Nkrumah and then proposed by Eric Williams of Trinidad, the Tunku Abdul Rahman and Mrs. Bandaranaiake, prime ministers of Malaysia and Ceylon (now Sri Lanka), respectively. It became clear that the newer members especially (sixteen of the then twenty members) wanted to make increasing use of the association and believed that a secretariat could facilitate this in many ways while moving away from the original fact and residual appearance of Anglo centricity to put emphasis on multilateralism and equality. The control of such limited machinery as the Commonwealth needed was removed by general agreement from the hands of any one national government and placed in those of a secretary-general, elected by, and responsible to, all the heads of governments collectively and with direct access to each of them individually. He is supported by a staff recruited from public services and professions in all parts of the Commonwealth. I had the great good fortune to be elected, from among the six nominees, to be the first secretary-general and was reelected for a second five-year term in 1970. I did not run for a third term and was delighted that my friend Shridath Ramphal, then foreign minister of Guyana, was elected to succeed me.

The general desire of member governments to make increased use of the Commonwealth, which prompted, and was facilitated by, the establishment of the secretariat, manifested itself in many additional ways. The value of any political instrument depends on what it is used for (or can be used for); on how effective it is (or can be made); and perhaps, not least, on the by-products of its use. The direct uses of the Commonwealth have, from the beginning, been in the fields of consultation, and in functional cooperation in selected areas in which members agree that such cooperation is feasible and desirable. The chief by-products have been, I think, the broadening of contacts, understanding, horizons, and friendships.

These fundamentals have not changed, but with increased membership, the consultation has, of course, widened; with diversification of membership among different races, continents, and economic stages not only has the subject matter been changed — to more far-reaching and more difficult issues — but the discussions have, in my judgment, deepened. In the past twenty years, the range of fields in which consultation and programs of cooperation take place has expanded dramatically.

Heads of the independent governments of the Commonwealth have been meeting for informal and wide-ranging consultations since the beginning of the century. They used to meet always in London, but the first one that I organized was in Lagos in January 1966. Since then, such meetings, which now normally take place every two years, have been held in Singapore, Ottawa, Kingston (Jamaica), Lusaka, Melbourne, several times in London, and the 1983 meeting was in New Delhi.

In 1966, the Commonwealth ministers of law and attorneys general began meeting regularly with the secretary-general every three years and had a legal division added to the secretariat. Health ministers began similar triennial meetings in 1965, and a medical unit was established. Commonwealth education ministers have met regularly since 1959. They had an executive unit that became a division of the Commonwealth secretariat in 1966 as did that of the Commonwealth Economic Consultative Committee, as the annual meetings of finance ministers of member countries were called. They had begun annual meetings in 1950 in the week before the annual meetings of governors of the International Monetary Fund (IMF) and the World Bank. There are also from time to time, though not on a regular periodic basis, meetings of ministers responsible for other portfolios and fields, such as trade, agriculture and rural development, or youth. And there are many meetings, some periodic and more ad hoc, of officials and experts, and of heads of member countries' law reform commissions, bureaus of statistics, auditors general and chief justices. Most of these meetings have profound effects on action, often resulting in agreements for cooperative programs of some sort.

But it is typical of Commonwealth meetings at most levels that the participants do not think of them essentially as occasions for negotiations but rather for consultations and exchanges of views. Methods of procedure at most intergovernmental Commonwealth meetings are very different from those used at meetings of the United Nations and its specialized agencies — or, indeed, at those of most of the great regional associations. They therefore merit some attention. There are no written rules of procedure, but there are conventions. Meetings are not open to the press; though of course, heads of government often give individual press conferences, and the secretary-general or his representative does so regularly. There is not a podium from which one representative speaks to the others. On the contrary, the practice is that all heads of government, or ministers of law (or whatever), sit around a table in a relatively small "committee room," with the secretary-general at the right of the Chairperson who is the minister of the host country and with only a few advisers (normally one or two) sitting behind them. They speak sitting as at a cabinet meeting, which was the model for Commonwealth meetings.

It is simply not proper to read a speech, treating the other representatives as a captive audience — as secretary-general I used to make it a practice to have this point understood by any heads of government or ministers participating for the first time. What with an election here or a coup there, it is normal to have one or two new members, and they welcomed the advice and usually got fairly quickly into the spirit of informality and first-name basis. I encouraged occasional questions and interjections, as did most chairpeople.

Sometimes, on particularly difficult or sensitive and potentially contentious issues, the heads of government and the secretary-general will meet alone for a few hours or a couple of days, with no advisers or recorders. On occasion only a small group of the seven or eight heads of government most directly concerned with the particular question meet with the secretary-general.

One instance of the former was the restricted meetings of heads and the "SG" (as the secretary-general is often called) under Sir Abubakar Balewa in Lagos in January 1966 on the Rhodesian crisis: it was agreed to impose sanctions and establish a standing committee of all members to supervise the situation. Another example is the two days of restricted meetings under Lee Kuan Yew in Singapore in 1971 on the issue of Britain's plan to make large-scale sales of arms to South Africa: As a result of these private meetings, it was tacitly agreed to drop the plan and brush the issue under the table. Though, in fact, Heath did sell a couple of helicopters to save face, his government was at last made to see that it would be strategic lunacy, as a number of us had been explaining to them, to try to counter a Soviet naval buildup in the Indian Ocean and the South Atlantic by a policy of military cooperation with South Africa that would alienate every other government and people who lived around the shores of those two oceans.

An important instance of the smaller meeting was that of the so-called "contact group" of eight that met during the weekend retreat during the 1979 meeting of the heads of government in Lusaka. The eight were Kaunda, the chairman and host; and Nyerere; Mrs. Thatcher and Lord Carrington; Malcolm Fraser of Australia; Michael Manley of Jamaica; the Nigerian representative, Adefope; and of course, the SG, "Sonny" Ramphal. They worked out the agreement that led to the constitutional conference in Lancaster House, the cease-fire, elections on the basis of one-person-one-vote, Commonwealth supervisory teams (both military and civilian), and independence based on majority rule for Zimbabwe. This agreement was unanimously approved a few hours later, during a barbecue supper that briefly turned into an "executive session" of all the heads and was made public in a special nine paragraph communiqué released that evening.[2]

The Commonwealth tradition of closed meetings (not open to the press) — though there are invariably many hundreds of media correspondents accredited to the biennial Commonwealth summit meetings — has, among other advantages, those of informality, of opportunities for a high degree of frankness, and, above all, it seems to me, of increased flexibility. It is much easier to compromise or change one's mind if you have not taken rigid positions on the public record. As Mike Pearson used to say, "nothing is harder for a politician to retreat from than a headline." The meetings of presidents and prime ministers with the secretary-general but no other ministers or advisers carry the opportunities for frankness and flexibility even further and, sometimes, facilitate spontaneous fresh ideas that help solve difficult and potentially con tentious problems.

As Lee Kuan Yew said to the press at the Commonwealth heads of government meeting in Ottawa in 1973:

> At other forums we tend to make set speeches, designed to impress, designed to gather votes. They are not really conducive to understanding the other person's point of view. We horse trade our votes. This is one forum where we can speak frankly and generate least rancour. . . . We have the same backgrounds, use the same terms of reference. We inherited basic institutions and concepts of government and society. We understand each other better than any other groups do. We use the same diction and concepts. It does not mean that we all stay put. We're all evolving and discovering our own personalities. . . . For this generation we have all been brought up in similar institutions with ideas and ideals which make it possible for us to speak with an informality and intimacy which is not possible elsewhere.

The distinction between procedures at Commonwealth meetings and those at the UN General Assembly and major council meetings (or of the annual assemblies of most of the specialized agencies) is significant for a number of other reasons. One is the method of taking decisions, which is not by voting but by "consensus." This can be a great advantage because of its flexibility and relative freedom from irresponsibility and abuse. In the UN General Assembly, UNESCO, and many other specialized agencies, it is theoretically possible to get a two-thirds majority and so carry a resolution, with the support of states representing less than 10% of the population of the world and less than 2% of the world's gross economic production or power. When abused, it can, and has tended to, weaken respect for, and the prospects of implementation of, resolutions. This is not in the best interest of any country.[3]

It is significant that in the vitally important negotiations on law of the sea, and those under way on key aspects of North-South relations and the international economic order in the UN system and outside it, there has been an increasing tendency for governments to agree to rely on the consensus system for decision-making because it is recognized that implementation is more desirable than adversarial propaganda.

In the Commonwealth, I was always careful never to give or allow any formal definition of "consensus." That would entail the loss of some of the desirable flexibility and the creeping in of an element of rigidity that could prove costly. Certainly consensus implies a large and representative majority, including enough to make the decision capable of effective implementation; certainly equal, it does not imply a veto. For example, the proposal to establish a fully multilateral development assistance fund—the Commonwealth Fund for Technical Cooperation (CFTC)—which was decided on by heads of government at their Singapore meeting in 1971, was opposed by Australia, one of the four "developed" member countries that had also taken no part in the Commonwealth Program for Technical Assistance that preceded the CFTC. But it was effectively established. Since contributions to it are voluntary, Australia was able to refrain from participating, but within two years, they became and have since always been a generous and major supporter. Equally, there are certain programs organized or serviced by the Commonwealth secretariat, such as those of the Commonwealth Science Council and the Youth Program, that have separate budgets and to which the great majority of, but not all, the member countries belong.

"Consensus" also avoids the rigidities of weighted voting systems. In effect members recognize tacitly, though without the need to quantify, that different members have differing weights in the need of help from, or in the ability to contribute to, the solution of various problems and programs. Thus, the views of the "front-line states" (Tanzania, Zambia, and Botswana) naturally carried particular weight, and they played a particularly important role in the discussions, over the years, on the problem of Rhodesia and its transition to Zimbabwe. But as Pierre Trudeau pointed out to the press during the Ottawa heads of government meeting (HGM) in 1973: "I think there is what I would almost describe as a beautiful equality. The people who get most attention are those who make the brightest interventions."

As there are no resolutions, as such, in Commonwealth meetings, decisions and conclusions are set out in communiqués, usually, but not always, one for each meeting, though on rare occasions special interim communiqués are issued by a meeting on particularly important decisions. The communiqués usually are written in relatively unponderous and informal language and express consensual views—though, occasionally, they may record that "most members were of the view that . . . but a few [or one sometimes named the member country] believed that. . . . " At times a communiqué may list a range of considerations put forward, without coming to any single conclusion. Commonwealth membership does not, as does that in the UN and many other international bodies, entail firm legal obligations. As Commonwealth finance ministers put it in their communiqué on their meeting in Cyprus in September 1970:

> It was recognised that the exchange of views among Commonwealth members was of great value in increasing understanding. It was recognised that a con-

sensus of views among all members might not always be possible, but where such an exchange of views led to harmonisation of policies or the emergence of a consensus, this would be welcome.

In emphasizing the difference between Commonwealth and UN procedures, I do not intend in any way to denigrate the latter. I have represented Canada at many UN General Assembly sessions and meetings of the Economic and Social Council (ECOSOC) and the Security Council and value them highly. The UN practice of making set speeches to other delegates or aimed over their heads at the press and public back home and, if possible, in other countries, too, is that used also by national parliaments and congresses. It is a necessary part of the molding of public opinion. Agreements are usually worked out "in the corridor." But heads of government, or ministers of foreign affairs or law, finance, education, or health, are naturally not prepared to be audiences for set speeches; they pay ambassadors to be "permanent representatives," while they themselves may attend for a day or two to make a speech and confer privately with a few opposite numbers. Commonwealth meetings, using what I have called the "smoke-filled room technique," do attract presidents and prime ministers, and at their own meetings, ministers of law, health, and so forth, precisely because of the informality of the discussions. It is significant, as Lord Caradon points out in a chapter in this book, that the UN Security Council now tends to have informal closed meetings before its official public meetings on important issues.

Weekend "retreats" (such as that in Lusaka referred to previously) have been traditional in the middle of the seven- or eight-day meetings of heads of government as occasions when presidents and prime ministers and the "SG," accompanied by their wives or husbands but without officials, spend two days together away from the conference. These provide valuable opportunities for the leaders to discuss issues and problems in small groups.

But it is significant that, unlike the common practice at the UN and specialized agencies, caucusing on the basis of race or region is virtually unknown at Commonwealth meetings. I have attended nine HGMs and some dozens of meetings of ministers dealing with various portfolios and have only known one occasion when there was a racial caucus—at the September 1969 HGM in London. There, all but one of the representatives of member countries in Asia, Africa, and the Caribbean met on a few mornings before the full meeting began. The purpose was not to gang up to pressure the white members, as some thought, but to dissuade Mr. Kapwepwe, who was heading the Zambian delegation, from leading his delegation in a walkout that would have created domestic political embarrassment and problems for all or most of the others. Kapwepwe was, I believe, also planning to build up support by a dramatic piece of political posturing to replace his President, Kenneth Kaunda. The caucus proved successful in its purpose. It is significant that one of the Asians avoided the racial gathering. Tunku Abdul Rahman, asked by the press, which was dramatizing as a misunderstanding the unusual procedure, to explain his boycott, quipped that he was "a Malaysian, not a Caucusian."

It is also not the practice to put formal resolutions at Commonwealth meetings, although memoranda of suggestions are sometimes circulated in advance by governments through the secretariat or memoranda by the secretary-general. And, of course, it is common for the secretariat to have background papers prepared and circulated on many of the issues on the agenda or likely to arise. The agenda is normally made up of very broad items – world political situations, social problems, and so on – though there are inevitably exceptions.

Sometimes heads of government will reach definitive agreement of substance after a discussion among themselves – for example, authorizing me, in 1975, to start a technical assistance program for Namibians, as I had requested in a memorandum circulated to them shortly before the meeting, announcing, also, in their communiqué that should the government of an independent Namibia wish Commonwealth membership, they would be welcomed into the association. On other occasions, they will ask that the issue be referred to a special meeting of representative senior officials of member countries. The top civil servants of each member country, usually either the cabinet secretary of the chief head of the office of the prime minister or president, meet for a few days with the secretary-general in the alternate years between the meetings of the heads of government themselves, which these officials also attend. Sometimes they meet separately in parallel under the chair position of one of the deputy secretaries-general to consider and make recommendations on items referred to them by the heads.

On other occasions, heads of government ask the secretary-general to appoint a group of experts, about six to ten, to examine and make recommendations on a subject, particularly one which is not very precise but has far-reaching implications. Various aspects of North-South relations have been prominent among problems examined in this way. It is a sensible practice for the members of such a group to be selected from a representative balance both of regions and of kinds of experience. Since the object is to help shape multilateral governmental agreements and to influence the policies of a number of governments, they are chosen from among persons with significant influence and reputations. These groups, which sometimes have included cabinet ministers and senior officials of individual governments, all however serving entirely in their personal capacities, tend to take decisions by consensus, as do meetings of Commonwealth representatives, and have avoided the adversarial pattern of many UN encounters. Their unanimity has proved influential and heartening in a divided world. Their influence is sometimes much wider than the Commonwealth.

For example, at the Jamaica HGM in May 1975, I was asked to appoint a group of "not more than ten" experts to identify practical measures that could be taken to create "a rational and equitable international economic order"—in effect, to suggest specific content for the increasingly current catch phrase about a "new international economic order" (NIEO). I was asked that their first report be ready within three months to help Commonwealth governments prepare themselves for the Seventh Special Session of the UN General Assembly on the subject later that year. The group, chaired by Alister McIntyre, then secretary-general of the Caribbean community, included the Tanzanian minister of finance, Amir Jamal, and several senior officials as well as a couple of university men. Their first report was formally presented to the UN special assembly and contributed significantly to the wide consensus achieved there. A somewhat similar group, chaired by Lord (Jock) Campbell of Eskan, was set up by my successor at the request of the 1977 IIGM and made practical proposals for the establishment of a common fund to help stabilize commodity prices. Their report helped movement toward consensus at a special meeting of Commonwealth ministers and, then, during the United Nations Conference on Trade and Development (UNCTAD) negotiating sessions of 1978–79, helped produce a more positive atmosphere that led to the final establishment of a fund.

One of the most impressive and, potentially, most valuable reports of a Commonwealth group of high-level experts appointed by the secretary-general to facilitate prospects for effective global negotiations is entitled *The North-South Dialogue: Making it Work*.[4] Commonwealth leaders at the Melbourne meeting in October 1981, naturally concerned at the stalemate in the dialogue, and, especially, in view of the crisis in the world economy, not only made a number of decisions to help progress on substantive issues but recognized that the lack of progress to date was, in part, the result of obstacles in the negotiating process itself. They asked for a study with recommendations on this and got a brilliant one. Under the chair position of Ambassador Akporode Clark of Nigeria, the group of nine was made up of experts of vast, and highly relevant, experience: William Clark, from 1968–80 Vice-President of the World Bank; Bernard Chidzero, Minister of Finance and Planning of Zimbabwe and former Deputy Secretary-General of UNCTAD; Singapore Ambassador Tommy Koh, the President of the UN Conference on the Law of the Sea; Professor Owen Harries, then Australian Ambassador to UNESCO; Sir Egerton Richardson of Jamaica; and Lloyd Searwar, Secretary-General to the 1972 Foreign Ministers' Conference in Guyana; India's A. D. Sengupta, Additional Secretary to Prime Minister Indira Gandhi; and Sri Lanka's Jayewardena, Ambassador to the EEC. Their advice on basic changes in approaches and attitudes to the negotiating process required of both North and South, and on changing some of the serious institutional and procedural obstacles that they identify, can, if heeded, contribute significantly to the prospects for recovery in the global economy and for practical cooperation for development.

Meetings of the Commonwealth ministers holding particular portfolios have been increasingly action-oriented in the past twenty years, both in facilitating agreement in more universal organizations on thorny issues tending to be polarized between rich and poor and in developing ideas and functional cooperative programs among Commonwealth countries themselves. An example of the former in the late 1960s and the early 1970s was the establishment by the International Monetary Fund of special drawing rights and then a "link" between their distribution and development needs — at first, the rich had insisted on distribution solely according to the quotas based on member countries' relative production and trade. The meetings of Commonwealth finance ministers that take place each year during the week preceding the annual governors' meeting of the IMF and the World Bank were, I think, decisive in working out the compromise agreement and the tactic of an IMF study of a "link" that made it possible for the representatives of both the poor and the rich to support the compromise and, in due course, enabled them to carry their governments in supporting the substance by which each part is "linked." In the past two years, the Commonwealth finance ministers' meetings have been in the forefront of the drive to increase substantially the resources of the Fund and the World Bank.

There are several forums in which the governments of the rich caucus among themselves — the "Group of Ten" in the IMF and the Organization for Economic Cooperation and Development (OECD) are examples. And there are many in which groups of poor countries caucus — the "Group of Seventy-seven," the nonaligned meetings, and several of the regional organizations are important in this regard. But the Commonwealth is one of the few associations that brings together, for frank informal and intimate discussion and sometimes "caucusing," representative members of industrialized, developing, and least-developed countries, including influential members of most regional organizations. This can prove increasingly important in countering the dangerous trends toward neoisolationism on continental or North-South lines.

But functional cooperation among Commonwealth members themselves is also of great value. Sometimes proposals for programs of this sort are put forward by the secretariat, sometimes by one or other member governments and sometimes by informal agreement between the two. For example, in the mid-sixties, when I first became secretary-general, I was concerned about developing some innovative and significant programs to use the Commonwealth more effectively to assist in economic development. I was impressed by what struck me as a strange gap in traditional aid programs, virtually all of which then were devoted either to training, building infrastructure, or increasing production — all worthwhile, but by no means comprehensive. At that time, little or nothing was being done to help developing countries earn more foreign exchange themselves by improving their export promotion and techniques. Meanwhile, there were influential civil servants among some of my richer client states who were keen to discourage what they called "any duplication" by the new Commonwealth secretariat. So on a visit to India in early 1966, I persuaded the Indian trade minister to propose, at a meeting of Commonwealth trade ministers that was called for that June, the establishment of a (multilateral) Commonwealth export market development fund and program. This won a lot of support, and there was agreement that a small team of experts from a representative group of member countries be set up to assist the secretariat in surveying member countries' needs in this crucial field and putting forward concrete proposals for actions. In due course, an export market development program (now a separate division of the secretariat) was authorized and established, and it has proved very successful. It organizes trade fairs and "buyer-seller" meets, in non-Commonwealth as well as member countries, of course; it assists developing member countries in design, quality control, and sales promotion, based on market research commissioned in potential importing countries outside, as well as within, the Commonwealth; it advises and helps train managers to process and upgrade raw materials in the Commonwealth country of origin before export; and so forth. The trade fairs alone have resulted in orders worth many millions of pounds for developing countries.

Commonwealth ministers of education, in the early 1960s, established a Commonwealth Scholarship and Fellowship Plan (CSFP) under which awards are given each year by some fifteen Commonwealth countries to postgraduate students or teachers from other member countries. These number about 500 per year and are normally for two-year periods. In addition, since the CFTC was established, awards have been given each year to some 1,500 young men and women, drawn from developing member countries to study or receive training — sometimes "in service" training — usually in other developing member countries. Teachers and trainers are also provided. The fact that the location of training places or the source of visiting teachers or trainers where these are required need not coincide with the source of the necessary financial aid is one of the many enormous advantages that the establishment of the multilateral CFTC has made possible. It also makes possible the development of centers of excellence in various fields in appropriate developing countries, vastly increases the supply of both training places and experts available for development cooperation, and incidentally decreases the risk of brain drain. Often the relevance of the experience of a visiting expert from a developing country is particularly great. This applies also, of course, in many fields beyond education. Now nearly two-thirds of the experts sent under the CFTC to developing countries come from other developing countries.

Commonwealth education ministers normally meet, as do their ministerial colleagues in other fields, to discuss problems rather than to undertake formal negotiations. This discussion often leads to broader and deeper perceptions of the nature and implications of the problems and, of course, to ministers learning from each others' successes and failures in trying to cope. It also leads them to agreements that various problems or topics should be discussed at an expert level and, frequently, that recommendations be worked out for possible solutions or cooperative programs. Thus, in between the triennial meetings of ministers, the secretariat arranges meetings of specialists from member countries on various topics such as technical education, science teaching, school inspection and administration, curriculum development, and non-formal education; and also, under the direction of, or with the concurrence of, governments, arranges seminars and courses in various fields.

Commonwealth discussions and cooperation in the educational, as in most other professional, fields go well beyond the governmental level. The Association of Commonwealth Universities brings together the heads of over 200 universities twice every five years; they discuss common problems and help universities recruit staff from other member countries and arrange exchanges. The Commonwealth Association of Science and Mathematical Educators deals with problems and cooperative opportunities in their fields. There are several hundred nongovernmental Commonwealth associations in various professional and "subprofessional" fields. The Commonwealth Foundation and the CFTC help them cooperate and assist in development programs.

Particularly during the past fifteen years, Commonwealth discussions on education have broadened out to stimulate discussions and programs for action on problems of unemployed school dropouts, on the drift from the countryside to the cities on a scale often well above the growth of urban job openings, and on problems of rural development. A meeting of ministers responsible for youth affairs, held in Lusaka in 1973, worked out guidelines for a Commonwealth youth program that heads of government, meeting in Ottawa a few months later, authorized the secretariat to establish. It works chiefly through three regional training centers in Zambia, India, and Guyana, training youth trainers and officials. Similarly, in 1975, a meeting of ministers responsible for agriculture and rural development arranged the establishment of a Commonwealth program in this field. Ministers of industry meeting in Bangalore, India, in March 1979 recommended that an industrial development unit be set up, and this was approved by heads of government meeting a few months later in Lusaka. It has given practical assistance in developing scores of industrial projects and diversifying and upgrading others. It advises and facilitates access to technology, equipment, markets, and sources of finance. The ministers of industry, in the discussions that led to the establishment of the unit, were guided by a report of a team of industrial specialists that the secretary-general had appointed after their earlier request for recommendations about harnessing Commonwealth expertise in an innovative way to accelerate industrial advance. The unit uses and is itself financed by CFTC resources.

The periodic meetings of Commonwealth ministers of law, health, and other fields, have similarly become increasingly action-oriented, discussing common problems and working out agreements when it seems useful for co-operation to pool information, organize research, and cooperate in training and other areas. Commonwealth meetings at other than ministerial or other governmental levels also work out and implement agreements for mutual co-operation in their respective fields — meetings, for example, of law reform commissions, or bar associations or the Commonwealth Magistrates' Association in the legal field — or the Commonwealth Medical Association, the Commonwealth Nurses Federation, and the Pharmaceutical Association in the health field.

Participants in Commonwealth meetings, especially at the head of government or ministerial or "senior official" level, seldom think of themselves as negotiating but rather as discussing; but the purpose is the exchange of views, and when it seems desirable and practicable, the result is agreements or undertakings, often informal but usually nonetheless effective, for harmonized and, often, for cooperative action. Because of the shared characteristics referred to earlier, the informality of Commonwealth procedures usually greatly enhances the effectiveness of this type of multilateral discussion.

This is largely true also in the case of Commonwealth activities in the "good offices" and mediation field and, essentially, for the same reasons. The secretary-general has little direct power — not because of any restrictions in the "agreed memorandum" by which heads of government set up the secretariat but because the various budgets that he administers are limited. The largest budget, that for the CFTC, being measured not in hundreds of millions but in tens of millions of pounds or dollars. The "agreed memorandum" is ambiguous, which I found to be a potential source of strength. The SG's role, like that of the Commonwealth itself, is based on informal conventions and precedent. Elected directly by the heads of government and responsible to them collectively but not, of course, individually, he has direct access to each of them and, therefore, to any other ministers or senior officials in the member countries. Once he develops the confidence and trust of the individual heads of government of a thousand million or more people in virtually all parts of the world, he is in a position to develop significant influence and opportunities to persuade. It is this plus the appropriate knowledge, common sense, and the necessary political intuition and instincts that are crucial to effective good offices and mediation.

The role of the secretary-general of the Commonwealth is, quite rightly, vastly less powerful than that of the UN secretary-general. Among other reasons, the Commonwealth's membership is only about a quarter of the world's countries and a quarter of its population: the UN's major problems are global and the superpowers matter considerably more. And the UN budget is, rightly, much greater. Nevertheless, the Commonwealth secretary-general (CSG) is in a sense freer, and can be less inhibited, in taking initiatives. This is partly because of the informality that is so fundamentally a feature of the Commonwealth and partly because there is nothing in the Commonwealth analogous to the UN Security Council, though there are a number of more junior standing bodies. The CSG can consult, when he wishes, with individual governments or with a group he selects for a particular purpose or with all. But he is breaking no convention if he takes a political initiative on his own and without consultations.

Such initiatives are usually, of course, with one or more Commonwealth governments. But they need not be so limited when circumstances seem to the SG to make it desirable to approach the head of another international organization or the government of a country or countries outside the membership of the Commonwealth. In my book, *Stitches in Time: The Commonwealth in World Politics*, I describe some of the issues I raised on various occasions with executive leaders of the EEC, the OAU, the World Health Organization (WHO), *l'Agence de Cooperation Culturelle et Technique*, the organization of Yaounde associate countries of the EEC, and the secretary-general of the United Nations. Here I will illustrate the general Commonwealth flexibility by a brief reference to initiatives I took with the leaders of Portugal and Frelimo, the liberation movement of Mozambique, in the early days and weeks after the overthrow of the Caetano dictatorship on April 25, 1974.

I was interested in the Portuguese revolution for several reasons. Primarily, the prospect of an independent African regime in Mozambique could help cut the exports and imports of the illegal racist regime of Ian Smith in Rhodesia and could help bring about democratic majority rule there, a goal that was very much within my Commonwealth responsibilities. Second, I supported personally the desire for self-determination by the people of Mozambique and hoped that this could be achieved without further bloodshed. Third, I did not like the implications of statements by General Antonio de Spinola, the head of the new Portuguese government, that deprecated the idea of independence for Portugal's African territories but suggested a willingness to envisage "a Commonwealth-type of system," implying that Commonwealth membership involved something less than full independence. I was also conscious of the Lusaka Declaration of 1973 (before the Portuguese Revolution), whose principal authors were Presidents Nyerere and Kaunda and in which the signatories undertook to urge the liberation movements "to desist from their armed struggle and to cooperate in the peaceful transfer of power from Portugal to the peoples of the African territories," if Portugal should change its policy and accept the principle of self-determination.

So I sent a message offering the prospect of substantial Commonwealth assistance if Portugal wanted a real Commonwealth-type solution and relationship with Mozambique. Spinola's foreign minister, Dr. Mario Soares, came to London on May 24 and we talked that day. I told him that the help of Tanzania and Zambia, on whose territories Frelimo forces were based, could be valuable if he was serious in seeking a negotiated settlement involving genuine independence. Portugal had no diplomatic relations at that time with these Commonwealth countries, but Soares saw the point and was keen to use Commonwealth channels to start negotiations with the Frelimo leaders. So I telephoned Dar es Salaam at once and President Nyerere's principal secretary, Dickson Nkembo, flew north that night with a foreign ministry official. Soares and his military colleague Colonel Bruno met with them in my flat the next evening and again two days later, and it was arranged that formal negotiations should start within the week in Lusaka between the Portuguese and the Frelimo leaders.

The talks in Lusaka went badly, Spinola hedging on independence and offering no firm timetable for self-government, talking only about a referendum on what type of constitution the people of Mozambique wanted. So they were broken off.

I therefore flew to Dar es Salaam, in early July, ostensibly to attend a Tanzanian anniversary celebration but really for private talks with the Frelimo President, Somara Machel, and his two principal colleagues, dos Santos and Chissano, which Nyerere had arranged at my request. I had a difficult two and a half hours. They thought the Portuguese leaders were merely stringing them along with no real intention of allowing independence. I took the line that the problem was Spinola but that Soares was sincere and that, in this situation, they would have nothing to lose and conceivably much to gain by offering some concessions such as a transition period, elections before independence, and some guarantee for Portuguese settlers and economic interests. One of Machel's colleagues said, deprecatingly, that this sort of negotiated route to independence might be a Commonwealth tradition but it was not part of Portuguese or Mozambique traditions. I said it had worked in Tanzania, Zambia, and several other parts of their continent and had become a successful *African* tradition. In the end, Machel agreed that I should transmit to the Portuguese what amounted to an ultimatum that if negotiations were not resumed within a fortnight, Frelimo would intensify the war; but if they were resumed on the basis of negotiating independence, he would envisage various guarantees and a transition period.

I transmitted all this to Lisbon with my views and those of some African Commonwealth leaders with whom I had visited, notably Kaunda. Spinola dismissed Soares. Spinola was removed almost immediately from the presidency, and Soares was reappointed foreign minister of a new and more like-minded government. The talks in Lusaka did resume and led to an agreed one-year transition to Mozambique's independence.

I raised other issues in my talks with Machel and his colleagues: my hope that they would undertake to cut all trade with Ian Smith's Rhodesia, cut all transit rights, and give maximum help to bring majority rule to that country. Machel said Mozambique's food came largely from Rhodesia, and its foreign exchange from Rhodesia's payment for freight transit through his country.

He would need help and time to consolidate administrative control. I promised him Commonwealth technical assistance also, and that I would try to get Commonwealth countries to urge international food and capital assistance programs through the UN. All this came about, and in the next six years, Mozambique contributed invaluably to the cause of the patriotic front and to the achievement of majority rule in Zimbabwe.

No international multilateral organizations or groups are as effective as is desirable to meet the problems we face in world politics — certainly not the Commonwealth. But not to use this rather unique association as *one* of the instruments to help men and women of different races and regions and stages of economic development move toward the global community that we need, in this age of proliferating atoms and threatened ecology, would be monumental folly.

NOTES

1. See Arnold Smith with Clyde Sanger, *Stitches in Time: The Commonwealth in World Politics* (Don Mills, Ontario: General Publishing Co., 1981; London: Andre Deutsch, New York: Beaufort Books, 1983), chapters 4 and 10; and Henry Wiseman and Alastair M. Taylor, *From Rhodesia to Zimbabwe: The Politics of Transition* (Elmsford, N.Y.: Pergamon Press, 1981).

2. Details of these three dramatic restricted meetings are set out in the author's book, *Stitches in Time*, 56–57, 217–18, and 239–40.

3. In *The We-They Frontier: From International Relations to World Politics* (Leeds: University Press, 1983), I support the desirability, and a relatively simple method, of improving the decision-making provisions in the United Nations and related assemblies by amending the Charter through an addition to the existing provisions that "decisions on important questions shall be made by a two-thirds majority of the members present and voting" (Article 18.2 of the UN Charter), of the new words "and representing over fifty percent of the world's population and over half (or over two thirds) of the contributions to the organization's budget." This, I suggest, would vastly enhance the prospect of implementation of the resolutions of our world societies, the effectiveness of which is increasingly needed in our interdependent planet.

4. Published by the Commonwealth secretariat, Marlborough House, London, 1982.

Editor's Comments on Inter-regional Negotiations

The chapter on the Commonwealth brings out the roles of a number of techniques too little used in other international forums. The Commonwealth consists of forty-seven states in all regions of the world. Essentially it is as varied an organization as the UN itself. This makes its contributions to dispute defusion potentially widely applicable.

The following contributions emerge:

1. Periodic summit meetings held in an atmosphere of informality can defuse crises and lesser difficulties among states.
2. High-level off-the-record meetings, without any formal rules of procedure, without voting and without resolutions, promote amicable international relations. The results of Commonwealth heads of government meetings are divulged to the public in agreed communiqués.
3. Discussion of intra-Commonwealth conflicts does not take place at the plenary meetings, but an atmosphere of general harmony and friendliness is created in which the heads of the governments-in-conflict are able to hold private discussions among themselves and move the conflict down from crisis levels.
4. Condemnation is avoided, unlike the language of UN resolutions. This springs from the realization that condemnation cannot conduce to an atmosphere of conciliation and, strictly speaking, has no place in diplomacy or negotiation.
5. Because of the general and continuing atmosphere of friendliness and informality among Commonwealth members, the secretariat is much more available than in most other organizations, as an instrument for promoting technical and training exchanges and even political discussions to resolve crises.

PART 4

THE SMALL-STATE FACTOR
IN DISPUTE SETTLEMENT

Chapter 6

Small States and the Peaceful Settlement of Disputes

Mircea Malitza

THE CHARACTERISTICS OF NEGOTIATION AND MEDIATION

The clearest and strongest argument for the peaceful methods that states can use to make a helpful contribution to the extinction of the hotbeds of tension or to appease litigations is supplied by Article 33 of the UN Charter. The listing of such peaceful means reveals a crescendo of the jurisdictional scope covered by the methods considered: negotiation, inquiry, mediation, conciliation, arbitration, judicial settlement, and resort to regional agencies or arrangements. Negotiation, at one end of the spectrum is the least governed by rules, the least formalized, and the least liable to institutionalization; whereas judicial settlement — suffice it to think of the rulings of the International Court of Justice — is formalized, served by elaborate techniques and with well-structured institutions. This has induced international law to deal primarily with the peaceful means at the lower end of the list, namely, those including jurisdictional procedures or proceedings within established international structures. The difficulty in the codification of norms for negotiation or mediation has brought about a distinction between diplomatic procedures — which, by mediating agreements between parties, resort only to the existing institutions and channels on the basis of practice and precedent and which could be termed gracious procedures — and more contentious ones, placing a dispute in a legal justiciable setting. Though rather clear-cut and lacking nuances, the distinction has the merit of pointing to the existence, apart from the category of explicit disputes, of another broad class subsuming political or unjusticiable disputes.[1]

Thus, negotiation and mediation, while less governed by rules and less served by institutions, enjoy the quality of having the maximum of flexibility, leaving a larger role for diplomatic innovation.

THEORETICAL STUDIES AND
REAL-WORLD NEGOTIATIONS

Arthur Lall rightly described this as "an era of negotiations."[2] Not only have negotiations become a frequent and important form of resolving litigations in international affairs, but a vast literature dealing with them has been published. Can diplomats benefit in practice from these theoretical studies?

Outside the studies of a historical, descriptive, and comparative nature, two schools assert themselves with more vigor. One, based on "games," seeks "solutions" and proceeds deductively. Through game experimentation and laboratory simulation of real situations, this school has worked out theoretical and even logico-mathematical models that have helped to achieve a better knowledge of human dialogue and, particularly, of negotiation. The most important feature of this school lies in assimilating negotiation to a game, that is, to a competition governed by rules. In contrast with pure competition (zero-sum games characteristic of other human activities, e.g., military actions, sports, contests), negotiation is assimilable to cooperative (non-zero-sum) games, in which the players are not solely separated by antagonistic goals and interests but are also linked by common interests and goals. Negotiation results in agreement, by which all sides should have satisfaction or gains.

The models based on game theory have increased the precision of the language used in negotiation analysis and have brought in some key concepts, current today, such as the number of strategies of each partner; the value ascribed by a party to a move (the crossing of two strategies), which is its payoff; the utility values employed in economic and mathematical studies; the concept of minimax, consisting in following a cautious strategy of ensuring the best outcome even in unfavorable situations; the saddlepoints and the Pareto solutions, which cannot be abandoned without a reduced payoff for at least one player. The penetration of these concepts even into diplomatic practice is remarkable: Diplomats will speak more and more frequently of strategies instead of alternatives, of utilities instead of preferences, of the successive phases of the game and of comparing the various equilibrium points leading to possible solutions.

The second school (social-psychological) is more inductive, based on experiments analyzed with concepts and variables that do not appear in game theory. It studies mainly the decision-making process, the interests, and the cognitive factors.[3]

The diplomat who looks at the literature dedicated to negotiations and their models observes that most of it considers two partners only. In reality few negotiations are purely bilateral, and on deeper analysis we may say there is hardly a conflict or a negotiation that would lead to a complete polarization around two sides. Though there are analytical studies and models dealing with *n* partners and with the coalitions they build, the social-psychological school has treated more extensively group negotiations and has provided useful concepts for multilateral negotiations and for conference diplomacy.

The contribution of models to negotiations in the understanding of political and social phenomena should by no means be underrated. Among the advantages of formal models to a diplomat is, first of all, the obligation to get to the root of phenomena and processes under consideration, the necessity to think exhaustively and ponder not only on the factors involved but also on their weight. Conflict situations were treated with quantitative formal methods, as in the case of the conflict in Cyprus.[4] In that instance, one may say that the treatment of the subject using game theory can make an indisputable contribution to a deeper understanding of its essence in a far more concise and rigorous way than many pages of traditional analysis.

MODELS AND REALITY: A CASE

To verify the usefulness of theoretical models and their concepts for diplomatic practice, we will take the case of the negotiations that led to the independence of Zimbabwe, culminating in the Conference of Lancaster House in 1979. Using the models presented in an issue of the *Journal of Conflict Resolution* (December 1977), we will confront the various concepts put forward there with the actual development of the Zimbabwe negotiations. These are the main conclusions analyzed more deeply elsewhere.[5]

1. The model of Bartos is based on the idea of equity, with reciprocity playing an important part and with a solution found usually at the middle of the road.[6] Openings in the process of negotiation are essential. Although the Zimbabwe negotiations confirm the importance of a minimal base of negotiations and the timely appearance of concessions, they did not start with a symmetrical situation and did not develop only according to an inner logic, without external influences and without an anticipation of the desired outcome.
2. For the model of Spector, the negotiation is a process in which values are modified according to the needs and compatibility of the personalities involved. Tensions, interactions, and transactions occur among the personalities. The model is purely psychological. The role of personalities cannot be neglected, but it is difficult to read the process of Zimbabwe negotiations simply in their terms.
3. Druckman introduces a useful notion, adding to the international interactions the international factors.[7] The diplomat finds himself at the boundary between the opponent and his own institutions. A boundary role conflict appears. Diplomats will recognize what they so often have experienced:

parallel with the dialogue with the opponents, they have to sustain a complicated dialogue with their own side. The observation is valid; the Zimbabwe negotiations still cannot be reduced to this factor.

4. Negotiation is a learning process, according to the model of Cross.[8] The Zimbabwe negotiations confirm the learning process in which a continuous adjustment of expectations took place, a gradual understanding of the others' strategies, true "discoveries" in the sense of modification of the initial images. An objection that can be made is that a learning process is more anticipative in nature than adaptive and that the increased awareness was addressed not only to the opponents but to the international environment as well.

5. Close to the learning model is the model of Zartman, considering negotiation as a collective decision-making process.[9] The key terms are "formula" and "detail." Zartman has made his idea clearer in a book that he has co-authored.[10] The Zimbabwe negotiations have shown that an initial formula or a framework of principle giving structure and coherence to the agreement subsequently detailed in the process was of paramount importance.

Applying these different tentatives of rationalization to the Zimbabwe negotiations, we learn that each one partially covers the real process, pointing up a fragment of the truth. For the diplomat, two concepts appear in the forefront: the central place of the search for a formula and the need to consider the context. We will develop these two ideas.

THE PRINCIPLE OF COMPREHENSIVE FORMULA

The decisive step in solving a problem that involves a confrontation of two positions is to find a broader and more comprehensive framework, containing a sufficient number of common interests, that can reduce the proportions of the conflictual component. Any situation can be represented as a pair of scales: one of conflict and the other of cooperation. For each element on the "conflict" side of the scale, common elements should be placed on the other scale so that the balance comes down definitely in its favor. The bringing in of such elements of cooperation is tantamount to multiplying the available strategies. It depends on the ability to formulate, in terms acceptable to both sides, broader interests than those in opposition.

That negotiator will fare better who is able to most comprehensively formulate the interests of both sides, to more rapidly translate their goals in accordance with a list of common values, and to define their expectations on a cooperative basis; and who, besides, is imaginative, generous, and in harmony with the fundamental tendencies of the international community. The Principle of Comprehensive Formula, as one might call it, is based on the fact that the interdependence of events and phenomena, the urgency of mankind's vital problems, and the need for mobilizing the techno-scientific resources, with a view to solving them, make it increasingly possible today to relate goals to a body of common interests, which will minimize the weight of conflicting interests and blunt their thrust. Translating the data of a situation into the language of the opponent's interests has been recommended by many, from Callieres to Deutsch. In light of the concepts supplied by the models, the idea is capable of improvement. The Principle of Comprehensive Formula involves: (1) referring the tables of values of the two sides to a common table so as to permit their comparison by the same yardstick — which is facilitated by the work of the United Nations and by the codification of the principles of international relations; (2) completing the existing list with new goals and strategies ("broadening the pie"); and (3) insuring a prospect of systematic collaboration in implementing the solution adopted, which involves some degree of institutionalization as a guarantee against risks, discontinuity, and erosion of the cooperative element. The Principle of Comprehensive Formula provides one of the best criteria for determining whether negotiations are conducted constructively and whether they are aimed at turning the rudimentary game of confrontation into a broad process of cooperation, increasing, rather than reducing, the number of options and seeking a solution in the extensive field of common interests.

THE CONTEXT

It is with justice that Oran Young notes:

> The existing models of bargaining generally deal with bargaining under conditions that can be described as isolated exchange. This means that the interaction must be regarded as divorced from any broader setting or environment, and this analysis will focus on the activities of essentially symmetrical players. In real-world situations, however, the assumption of isolated exchange tends to abstract away a variety of international factors. In fact, informal discussions of bargaining often emphasize heavily factors of this kind, and some writers have gone so far as to argue that the concept of bargaining cannot be meaningfully defined without reference to these factors.[11]

We shall sum up the current shortcoming of the analytical models of bargaining as a factor in the peaceful resolution of conflict by pointing out that such models often neglect, rule out, or ignore the more general context. It has been almost a working premise of formal models to discard exogenous actors or give them subsequent treatment, after the process mechanism is completed. As a result of neglecting the setting — a concept of paramount importance in international phenomena and all the more so in conflictual situations — there has been little research done on the role of third parties and of the political environment in resolving disputes. The more rational the models are, the broader the setting should be. This was realized by the great ancient

Greek playwrights: their situations are highly rational and explicit, and mathematical modeling is readily applicable to them. But their solution was to add another hero above the characters themselves, namely, the choir, which used to sum up the context, so to speak.

The context is so overwhelmingly decisive for the successful operation of peaceful means, that in a hostile context even good solutions cannot work, while in a favorable context even hard solutions may succeed. In developing such an international context, the necessity of which has been revealed at the present stage of research, the smaller countries play a role that goes beyond the limits of phenomena dealt with in the traditional literature, which concentrates on the explicit roles played on the basis of jurisdictional qualifications.

SMALL STATES AND INTERNATIONAL CONTEXT

In speaking of the role the small- and medium-sized countries may have in resolving specific disputes, we should consider not only their direct intervention but also the impact they make through the context in order to render the use of peaceful means more effective. To examine this contribution, we must specify that the consideration, in this study, of the role of small- and medium-sized countries in resolving conflicts does not in any way lessen the role of the generally acknowledged big powers. The role of big powers has already been studied in great detail. In the resolution of conflicts, they owe the impact of their potential intervention to the authority they enjoy, also confirmed by their special position in such peacekeeping bodies as the Security Council. In these studies, emphasis was placed on the fact that the larger countries have the means to control the implementation of the agreements resulting from the resolution of conflicts, and they also possess the resources to compensate for the possible losses or damages suffered by the interests of a given country in the wake of a conflict resolution. However, the preservation of peace is not the exclusive domain of the big powers.[12]

Though lacking the same means of control and implementation, the small- and medium-sized countries can turn their specific circumstances into advantages. Being less involved with strategic and global interests, they are more open to a sympathetic understanding of the specific criteria and angles of the parties to a conflict or to the peculiarities of a limited region. Hence the credibility attached to their participation in the resolution of a dispute or conflict. The second advantage is that of suppleness. Indeed, the decisions of the medium powers can be made without involving complicated and lengthy processes. Some have even likened the freedom of movement of medium powers to small-sized towboats that can readily carry out complicated maneuvers in the harbor areas for the benefit of large liners whose real performance is on the high seas.

Therefore, the basis for a possible intervention of medium-sized countries aimed at improving the context for the resolution of conflicts lies in their credibility, resulting from an absence of vested interests in strategic implications, and in their fast and flexible maneuverability in complicated situations. These features are not emphasized just to offset the role that the great powers have to play, alongside the smaller ones, in the resolution of conflicts that require solidarity of all factors, whatever their size or interests. Likewise, the size and status of the small- and medium-sized countries do not make them more devoted to the cause of peace or peaceful conduct, as can be seen from the alarmingly large number of local conflicts in different parts of the globe. For all that, the small- and medium-sized countries are a factor that can influence the balance of general peace and promote peaceful methods for the termination of conflicts to a far greater extent than they are currently credited with.

The role of these countries is emphasized also by their greater participation in international activities and in global debates not so much on the issues of peace and security but rather on economic and social matters and on other aspects of international cooperation. It might be noted that the negotiations on a new international economic order, on the resolution of the pressing problems of food, energy, resources, urban planning, seas and oceans, population, health, human resources, and cultural cooperation, are actually setting into motion and promoting precisely those instruments that are called upon to solve more significant political problems, as well. These vital issues have always been a remarkable school for the development of participation and involvement in decision making not only in respect of the practical bargaining with which they are directly concerned but also in the field of peace and security into which their lessons carry over.

THE PREMISES OF THE POLITICAL APPROACH

In studies on peaceful means, we constantly come across hard-and-fast classifications that have led to the neglect of the considerable scope of some subtler judicial possibilities and nuances. Just as judicial literature has neglected negotiations and nonjusticiable cases, and theoretical studies have overlooked the procedures that are nonformalizable or unsuitable for analytical treatment, so too, the classical enumeration of peaceful means only distinguishes between means usable by the parties concerned and those involving third parties. Indeed, according to the formulation of the classical legal doctrine, negotiation proceeds among conflicting parties. The way left open for the intervention of a third party is either to have a direct mediatory, conciliatory or arbitrational role, or to take part in institutionalized collective regional or world forums for peacemaking and the termination of conflict. There are many situations when conflicting parties cannot undertake direct negotiations, but they do not consider it proper to submit their dispute to an institution with a markedly legal character or else to resort to the involvement of a third party in ways consecrated by practice.

The international situation at the moment points to the fact that the time is ripe for a theoretical and practical exploration of intermediate ways and mixed solutions.

Mediation is viewed by some authors as an accessory to the negotiation.[13] We shall not go deeper into its classical forms, which have proved, more than once, to be too rigid because of an overemphasis on their jurisdictional and institutional elements; we would prefer to emphasize those peaceful means that we are going to call by the general name of "the political way," which is a blend of negotiation, mediation, and sometimes, the conciliatory process.

Complete attachment to the doctrine of peaceful resolution of conflicts does not go beyond the specific obligations laid down in the charter. This attachment implies renunciation of the doctrine of force and support for the principles of nonrecourse to the use or threat of force. The political way excludes, from the beginning, war, armed clashes, and violent confrontations as means to solve conflicts. No justification of a recourse to weapons is admissible, save in the obvious cases of legitimate self-defense in order to safeguard a country's national existence. In all other cases, recourse to arms is inadmissible. The only ground for conflict resolution is that offered by the existing system of rules of international conduct, which requires constant improvement, incorporated in the unanimously recognized documents or established as such by long historical practice.

The premises of a country's participation in the political resolution of an interstate dispute has the following essential components:

1. Not only is the path of violence ruled out but also the belief that violence can lead to no durable advantages is subject to no revision. The medium-sized countries can strengthen the idea that in our time, solutions based on force can only be false and temporary.
2. Another current fundamental finding is that an unresolved, long-drawn-out conflict erodes the material, moral, and human resources of a country and that the damage done may in some cases be irreparable. In many medium-sized countries, there is a constructive climate for efforts aimed at implementing economic, social, and cultural programs as true national priorities. It is this very climate that leads to the idea that involvement in conflicts necessarily damages one's position within the world economy, that it amounts to a huge step backward at a time when mankind is striving to solve basic issues related to food, environment, energy and material resources, science, technology, and so forth.
3. Another component of the philosophy of the political way is the realization of the risks of escalation. Most of the countries have completed a long process aimed at reducing and removing their dependence on outside powers, colonialism being the most brutal form of such dependence. Con-

flict, by its logical involvement of the allies, has the tendency to extend beyond local and regional confines and, eventually, to develop into a world problem, as is evident in almost all contentious cases. This growth in scope is accompanied by diminished independence and by the acceptance of a high cost for the political and economic future of the country.

4. An argument to which the medium-sized countries are particularly sensitive is the idea that involvement in a conflict diminishes a country's international status and cripples its potential participation, on equal terms, in the increasingly varied fields of international cooperation. Indeed, the involvement in a conflict, while channeling all forces in one direction, casts a special light on all the actions of a country, whose credibility is impaired and whose standing in the international community is lessened as it has to face attitudes ranging from disapproval to explicit condemnation.

PRACTICAL CONTRIBUTIONS

These are premises opening practical ways for medium-sized countries to make an active contribution to the termination of conflicts. The following serve as examples:

1. The contribution of a medium-sized country to the peaceful resolution of disputes depends on the links it has with all parties to a conflict. Indeed, the chief means for a third country to take an initiative and to participate in conflict resolution is to possess open communication channels. That is no easy thing to do in a world in which discontent or disagreement frequently result in the breaking of diplomatic relations and other channels of communication. The political way cannot do without channels (fully unobstructed and in operating condition) to convey ideas and possible solutions.

2. The very maintenance of simultaneous ties with the parties in contention, the effort to listen to the arguments of each party, and the explicitly stated intention to keep a stance of objectivity — which does not rule out disagreement with unfounded positions or disapproval of inadmissible procedures — stimulate possibilities to restore normal relationships among the parties to a conflict and to seek solutions in a peaceful dialogue. Here we have to deal with a known transitivity property: If A has a dialogue with B, and C has a dialogue with B, then A, too, can communicate directly with C. It is known that irreconcilable positions are generally characterized by complete intransigence toward uncommitted parties and by a polarization of the parties around the idea of *non datur tertium*, while real solution seeking is enhanced by those elements.

3. The third contribution of a medium-sized country to conflict resolution is to work out a framework of common interests, the scope of which transcends that of the conflict. It is a duty of the third parties to stress,

emphasize, and prove the absolute priority of those interests whose significance is above the current stakes and to elaborate a comprehensive formula that is distinct from a mediator's task. Third parties play a constructive role by facilitating the parties' own efforts to find a solution and remove the obstacles from the way leading to it. While it is not formalized by a definite mandate, it is meant to assist the direct negotiation between the parties, and consequently, it can be exercised more credibly and more profitably.

Regional organizations have made the geographical point of view, regional or continental, carry greater weight. Regional peaceful projects such as the economic and industrial ones, the development of complex operations along rivers that flow through several countries, the trade or tariff agreements, and joint ventures — all such forms of cooperation — are by their essence, apt to oppose the expansion of conflicts.

4. Conflicts are generally accompanied by a bitter propaganda war, with an aim to humiliate, discredit, and morally defeat the opponent; a war sometimes waged more fiercely than military conflicts themselves.

The role of medium-sized countries is to help the conflicting countries get into dialogue and negotiation by containing the psychological war and discouraging noisy name calling and condemnation.

THE UN DECLARATION OF 1982

At the Thirty-fourth Session of the General Assembly of the UN, Romania introduced a document on the peaceful solution to disputes between states, which stresses the imperative to find solutions at the table of negotiations.[14] The document proposes the adoption of the Declaration on the Peaceful Settlement of International Disputes and other measures to improve the existent procedures, making them more appealing and useful to the states. It pronounces the belief that "durable, really viable solutions to all disputes, no matter how complicated they may be, can only be found by direct talks among the parties concerned at the negotiating table." In this spirit the idea of a permanent commission of the General Assembly for good offices and conciliation, open to participation by all states was advanced. Behind the Romanian initiative was the conviction expressed by President Nicolae Ceausescu that, "More than ever before are the democratization of international relations and a greater role of the UN and other international organizations required since they provide an organized framework for the active participation of all states, of the small- and medium-sized countries, of the developing and non-aligned states, in the resolution of the complex issues of the world today."[15]

At the Thirty-seventh Session of the General Assembly the Declaration worked out by experts at Manila was adopted by consensus.[16] It is an important document meant to enhance the application of the principle of the peaceful settlement of disputes. Speaking on behalf of African countries, the representative of Kenya called the adoption of the Declaration "a milestone in the history of the UN." Underlying the adhesion of African states to the principle, he mentioned the existence in the framework of the OAU of a Mediation, Conciliation, and Arbitration Commission.

Beyond any doubt, this document will stimulate the study and the application of the basic peaceful methods of the Charter, among which negotiation is the first one. Article 10.I of the Manila Declaration affirms:

> States should, without prejudice to the right of free choice of means, bear in mind that direct negotiations are a flexible and effective means of peaceful settlement of their disputes. When they choose to resort to direct negotiations, states should negotiate meaningfully, in order to arrive at an early settlement acceptable to the parties. States should be equally prepared to seek the settlement of their disputes by the other means mentioned in the present Declaration.

CONCLUSIONS

Diplomats can improve efficient recourse to the tools of peaceful means by consulting the literature of models. They will not find panaceas, but they may acquire useful concepts such as those of "context" and "formulae." These two guiding ideas illuminate the role of small- and medium-sized states in participating in attempts to reach solutions. The political way means blending negotiation and mediation, the less formalized and institutionalized ways of handling conflict situations and crises; excluding recourse to force; and committing all countries, on equal terms, to the creation of settings favorable to the application of peaceful means. The rules of this contribution can be outlined and recognized in cases that the experience of the last few decades has provided. A country's capacity to maintain contacts and retain the confidence of the conflicting parties is the crucial element, proving, by the compatibility of simultaneous relations, that the parties concerned are also able to move into a zone of agreement. At a time when there are many still unresolved conflicts in the world, a more frequent recourse to negotiation is an encouraging development. It should urge political science to go deeper into the questions of peaceful means and the role of third parties; to consider them from a new angle, freed from the tribute paid to older models; to improve their efficiency; to strengthen the normative basis of international conduct; and to facilitate recourse to peaceful instruments.

One of the resources insufficiently considered so far is that of the possible contribution of the medium-sized countries, which have been erroneously believed to be doomed to take part in conflicts only as allies of one party or another, as a result of the growing polarity in the world. The capacity of a country to maintain an independent attitude serves the interests of peace, keeps conflicts under control, and assists the parties in starting peaceful negotiations on disputes that may otherwise develop into dangerous hotbeds of tension and threats to world peace.

NOTES

1. Mircea Malitza, *Teoria si practica negocierilor* (Bucharest: Editura Politica, 1972).

2. Arthur Lall, *Modern International Negotiation: Principles and Practice* (New York: Columbia University Press, 1966).

3. Daniel Druckman, editor, *Negotiations: Social Psychological Perspectives* (Beverly Hills and London: Sage Publications, 1977).

4. Malvvern Lumsden, "The Cyprus Conflict as a Prisoner's Dilemma," *J. of Conflict Resolution* 17, no. 1 (March 1973).

5. Mircea Malitza, editor, *Negocierile in Mecanisme de reglementare pasnica a diferendelor dintre state* (Bucharest: Editura Politica, 1982), 50–82.

6. O. J. Bartos, "Simple Model of Negotiation: Sociological Point of View," *J. of Conflict Resolution* 21, no. 4 (December 1977).

7. Daniel Druckman, "Boundary Role Conflict: Negotiation as a Dual Representation," *J. of Conflict Resolution* 21, no. 4 (December 1977).

8. J. G. Cross, "Negotiation as a Psychological Process," *J. of Conflict Resolution* 21, no. 4 (December 1977).

9. William Zartman, "Negotiation as a Joint Decision-Making Process," *J. of Conflict Resolution* 21, no. 4 (December 1977).

10. William Zartman and Maureen R. Berman, *The Practical Negotiator* (New Haven and London: Yale University Press, 1982).

11. Oran R. Young, *The Analysis of Bargaining: Problems and Prospects in Bargaining, in Formal Theories of Negotiations* (Champaign, Ill.: University of Illinois Press, 1975), 399–400.

12. Jacques Freymond, "How the Small Countries Can Contribute to Peace in Small States in International Relations," *Nobel Symposium 17*, edited by August Schou and Arne Clav Brendtland (Stockholm: Almqvist and Wiksell, 1971), 177–85.

13. Grigore Geamanu, "Theorie et pratique des negociations en Droit International," *Collected Courses of the Hague Academy of International Law*. I Tome 166 (Leyden: Sijthoff, 1981), 369–447.

14. United Nations, GA Doc. A/34/143 of July 13, 1979.

15. Nicolae Ceausescu, "Address to the Solemn Session of the National Assembly," Bucharest December 1, 1978.

16. United Nations, GA Res. A/RES/37/10 of November 10, 1982.

Editor's Comments on Peaceful Settlement of Disputes

This chapter makes its first significant point in regard to the processes of negotiation by analyzing some of the main methodologies developed by scholars in the field of negotiation. The author draws attention to the games approach, which is deductive. Paradigms are fleshed out in the games, which can then be applied to real situations. The second methodology to which the author draws attention is the inductive approach based on experience. From his analysis, the author concludes that the games approach might give the diplomat a more precise and analytical tool than traditional diplomacy. He substantiates this view by looking at the Zimbabwe negotiations (Lancaster House phase).

The author suggests that a realistic and fruitful approach to negotiation would be to apply what he calls the Principle of Comprehensive Formula, which involves bringing into the negotiation as broad a scenario of factors as possible so that there is no exclusive focusing on the issue in its narrowest terms. In a highly interdependent world — politically, strategically, economically, socially, and communication-wise — it is clear that the broad view is a must in negotiation, argues the author. It increases the options and, hence, aids the search for a solution.

In this light, the author sees a considerable scope for the small- and medium-sized countries to contribute constructively to the solution of problems between states that might appear to concern only the parties to the dispute or conflict. To fill this role a small- or medium-sized country must be completely attached to the renunciation of force in international affairs. It can then help what the author terms "the political way" of resolving conflicts.

PART 5

DISARMAMENT NEGOTIATIONS

Chapter 7

Multilateral Forums

Inga Thorsson

This chapter deals with an area of multilateral negotiations in which genuine progress and constructive results are glaringly missing and a dramatic break-through is urgently needed.

In the first part of the chapter, I shall give a brief background review of some earlier disarmament negotiations in order then to continue with an account of what has been achieved since the Geneva negotiations started in 1962. Some conclusions will be drawn from this experience. Following that, I shall make case studies of two disarmament issues given "highest" and "high" priority, respectively, by the United Nations General Assembly when charging the Committee on Disarmament (CD) with negotiating them. Some final conclusions will then be given.

> To this project, which is formed with great purity of intention and displayed with spriteliness and elegance, it can only be objected, that, like many projects, it is, if not generally impracticable, yet evidently hopeless, as it supposes more zeal, concord and perseverance than a view of mankind gives reason for expecting.
>
> Samuel Johnson, ca. 1775

BACKGROUND

At the turn of the century, when the industrial revolution gained speed in spreading technical know-how and industrial capacity, the major powers were entangled in an unstable political situation marked by imperialism and competition between military alliances. Political and economic conflicts paved the way for an unabated and destabilizing arms race, limited only by the then existing level of technology and the resources available to the nations involved.

In the same period, however, a first effort toward security and disarmament took place within the international peace conferences in the Hague, convened in 1899 and 1907. Although certain rules of war — wars the conferences accepted as inevitable — were codified, at least as far as declared wars between "civilized" countries were concerned (colonial wars being regarded as internal conflicts), all initiatives in disarmament failed. It is, however, important to note that the very idea that international security and disarmament are of direct interest to all nations, and that collective action is required, was founded by the Hague conferences. Alas, war stopped a third conference planned for 1915.

In the four peace treaties of 1919, the victors stipulated unilateral and compulsory reduction of armaments by the defeated powers and the demilitarization of certain areas. The Allies drew the lines of a new map of Europe and adjacent areas (e.g., in the Middle East), essentially, in accordance with their own perceived security needs.

A Treaty of Mutual Assistance, which was a general pact of nonaggression, condemning aggressive war and guaranteeing mutual assistance against any aggressor — drafted within the League of Nations in 1923 — never got off the ground because Great Britain, Germany, the United States, and the Soviet Union rejected it. A protocol for the Pacific Settlement of International Disputes of 1924 was killed when the US Senate refused to ratify it.

In the interwar period, efforts toward disarmament and arms control were renewed. Beginning in the 1920s and culminating in the London Naval Conference, 1930–35, attempts toward numerical and technological limitation of a naval buildup failed because Japan refused to enter into any obligations.

Although Germany had ratified the Hague Convention of 1899, the German army used asphyxiating gases, for the first time in modern warfare, in the Battle of Ypres in 1915. The public reaction of repugnancy toward the usage of about 110,000 tons of antipersonnel chemical-warfare agents during World War I, and well over 1 million poison-gas casualties, paved the way for negotiations after the war and within the League of Nations on banning chemical warfare. The first important agreement on chemical weapons, which is still by and large enforced, is the 1925 protocol prohibiting the use of chemical and bacteriological weapons in war. Many states have expressed reservations, however, limiting the prohibition to "first use" only. The use in conflict of chemical weapons has not been significant since the primitive, but widespread use in World War I. It is important to note that in spite of extensive stocks of chemical munitions, these were not used during World War II, neither in Europe nor in the Far East. The reason was most probably fear of reprisal in kind.

In 1932, a conference was convened in Geneva on the "Reduction and Limitation of Armaments." Here the Soviet Union put forward proposals aiming directly at general and complete disarmament, while Western powers proposed a wide variety of more restricted arms-limitation measures. Germany reserved the right to rearm unless other nations disarmed to its level, and, after Hitler came to power, Germany withdrew from the conference and the league in 1933. The Geneva Conference was eventually dissolved in deadlock after having failed to reach any agreements. From 1933 on, and in the political climate created by Hitler's Nazi Germany, the world witnessed a period of general rearmament and intense preparations for war, leaving no room for disarmament measures.

A series of commissions and conferences on disarmament were convened within and under the auspices of the United Nations during the first two decades of its existence. The very first UN General Assembly resolution (GAI/1) adopted on January 24, 1946, dealt with nuclear weapons and all other major weapons of mass destruction. From this time until 1961, fruitless talks took place successively in forums such as the Atomic Energy Commission, the Commission for Conventional Armaments, the Disarmament Commission, and the Ten-Nation Disarmament Committee. Myriads of proposals and counter proposals were submitted on various issues related to general and complete disarmament. Mistrust and global competition between the United States and the USSR dominated the period. A relative relaxation of relations between the new military alliances, NATO, and the Warsaw Pact, did not improve prospects for real disarmament measures, general or limited. Nations did not enter into disarmament discussions in a serious spirit of good faith; plans and counterplans were considered instruments of propaganda rather than means of achieving some measure of disarmament, if any at all, through concrete multilateral negotiations. Negotiations broke down over issues that still have a familiar ring: the West charging the East with avoiding questions of preliminary, gradual measures and verification; the East accusing the West of avoiding the question of general and complete disarmament.

This was the situation when the presently ongoing round of disarmament negotiations was made possible by a joint United States/USSR statement (the Zorin-McCloy Agreement) in 1961 on certain basic principles relating to disarmament.

The two governments agreed to recommend that negotiations should achieve general and complete disarmament and that war be renounced as an instrument for settling international disputes. States would only be permitted such nonnuclear arms and forces agreed to be indispensable for internal order. The armed forces of nations would be eliminated; military establishments, including bases, dismantled; weapons production stopped or converted to peaceful use; all stockpiles of weapons of mass destruction and their means of delivery eliminated; and all organizational military efforts of states abolished and, thus, military expenditures discontinued.

These measures would be carried out in agreed steps, with verification in each stage. All measures should be so designed as not to imply diminished military security for any state and be placed under effective international control by a UN disarmament organization, employing inspectors with unrestricted access, without veto, to all places necessary for verification.

In 1961, the UN General Assembly unanimously endorsed an agreement, reached bilaterally between the United States and the Soviet Union, on the actual establishment of a new Eighteen-Nation Disarmament Committee (ENDC) by enlarging the Ten-Nation Committee by adding other members of the UN not belonging to either of the two major military alliances. The task assigned to the committee was to negotiate an agreement on general and complete disarmament, on the basis of the Zorin-McCloy Agreement and to report to the General Assembly as soon as such an agreement was reached.

The committee almost immediately arrived at a deadlock over its main task; general and complete disarmament.

Although the phrase "general and complete disarmament" may still figure as the ultimate goal, no one regards it as a matter of any current interest. Instead, the ENDC (later transformed into the Conference of the Committee on Disarmament [CCD] with thirty-one members, and finally into the present forty-nation body, the Committee on Disarmament [CD], created after the First Special Session of the General Assembly on Disarmament in 1978) has concentrated on, at least theoretically, more limited objectives, intended to initiate a step-by-step approach to general and complete disarmament. As the projects dealt with so far have contributed very little or not at all to real disarmament, they are commonly called arms control measures or collateral measures of disarmament.

WHAT HAS BEEN ACHIEVED

Let me scrutinize a few products of multilateral arms-control negotiations since 1961. A conference of twelve countries drafted an international treaty, which was signed in 1959 and entered into force in 1961 and which established the Antarctic as a demilitarized zone. No military forces were present at that time, and the treaty thus stipulates continued nonpresence. The twelve signatories and other parties executing substantial polar research have the right to verify compliance by national means. The relevance of this treaty reflects the fear of the countries nearest to the Antarctic that a hostile nation could establish military bases there; the fear that hostile nuclear submarines might hide in Antarctic waters; and most important, the fear that the nuclear launching installations might be installed. Sooner or later general technological progress would make such endeavors feasible. The treaty was adequate at the time, but it does not address the territorial claims of various nations, and all economic activities are omitted, which, in view of accelerated prospecting for minerals, may well cause future rivalry among states for the control of resources.

By 1953, both superpowers had conducted thermonuclear tests. After the accident on March 1, 1954, in which radioactive fallout from a fifteen-megaton US test in Bikini hit the crew of the Japanese fishing vessel "Lucky Dragon," the Japanese parliament formally called for international control of nuclear testing. This thought was picked up by Prime Minister Nehru of India in a statement on April 2, 1954. India later brought the idea to the UN General Assembly, thereby stimulating a six-year period of negotiations between the United States, the USSR, and the United Kingdom. The three powers agreed, following extensive technical and political negotiations and after failures to uphold a moratorium on testing, on a text banning nuclear weapons tests in the atmosphere, in outer space, and underwater. They reached this result as the members of an ENDC subcommittee. The draft treaty was discussed extensively in the ENDC during the spring of 1963, followed by final talks among the three powers that summer. This led to the signing in Moscow on August 5, 1963, of the partial nuclear weapons test ban treaty, which having entered into force the same year, has been ratified by some 110 states. The parties undertake "not to carry out any nuclear weapons tests, or any other nuclear explosion in the atmosphere, underwater or in outer space, or in any other environment if the explosion would cause radioactive debris to extend beyond the borders of the state conducting the explosion." Since this provision in no way hampers further modernization of warhead technology, not even theoretically, it must be labeled as primarily an international environmental protection measure and not as an element of nuclear disarmament, *stricto sensu*.

The 1968 Non-Proliferation Treaty (NPT), entered into force in 1970, stipulates that non-nuclear-weapon states shall remain nonnuclear and the nuclear-weapon states prior to January 1, 1967, shall not share their weapons with anybody else. "In return," cooperation in the peaceful uses of nuclear energy is provided for under international safeguards and control, and the nuclear-weapon states "undertake to pursue negotiations in good faith on effective measures relating to the cessation of the nuclear-arms race at an early date and to nuclear disarmament and complete disarmament under strict and effective international control."

Unfortunately, a number of states, in different stages of development but having a technological and economic basis for making their own nuclear weapons, did not sign the treaty. Two nuclear weapon states, France and China, have continuously refused to adhere to it.

In accordance with the stipulations in Article VIII, para. 3 of the Treaty, a review conference was held in Geneva during May 1975. On that occasion it became apparent that the treaty was still politically the best possible instrument to serve its nonproliferation purpose; but, on the other hand, deep tensions between various groups of states were evident. The non-nuclear-weapon states accused the three nuclear-weapon states of continuing the nuclear-arms race in spite of the undertaking contained in Article VI; some non-nuclear-weapon states referred, adamantly, to the treaty as discriminatory. Developing states were opposed to what they felt to be the noncompliance with Article IV, which intended to guarantee to all states the free access to nuclear energy and its technologies. At the end, and in spite of many difficulties, the conference adopted a final document, establishing guidelines for the future implementation of the treaty and calling for a new review conference in 1980.

The Second Review Conference, taking place in August-September 1980, revealed the same tensions and difficulties, particularly regarding Articles IV and VI. This time, Article VI came in the forefront, the nuclear-weapon states maintaining, with apparent sincerity, their compliance with this article as they had met the only undertaking which, in their view, was contained therein, that is, to negotiate in good faith. The non-nuclear-weapon states opposed this argument strenuously, recalling that the article, adopted in 1968, referred to negotiations to reach a cessation of the nuclear-arms race "at an early date" and that, to the contrary, the nuclear-arms race had been pursued and intensified relentlessly. Although some progress was made toward an agreement concerning Article IV, and although the United States at the very end made some minor concessions in the nuclear-weapons field — considered by the non-aligned nations to be too small and to come too late — the Second Review Conference showed itself unable to agree on a substantive final document, deciding only to call a Third Review Conference in 1985.

The great need for a NPT is generally acknowledged, as is the need for its further strengthening and its adherence becoming more universal — its membership now being 115 states but still not including a number of technologically advanced "threshold" states. It is, however, important to state that the treaty suffers from various deficiencies, most of them signs of the fact that the drafts submitted to the ENDC in Geneva were the products of bilateral United States-Soviet Union talks, reflecting the concerns and needs of the superpowers. Only through the insistence and hard work of the neutral and nonaligned members of the ENDC was Article VI finally agreed upon, and the review conferences, as indeed the developments of the arms race in the 1970s and the early 80s, have shown quite clearly the inherent weakness of this multilateral contribution to the treaty. But there are several other weaknesses in the treaty. The main nuclear-weapon states continue to spread stockpiles of their nuclear weapons to nonnuclear countries within their security systems; they abuse the right of innocent passage and freedom of the high seas to introduce nuclear weapons to ever vaster stretches of international waters; the treaty covers nuclear warheads, but not delivery systems, and it does not prohibit or restrict consultations, planning, and preparations for nuclear war, nor ban deployment of nuclear weapons on the territory of alliance members. In short, the disarmament content, what has been called the vertical nonproliferation element, is weak and almost nonexistent.

In 1966, and after several years of initiatives by various member states and debates at the United Nations, the United States and the Soviet Union submitted identical draft treaties on another "nonarmament" matter: the outer space treaty. The treaty bans nuclear weapons or other weapons of mass destruction on all celestial bodies, with two fundamental exceptions: the Earth as a celestial body and the Intercontinental Ballistic Missiles. In spite of the aggressive research and, hence, resulting technological advances in the field of military use of space, the treaty provides no specific provision for expanding its scope with regard to military activities in orbit around the Earth.

Within the context of the Law of the Sea, the delegation of Malta to the UN proposed in 1967 that all activities on the seabed should be permanently peaceful. As a result, the General Assembly that year included in its agenda an item entitled, "Examination of the question of the reservation exclusively for peaceful purposes of the seabed and the ocean floor, and the subsoil thereof, underlying the high seas beyond the limits of present national jurisdiction, and the use of their resources in the interests of mankind." The following year the General Assembly established an ad hoc group to study the matter. Consequently, both the Soviet Union and the United States proposed to the disarmament committee in Geneva (ENDC) an international agreement on the limitation of military use of the seabed and ocean floor, in order to "prevent an arms race before it has a chance to start." The Soviet Union and the United States submitted separate drafts in 1968 and 1969. The Soviet Union had a strong interest to secure, if at all possible, the prohibition of the use of antisubmarine detectors that might reduce its naval power instead of leaving unaffected the freedom of its own submarines and vessels. The United States, Britain, and other NATO countries had a diametrically opposite interest. The smaller nations, apprehensive over increasing superpower naval and marine activities, mostly wanted to see a total and complete prohibition of any kind of military activity on the seabed. In 1970, the Soviet Union and the United States submitted a joint draft treaty prohibiting the emplacing of nuclear weapons or other weapons of mass destruction on the seabed and the ocean floor beyond a twelve-mile coastal zone. It had then been revised three times in response to suggestions in the CD in Geneva (then the CCD). The superpowers had aimed at a quick fix of the situation, as it presented itself. Many nonaligned and neutrals considered that probable future technological advances might endanger the scope of the draft treaty and, therefore, proposed that continued negotiations would secure the prevention of an arms race on the seabed and that the treaty should be periodically reviewed. Despite the fact that years have passed since the entry into force of the treaty in 1972, no such promised negotiations have taken place. At a review conference in 1977 the big powers maintained that the treaty had not been violated and that no technological development, relevant to the treaty, had taken place. They also resisted another review conference. Nonaligned and neutral countries, however, managed successfully to press for a Second Review Conference not later than 1982 and for an appraisal of technological developments, relevant to the treaty, to have been performed by that time.

The seabed treaty bans what no one intended to do had there been no treaty. Stationary nuclear-weapons installations on the seabed are not judged to be militarily interesting. Free-swimming submarines and "crawling" nuclear mines just off the seabed offer much better warfare possibilities. The treaty has not even removed motives for research and development to improve possibilities to emplace nuclear weapons on the seabed. Its main merit may be that the parties de facto have undertaken to monitor their own territorial waters in order to prevent preparation of hostile activities directed toward a third party.

There is not much to say about the convention on the prohibition of military or any other hostile use of Environmental Modification Techniques (ENMOD). It is one of several nondisarmament treaties. It was proposed to the UN General Assembly in 1974 by the Soviet Union, and its scope was contentious from the outset. Western countries maintained that the examples given were unrealistic as weapons, and scientifically-technologically improbable. After a period of consultations, the United States and the Soviet Union, in 1975, submitted to the CCD identical texts of a draft convention banning environmental modifications having "wide-spread, long-lasting or severe effects."

This is a threshold definition, which indicates that what is not explicitly prohibited may be taken as implicitly permitted. Also, a clear definition of the terms "wide-spread, long-lasting or severe" has never been given. This fact, taken together with the convention's inadequate complaints procedure — which to some extent was improved in the course of the CCD negotiations, introducing the establishment of a consultative experts committee — makes it highly unlikely that any action, for example, large-scale use of defoliants in a conflict, would ever be formally declared a violation of the treaty. Another disputable matter is whether hostile action below the undefined threshold would be permitted. In fact, the relevance of the whole convention is at issue. Some states maintain that modification techniques will never be practical as weapons against any enemy in a conflict; others hold the view that conventions of this type may have considerable value as a tool in defense planning since the eventual development of this type of weapon might be discounted.

Having said this, I should not like to belittle the damaging importance that ENMOD or, for that matter, most kinds of modern warfare methods will have on the human environment. This is an aspect of the dangers of war that will require continuous and effective examination by the international community.

I have already referred to the fact that an important ban on the (first) use of chemical and biological weapons was agreed upon in Geneva in 1925. Efforts between the two world wars to further strengthen the protocol failed, and the subsequent development of nuclear weapons overshadowed the importance of other mass-destruction weapons systems. Provisions for the abolition of chemical and bacteriological weapons (CBW) were included in the Zorin-McCloy Agreement in 1961 but not as a priority item for either of the superpowers. The allegations against lavish American use of chemical agents in Vietnam again shifted the attention of the United Nations and the disarmament community to the question of CBW. In the lively debate in 1966, the United States maintained that substances used by US troops were riot-control agents, employed for humanitarian reasons. The United States also maintained that defoliants were not chemical-warfare agents. The Soviet Union preferred to keep silent. Although many UN members did not appreciate the context in which proposals for CBW prohibition were put forward at that time, there was strong support for a UN General Assembly resolution calling for the strict observance of the Geneva protocol.

Toward the end of the 1960s, negotiations were reopened in the CCD in Geneva on the prohibition of the development, production, and stockpiling of CBW and on their destruction. For Western countries, the starting point was that it would be easier to first work out a separate biological convention since the question of verification of a prohibition of chemical weapons clouded prospects for progress. The nonaligned and neutrals, as well as socialist countries, wanted both kinds of weapons to be covered in a single treaty. These positions blocked the work for several years, although the United States, in 1969, unilaterally renounced biological warfare and bacteriological weapons (BW) stocks were ordered to be destroyed. The deadlock did not cease until the Soviet Union suddenly abandoned its original position and, in 1971, declared itself ready to negotiate a ban on biological weapons only. The United States and the Soviet Union then bilaterally prepared and submitted separate but identical draft texts. The resulting Convention on Biological Weapons concluded in 1972 and entered into force in 1975 is, in fact, the first real disarmament step taken during the whole postwar period; the only one involving any measure, however minute, of military "sacrifice." But all requirements for verification and control had been totally abandoned. As no control measures are prescribed in the treaty, there is in essence no clear assurance that the convention will be implemented. The complaint procedure, which requires complaints to be launched in the UN Security Council, is designed to give the five permanent members the power to veto any investigation into alleged violations or suspected activities. At and following the 1980 Review Conference, Swedish and other neutral-nonaligned initiatives to strengthen and make more democratically acceptable the verification and complaints procedures of the convention have so far been effectively stopped by the superpowers. A more flexible, more objective and less discriminatory pattern of verification and complaints procedure, clearly separating fact finding from the political power game of the superpowers in the Security Council would set an important precedent for prolonged discussions on chemical weapons. These discussions will be subject to review in the fourth part of this chapter.

Since 1980, and following the submission to the CD in 1979 of identical texts of a draft convention banning radiological weapons by the United States and the Soviet Union, negotiations have been conducted in an ad hoc working group of the CD on this issue. Although the two superpowers have shown great fervor in insisting on the rapid conclusion of the negotiations and the forwarding of a draft text to the UN General Assembly for its approval, many CD members have not been able to mobilize the mental involvement needed. The reason is a general feeling that, again, the CD is presented with a non-disarmament issue instead of being required to negotiate the highest priority items on its agenda, given this rank by the General Assembly. Regarding the views of the Swedish government — and my own — on this issue, I can do no better than to quote relevant parts of a statement that I gave in the CD on July 9, 1981:

> They (the superpowers) have not hesitated to put before the Committee a draft Radiological Weapons Treaty which has, during our negotiations, been convincingly shown to be completely lacking in substance. . . . As matters now stand, we entertain grave doubts about the usefulness of going forward with the deficient text originally provided to us by the United States and the Soviet Union as we do not think that it would add to the already suffering credibility of the Committee on Disarmament.

In the field of reduction of conventional weapons, there has been no progress whatsoever. Historically, each new type of weaponry, which has revolutionized established methods of warfare, has been regarded as nonconventional. In present-day nomenclature, all weapons except nuclear, chemical, biological, and the somewhat nebulous category of weapons defined as "new weapons of mass destruction" are called conventional.

As early as February 1947, the UN Security Council established a Commission for Conventional Armaments. Its aim was ambitious: within three months, proposals for general measures of regulation and reduction of armaments and forces would be put forward, together with practical and effective safeguards in connection with implementation of these measures. The commission failed to reach its objective, did not meet after early 1950, and was dissolved in 1952. Western countries, which dominated the committee, requested reliable and verifiable data on existing levels of armaments and forces. The Soviet Union resisted the separation of conventional weapons from "weapons of mass destruction," and rejected the notion that security must precede disarmament, which it called a "militaristic thesis."

Since then, new proposals have been few and sparse. In the 1970s, the United States suggested ideas on conventional control on a regionalized basis in the CCD and bilaterally with the Soviet Union. Japan, Belgium, and Denmark have also shown interest in the matter at the UN. Proposals have been made to regulate the international arms traffic and the growing militarization of Third World countries. Many developing countries, which for various reasons (in fact usually because of superpower rivalry in the region) consider that their security needs justify important and major arms, have persistently and successfully opposed these attempts.

CONCLUSIONS

The main conclusions drawn from a review of multilateral disarmament negotiations, of which I have been a partner since late 1973, will be given in the fifth and final part of this chapter. Here I shall only present some views on the concrete results achieved since 1962: the beginning of the work of the ENDC, followed by the CCD and, in January 1979, the CD.

It would not be fair, or an indication of good judgment, to apply what I have just quoted as well-founded views on the draft Radiological Weapons Treaty or on the various conventions and treaties adopted over the years. The fact remains, however, that with the exception of the convention on the prohibition of the development, production, and stockpiling of bacteriological (biological) and toxin weapons and on their destruction, no agreements on genuine disarmament measures have been concluded in the period 1962–1981, a period characterized by an incessant and intensified arms race, both quantitatively and qualitatively, both in the conventional and in the nuclear-weapons field.

Moreover, it should be emphasized that the convention referred to above is generally considered to have been successfully concluded only because use of the weapons thus banned was considered, by military and political leaders, to be of a completely insignificant military value. The arms-control measures agreed upon, such as the partial test ban treaty of 1963, the NPT of 1970, the Seabed Treaty of 1972, are all of a nature not to impose any restrictions whatsoever on the further development and refinement of the terrifying arsenals of major military powers—the NPT because of the interpretation that the major nuclear powers give to its Article VI (see page 98). As far as the letter and the spirit of the Outer Space Treaty of 1967 is concerned, most recent events in the exploitation of outer space seem to indicate that at least the spirit of the treaty is seriously threatened.

Thus, multilateral disarmament negotiations have so far touched upon very restricted areas of weaponry and have addressed those aspects of decision making that placed no restrictions on the freedom of the militarily strong and mighty to continue the arms race, to the detriment of the rest of the world as well as to themselves.

THE FIRST SPECIAL SESSION OF THE UN GENERAL ASSEMBLY DEVOTED TO DISARMAMENT, MAY-JUNE 1978

It is indicative of the dismal developments of our times in the armament/disarmament field that thirty-two years after the adoption by the UN General Assembly at its first session in January 1946 of a resolution on disarmament (GAI/1) there was a clear need for a special session of the assembly on disarmament. At the initiative of the nonaligned countries, the first such session was held from May 23–July 11, 1978.

There may have been those who had hopes for progress toward disarmament on that occasion. They were ill-advised. The time was not ripe, the place was not right. But the session took on an importance of its own. The final document, adopted after arduous and exhausting negotiations, establishes the fundamental political basis for the common worldwide quest for peace and security. Both in its declaratory part and in its Programme of Action, it is a good solid document. The trouble is that five years after its adoption not a single measure contained in the Programme of Action has been implemented.

Paragraph 28 contains an important statement expressing worldwide interest in disarmament and peace. As it is of some relevance to one of my main conclusions at the end of this chapter, I quote it in full:

> All the peoples of the world have a vital interest in the success of disarmament negotiations. Consequently, all States have the duty to contribute to the efforts in the field of disarmament. All States have the right to participate in disarmament negotiations. They have the right to participate on an equal footing in those multilateral disarmament negotiations which have a direct bearing on their national security. While disarmament is the responsibility of all States, the nuclear-weapon States have the primary responsibility for nuclear disarmament and, together with other militarily significant States, for halting and reversing the arms race. It is therefore important to secure their active participation.

In the Programme of Action, all conceivable aspects of the arms race and the need for disarmament are dealt with. It is, for example, worthwhile to note that, in paragraph 45, conventional disarmament is listed as a third-priority issue, something which represents an important new approach within the United Nations, particularly since the following paragraph states that nothing should preclude states from conducting negotiations on various priority items concurrently. It should be added, however, that since 1978, it has not become easier to start real and substantive work of any kind related to conventional disarmament. Also, for the first time the Programme of Action takes up, in paragraph 85, the need for limitations of all types of international transfers of conventional weapons and calls for consultations among major arms suppliers and recipient countries to that end.

The main emphasis is, however, on the need for a cessation of the nuclear-arms race and nuclear disarmament. The Programme, in the well-known paragraph 50, calls for a step-by-step approach to this goal, including a comprehensive/phased program for progressive and balanced reduction in stockpiles of nuclear warheads and delivery systems. Thus, the fight against the nuclear-arms race is still given highest priority, in accordance with demands put forward by neutral and nonaligned countries.

Another important decision was to replace, as of January 1979, the thirty-one-member CCD by a larger body, the CD, with a membership of the five nuclear-weapon states, as well as permanent members of the UN Security Council, and thirty-two to thirty-five other states — the end result being, as a matter of course, thirty-five. This provided an opportunity to remove the prerogative of the co–chair position exercised since 1962 by the two super-powers — something that several members of the CCD, among them Sweden, had requested for years — and let the chair position rotate in alphabetical order on a monthly basis. This arrangement allowed France, *inter alia*, to take its seat at the multilateral disarmament negotiating table for the first time in January 1979. One year later, China also entered the CD, bringing its membership to forty.

The special session of the General Assembly also decided that a Second Special Session on Disarmament (SSOD-II) should be convened at a date to be decided by its next regular session. In autumn 1978, the date was set for 1982.

TWO CASE STUDIES

In this part of the chapter, a special review is made of the multilateral negotiations — or rather the absence of multilateral negotiations — on two top issues on the agenda of the CD, assigned the highest and high priority, respectively, by the UN General Assembly. These issues are a comprehensive nuclear weapons test ban treaty (the CTBT) and a convention on the prohibition of the development, production, and stockpiling of chemical weapons (CW) and on their destruction (the CW Convention).

Earlier in this chapter reference was made to the so-called partial test ban treaty of 1963. In its preamble, the commitment of the parties is explicitly spelled out as: "Seeking to achieve the discontinuance of all test explosions of nuclear weapons for all time." This commitment was confirmed in a preambular article in the non-proliferation treaty of 1968, where the parties recall the determination expressed (in the partial test ban treaty) to seek to achieve a CTBT.

What has happened during these twenty years? On the one hand, underground nuclear testing is continuing unabated and has even been intensified by some nuclear-weapon states, amounting in 1980 to roughly one test every week somewhere in the world. This has made possible successive development, modernization, and refinement of warhead technology. This was revealed in a report issued in 1976 by the US Energy Research and Development Administration (now integrated into a Department of Energy), in which, for the first time, a few results of thirty years of US testing were given: seventy-four different types of nuclear warheads had been tested, fifty of them accepted in the stockpile at one time or another, twenty-six of them were at that time in the stockpile of thirty-three different weapons systems. Since 1976, as stated above, nuclear testing has been performed at a continuously high level. Apart from observed tests, we have no similar insight into nuclear-weapons development in the Soviet Union. Taking into account the intensity of their testing, there is no reasonable alternative but to assume that both superpowers vigorously pursue similar policies of aggressive development, production, and stockpiling of nuclear warheads. This happens in spite of the countless appeals to these states to reduce their testing activities, of which just one example may be given: in the final document of the first NPT Review Conference in May 1975, a call was made to them with consensus and their own agreement "to limit the number of their underground nuclear-weapons tests to a minimum" pending the conclusion of a CTBT.

At the same time, there is the commitment of the superpowers and the United Kingdom in the partial test ban treaty, "seeking to achieve the discontinuance of all test explosions of nuclear weapons for all time, determined to continue negotiations to this end." Any handbook on the history of disarmament clearly illustrates the so far futile attempts at such negotiations over the years and the continued absence of multilateral negotiations. Resolutions adopted annually by the UN General Assembly, powerful criticism from neutral and nonaligned countries, as well as constructive proposals elaborated in great technical details by several members of the CD have not been able to influence the situation.

On some occasions in the past, members of the committee have suggested various types of a threshold test ban, to be supported by a voluntary moratorium on tests below the threshold and/or a gradual phasing out of such tests. The superpowers declared themselves opposed to any such ban, confirming this position at the 1973 session of the UN General Assembly, just before they made their move of conducting secret and bilateral negotiations on such a type of test-ban treaty. These led to the superpowers signing, on July 3, 1974, the Treaty on the Limitation of Underground Nuclear Weapon Tests, in which they agreed to limit the yield of underground tests to a maximum of 150 kilotons and committed themselves to reduce the number of such tests to a minimum. This agreement, which was a completely bilateral affair between the two powers, has not entered into force, although it has been understood that the parties would abide by its basic stipulations.

Before I turn to the history of the most recent years of pressure and efforts to reach a CTBT, mention should be made of the positions toward such a treaty of the two remaining nuclear-weapon states: France and China. France will not accept, and will not adhere to, such a treaty, as it does not agree that it would constitute an important obstacle to nuclear-weapon proliferation and further nuclear-weapon refinement. Clearly, France wants to continue its own testing program. China maintains its opposition to any isolated treaty banning tests unless it is linked to a complete prohibition and destruction of nuclear weapons. Note should also be taken of the fact that by not adhering to the 1963 partial test ban treaty, these two countries have not made the formal commitment to a CTBT contained in the 1963 treaty.

Following some favorable developments in the CTBT field, whereby in late 1976 and early 1977, steps were taken by both the United States and the Soviet Union toward talks on a CTBT — the so-called trilateral negotiations — started in the summer of 1977 among these two powers and the United Kingdom, the period 1977–1981 represents a strong and dismal part of the CTBT history.

During the autumn of 1977, general feelings of optimism reigned concerning the trilateral talks, even if some delegations of the CCD, including Mexico and Sweden — the latter having submitted to the 1977 session of the CCD a draft CTBT text — emphasized the need to establish a CCD working group to start multilateral negotiations, with a view to submitting the approved draft text to the 1978 special session at the UN General Assembly. The GA Res. 32/78, urging the trilateral negotiators to bring their talks to a positive conclusion at the earliest possible time and to transmit the results for consideration by the CCD, and requesting the CCD to take up the agreed-upon text with the utmost urgency in order to have a draft treaty submitted to the GA 1978 special session, was adopted with the affirmative votes, without any reservations, of the three nuclear-weapon states' negotiators.

Then trouble began. There was evidence of pressure groups with the political, scientific, and technological communities in the United States, working against the adoption of a CTBT. As is almost always the case, it was never possible to get evidence of the presence of corresponding forces in the Soviet Union. However, the trilateral talks dragged on and annual reports were given to the CCD, then the CD, by the United Kingdom as spokesman for the three in the summers of 1978–1980. The first two reports were of an extremely general character, while the last one went into greater detail to explain the reasons for the continued delay. These reports, however, failed to satisfy many of the other delegations, and draft resolutions have been tabled all these years, at successive sessions of the General Assembly.

Contrary to the sense of the votes cast by the trilateral-negotiating states' manner of action at the 1977 session of the General Assembly, the United States delegation at the 1979 session of the assembly, while voting in favor of a similar draft resolution, stated that this could not be taken as indicating readiness to conclude the tripartite talks with any particular provisions or by any deadline.

The next in the sequence of events in the dismal history of the CTBT was the announcement in the summer of 1980 by a member of the then United States administration that the tripartite efforts were aiming not at reaching a treaty of unlimited duration, as pledged in 1963 and repeated in 1968, but at a limited agreement of a mere three-year duration. Such a treaty would probably remain limited to the original three parties and would hence not promote worldwide adherence so badly needed as an effective means to prevent horizontal proliferation. It could well stall multilateral negotiations on a

CTBT "for all time" and would consequently have a negative impact on joint efforts within the CD to achieve and maintain an international verification system.

In February 1981, I had the following to say in the CD on the subject:

> In practice, a three-year CTBT would not be a treaty in the same sense as the commitments made in 1963, but would amount to a moratorium on nuclear tests. When we shall achieve it, I think that we should all consider it as such in a positive spirit. If it were agreed to accept a three-year moratorium, remaining problems of verification between the tripartite states would not be of immediate concern and could well be solved within the moratorium period. We have, of course, been told ad nauseam that a CTBT, and hence a moratorium, cannot at present be adequately verified through national means only. But I think that we have been able to demonstrate satisfactorily that the likelihood of detection of clandestine nuclear testing is very high. The danger of the loss of face and credibility would no doubt constitute a sufficient deterrent.

During 1981 and as a result both of the change in the United States presidency in January 1981 and increasing tensions between the two superpowers, no tripartite talks were held and no report was consequently given to the CD at its 1981 summer session.

In 1980, the Soviet Union changed its position and declared itself willing to participate in multilateral negotiations of the CD, provided that all five nuclear-weapon states would join in the negotiation and the obligations of a CTBT. Considering the declared positions of France and China (see page 106), the attitude of the Soviet Union does not seem to be helpful in the CD's efforts to achieve such a treaty.

The CD itself, and particularly its Group of 21, that is, its neutral and non-aligned member delegations, has meanwhile been increasingly active in the CTBT field, so far, unfortunately, without any results. Numerous working papers have been submitted, and statements have been made adamantly criticizing the dominant powers, particularly since, in spring 1980, agreement was achieved to establish ad hoc working groups of the CD in four areas but not including a CTBT and nuclear disarmament. The latest developments so far are the submissions of Working Paper CD/181 of April 24, 1981, proposing an ad hoc working group for the multilateral negotiation of a CTBT and of Working Paper CD/192 of July 8, 1981, requesting a decision to be taken on that proposal, followed by a statement by the CD on July 14, 1981, that, due to the continued resistance of the United States and the United Kingdom delegations, no consensus could be found on the proposal by the Group of 21.

This is the history so far of an item that has been on the agenda of the disarmament community discussion for 25 years, which is the highest priority item of the UN General Assembly and item no. 1 on the CD's agenda. What can be learned from this is that the commitment to a comprehensive nuclear weapon test ban for all time — however legally binding since the 1963 and 1968 treaties—has been transformed into superpower rhetoric, and the sincerity of their political will to stand by their commitment must be seriously questioned. The effect is that so far the CD has been denied the possibility to achieve one of its main duties.

The subject of the second case study is the more than a decade-long effort to reach a complete ban on CW. Reference was made in the early part of this chapter to the Geneva protocol of 1925 prohibiting the use (first use) in war of CBW (see page 94). A review has also been made of the early efforts to reach a ban on the production of CBW (see page 100–101), resulting in a convention on biological weapons in 1972 and continued effort in the CW field since then.

In the course of the 1970s, several draft texts of such a convention were submitted to the CCD, by the East European states, by Japan (1974) and by the United Kingdom (1976). Hundreds of statements were made, working papers were submitted and expert meetings held within the CCD without leading to any progress in this field accorded high priority year after year by the UN General Assembly. Admittedly, the problem of verification of compliance with the stipulations of the convention offers particular difficulties when it comes to a kind of weapons which emanates from a rapidly expanding chemical industry, beset by industrial secrecy, and producing thousands of chemical agents, poisonous or nonpoisonous, for peaceful, wartime, or double use.

In 1977, the United States and the Soviet Union initiated preparatory bilateral talks on a convention in this field. Since then and up to 1980, the CCD, now the CD, received fairly meaningless reports on these bilateral talks. During the summer of 1979, the CD had, by consensus, decided to devote two weeks in July to the consideration of this item. Not until then did the superpowers convene a meeting in Geneva of their CW experts to draft an annual report. Because of differences of opinions and a delay in the final approval of the report, it was only submitted to the CD after the end of the two-week period. Then the CD was, as supposed by the superpowers, to take approving note of it.

The situation was somewhat changed when, in the spring of 1980, the superpowers agreed to the establishment of an ad hoc working group in this field, although with the limited mandate of "identifying elements" to be in a future CW convention. During the 1980 and 1981 sessions of the CD, intensive work had been ongoing in the ad hoc working group, including the convening of expert meetings on specific issues. In spite of concentrated negotiating efforts it, however, has not been possible so far to reach an understanding with the superpowers on an extension of the mandate of the CD ad hoc working group to include actual negotiations on a treaty text.

As is the case regarding the tripartite preparatory negotiations in the CTB field, the bilateral preparatory talks between the United States and the Soviet

Union on a CW convention have been in recess since the coming into power of a new administration in Washington in January 1981.

Meanwhile, suspecting the Soviet Union of keeping considerable supplies of CW and maintaining a "chemical warfare capability," the United States, in the summer of 1981, intensified its preparations for chemical warfare, including the production of nerve gas and so-called binary chemical weapons. This would indeed seem to indicate neither a revival of the bilateral United States-USSR talks, nor a belief in progress in the ongoing multilateral talks on "identifying elements" of an international convention.

FINAL CONCLUSIONS

The multilateral disarmament negotiations and, particularly, the blatant lack of results of these negotiations reflect the existing power structures of the world, technologically, economically, militarily, and politically. They also, of course, reflect the competition between the main actors. Sometimes we look for signs of a deteriorating capacity to exercise power by the Great Powers in any of these fields — and from time to time there are some — deeply frustrated as we are in the overwhelming majority of small- and middle-sized states by the use that the Great Powers are making of their position. In the next moment, we may consider the possible effects, positive or negative, of any change in a situation that might be conceived as a "balance of power," indicating some kind of equilibrium. On the other hand, if a kind of "balance of power" — a doubtful concept in our era — is exercised mainly through the horrible state of a "terror balance," we should remember that this is a dynamic state, particularly susceptible to a change that might only too easily be transformed into what very aptly has been called "terror without balance."

One of the key problems here is the different ways in which states conceive the concept of "security," which, due to technological advances and geopolitical changes, is subject to continuous and active consideration of governments. In paragraph 29 of the final document of the UN General Assembly's First Special Session on Disarmament (SSOD-I), it is stated that:

> The adoption of disarmament measures should take place in such an equitable and balanced manner as to ensure the right of each State to security and to ensure that no individual State or group of States may obtain advantages over others at any stage. . . . At each stage the objective should be undiminished security at the lowest possible level of armaments and military power.

This paragraph, in itself, contains a beautiful statement on the key word of security. The problem is that neither in this paragraph, nor in any other part of the whole final document is the concept of "security" or "national security" clearly defined. And each state defines the concept in its own way. Small- and medium-sized countries tend to regard security in its traditional meaning as the absence of direct military threats. Larger states, and particularly the superpowers, consider themselves threatened by events, more distant in time, space, and content. By experience, security shows itself to be a stretchable concept, closely related to the means of power available. The greater a state's military power and the more ambitious its intention to exercise this military power, by actual use or by threats of use, the more extensive its concept of "security." Statements from both superpowers indicate that not only military factors but also phenomena of economic, ideological, or religious nature are perceived as threats to "national security." This brings indeed a new and dynamic dimension to the key issue of "security," adding new aspects and new problems to the task of ending the arms race and starting a disarmament process. Indeed, the result of these dynamic processes seems to be that the superpowers and, to some degree, the other nuclear-weapon states impose their perceptions of international and, first and foremost, national security on all other nations in the world.

There are fundamental political differences between the goals of disarmament and the results achieved at present in some areas of "arms control." "Arms control," or even "arms limitation" presupposes the continued value for international security of military force at different levels, while "disarmament" at least in the final analysis, rejects the very value of military strength as a factor in relations between nations. Arms control and disarmament are, in fact, two different dimensions of activities, and as such, they are frequently counteracting. In the very recent past, during the first half of 1981, we have indeed seen these forces at play. At the very best, one of the superpowers would, under certain defined conditions, agree to the resumption of some kind of arms-control talks. The other superpower rejects any such preconditions, which it considers constituting an unacceptable measure of dictation. At the time of writing, this indicates the presence of a deadlock in talks and negotiations between the superpowers, which has its evident effects on multilateral disarmament negotiations.

These negotiations, by necessity, have to be carried out under the principle of "consensus," that is, in theory, the veto right by any member of the negotiating body but, in practice, the veto right of the great powers. Under present power structures, the CD is, in fact, working on the terms of the superpowers; the way in which they define their security needs and interests dictates the conditions of work of this forty-nation multilateral negotiating body, the only official negotiating body for disarmament in the world.

No wishful thinking concerning the abolition of the consensus principle can do away with these obvious facts of *realpolitik*. The way in which the work of the CD is proceeding seems therefore to lead to the following conclusions regarding the superpowers' attitudes toward multilateral disarmament negotiations:

1. a decisive disregard of such negotiations and a corresponding preference for direct and secret bilateral talks;
2. such bilateral talks leading either to direct results (e.g., SALT or the Threshold Test Ban Treaty of 1974) or the submission of draft texts to the multilateral body for — as is their desire and intention — its service as a mailbox for transmission to the UN General Assembly (e.g., the ENMOD Convention, the draft text on a Radiological Weapons Convention);
3. a refusal to participate in the work of the CD and, thus, preventing the CD from working in conformity with UN resolutions, even those supported by them (e.g., the CTBT);
4. when agreeing to establishing machinery within the CD on the negotiations of disarmament measures, limiting the mandate of such machinery so as to be able to control its effectiveness (e.g., the CW Convention);
5. finally, a general disregard of legally nonbinding but politically and morally binding commitments to multilateral disarmament negotiations voted for, or agreed upon by consensus, in the UN General Assembly (e.g., the final document of the General Assembly's SSOD-I).

The case studies of the history of the multilateral negotiations in the CTBT and the CW Convention are, in my view, indicative of the attitude of the superpowers to truly multilateral disarmament negotiations as described above, which reveal the reasons for their somber failures. Behind this attitude, leading up to these failures, the following realistic matters of fact can be listed:

1. the establishment of disarmament units nationally and of the negotiating machinery internationally have so far not accelerated the achievement of results; and it might even be said that, in some cases, they have even tended to direct attention of planners and of research and development efforts toward areas that, up to that point, had not been objects of military competition ("bargaining chips");
2. with the exception of the BW Convention, no agreement on real disarmament has been reached;
3. when arms-control measures have been agreed upon, a number of important states have not adhered to them (e.g., the partial test ban treaty, the non-proliferation treaty);
4. several arms-control efforts were fairly obsolete when signed;
5. disarmament efforts have only marginally, if at all, affected the arms race;
6. military force is a factor of ever-growing importance in international relations;
7. states had better be judged by their acts rather than their rhetoric for a worldwide arms race and continued militarization of societies are historical facts; not restraint, nor cessation or control of the arms race, nor disarmament;

8. the Soviet Union and the United States deliberately propel the race for arms, beyond reason, conditioned by their unilaterally formulated principles of "security" and "interest;" thus, the superpowers, in fact, weaken and degrade multilateral disarmament efforts.

These are realistic and pessimistic matters of fact in an evaluation of many years of disarmament efforts. It is no wonder that people who have devotedly and skillfully involved themselves in these efforts are now trying to find new ways and new approaches. As I have already said, the idea of abolishing the consensus principle in international negotiations seems, unfortunately, only to be wishful thinking. No majority vote in the CD taken against all or some nuclear-weapon states will, for example, bring a CTBT into real life and put an end to nuclear-weapon testing. It is, on the other hand, my convinced view that the superpowers would do well to agree to majority votes in matters of procedure, so as not, as is at present the case, to prevent the CD from taking such procedural decisions that would enable it to conduct negotiations on the highest priority item, not only on its agenda, but on that of the international community.

But the decisive facts of life remain. With the present power structures within the international community, there will be no effective disarmament measures until the leading powers, and particularly the two superpowers, reach a new understanding of their real and true national security interests and link them with the real and true international security interests of the whole world of our era – a world in possession of nuclear technology or its application; a world of rising political, religious and ideological, social and economic tensions; a world in desperate need for interdependence and cooperation instead of confrontation and military might.

Will this be possible in the time available? Perhaps not without a change in the present power structure, which will require a fundamental break with the past and the present. Taking into account the political and military dominance of the superpowers will not be easy, nor achieved early enough; the superiority is too great. But in the technological and the economic fields, the position of the United States is being threatened; the writing on the wall is seen both in Japan and in the European Community, and perhaps in the newly industrialized countries of the South as well. The same threat can, of course, be directed toward the Soviet Union, already in considerable economic trouble. If the position of the superpowers can be challenged, to whatever intent and for whatever purpose, perhaps their dominant influence may crumble.

All this is a matter for the future. But, of course, in the field of the arms race, the political and military superiority of the superpowers, together with their mutual relations and their attitudes toward the rest of the world, makes meaningful disarmament negotiations so difficult, something must happen sooner than that.

Perhaps the phenomenon in the spring and summer of 1981 called the "new wave of disarmament," to be found in Western Europe and the United States, and the call for a European disarmament conference, involving parliaments and governments, might be new and powerful factors. A rapidly growing number of people refuse to be drawn into what they conceive to be a super-power conflict. For them, the arms race has turned from being an issue of deterrence, of military balance, of inferiority or superiority, to being an issue of survival. In any case, it is, in my view, a serious mistake, psychologically and politically, to dismiss the arms-race resistance movement as a new wave of "neutralism," however unrealistic and irrational their arguments and slogans may sometimes be. Growing increasingly stronger, it should instead be considered a memento to be taken very seriously, particularly by the CD delegations, the governments of which have formed and continue to form such decisive obstacles to effective multilateral disarmament negotiations.

We others should do well to enter a dialogue with the new wave of disarmament. Perhaps we could then disprove the statement by Samuel Johnson as applicable to the cause of disarmament, which is quoted at the beginning of this chapter. Mankind may, after all, have the zeal, concord, and perseverance needed for that purpose.

Chapter 8

The Search for Common Ground Among the Superpowers

Adrian S. Fisher

In writing about the principles and practices of modern international negotiation, I will direct my remarks primarily to the field of international negotiations dealing with arms control and disarmament for the primary reason that this is the area of international negotiation in which I have had the most experience. I do so without any apology because negotiations in the field of arms control and disarmament, involving as they do critical issues of national security, present the problems implicit in modern international negotiation in their starkest form. It is obvious but useful to start by analyzing the various interests of the parties in an international negotiation involving arms control and disarmament.

The countries involved may be divided into four categories. The first are the superpowers, the United States and the Union of Soviet Socialist Republics, the states with the greatest nuclear arsenals and the most readily available conventional forces. The second group includes the other nuclear-weapon states: either those with an avowed nuclear capability, such as France, England, and China; or those that are known to have or are very close to having, a nuclear capability, such as India and Israel. The third group consists of those countries that have an industrial base sufficient to develop a nuclear arsenal and substantial conventional forces but have not yet developed nuclear arsenals. Finally, there are the other countries of the world, with varying arms potential and political alignment, that would all be jeopardized in the event of a world war and would also be exterminated by a nuclear holocaust.

These varying interests have their initial, and most obvious, reflection in the formal structure that has been created for negotiations on arms control and disarmament. It would not be useful to take a detailed examination of the various forums in which arms-control negotiations have taken place since then. They extend from the original International Atomic Energy Commission (members of the Security Council plus Canada, when not a member) to the current forty-nation CD, consisting of the five avowed nuclear powers, members of NATO and the Warsaw Pact, and various other countries of the world. It also consists of a revived UN activity, including a special session of the UN devoted to disarmament, a dedication of the First Committee of the UN General Assembly to disarmament and related international security matters and a reactivation of the UN Disarmament Commission, now consisting of the entire membership of the United Nations.

Throughout these various structures, there run a variety of themes that reflect the varying national interests that have been discussed above. The first is that, notwithstanding various institutional changes with respect to the United States-USSR relationship (the creation of the cochair position of the United States and the USSR in 1962 and its abolition in 1978), the relationship between these two powers is critical to any progress in arms control and disarmament. The few agreements in the field of arms control and disarmament that have been reached (the limited test ban treaty, the NPT, the seabed treaty, and the Strategic Arms Limitation Talks [SALT]) were all preceded by United States-USSR negotiations. There is, furthermore, very little hope for a comprehensive test ban treaty, SALT II, or a comprehensive treaty dealing with CW, unless the foundation has been laid by an agreement between the United States and the USSR.

Agreement between the United States and the USSR may be a necessary condition for a successful arms-control agreement. It is not, however, a sufficient condition. Agreements reached by these two states are subject, in varying degrees, to being rendered ineffective by other countries that have the power to do so and may, perhaps, even be induced to do so by an adverse reaction to what they regard as an attempt by the "superpowers" to force them to adhere to an agreement in the negotiation of which they had no significant role. This has been particularly true in the case of the NPT, the limited test ban treaty, and less acutely so, in the case of the seabed treaty and SALT I. It will clearly be the case in the event of a comprehensive treaty dealing with CW and the comprehensive test ban treaty. It will also be true in the case of further negotiations with respect to SALT because the United States and the USSR are not the only countries that have the capacity of, or a substantial interest in, nuclear-delivery systems.

The contrapuntal problem presented by the relationship between the United States and the USSR, when their respective allies and friends are involved or interested, has been one of the most vexing ones affecting arms-control negotiations. One reason it is vexing is because of the substantially different approaches of the United States and the USSR to the issue of consultation. Part of this difference in approach is due to the different structures and procedures between NATO and the Warsaw Pact. While recent events have made it clear that Soviet control over Warsaw Pact decisions is not as direct or immediate as it was once considered to be, it is still clear that the Soviet Union does not consider itself under the same obligation to consult its Warsaw Pact allies as the United States feels to consult NATO.

This same approach carries through to the countries in the nonaligned world. Here the difference, which also may be slightly overstated, is that the Soviet Union takes the position that if it and the United States agree, the two can persuade (with a reasonably strong arm) the other countries to go along. The United States normally takes the position that it should sound out the other countries' reactions to its position before coming to an agreement that it would try to sell to the world. The Soviets tend not to use this tactic. It is my impression that when they have come to an agreement with the United States, they have twisted as many arms as they could and as hard as they could in order to get international acceptance for it.

Both the Soviet Union and the United States agree on the result, however. Both agree that it is necessary to get the widest possible consensus for arms-control agreements, including that of those countries whose military and economic status is such that they could not upset the particular accord. The expressions of the organized opinions of mankind through the United Nations and related bodies, has a substantial binding effect even though many of the countries who participate in this expression do not have the actual power to take action inconsistent with the arms-control measure under discussion.

Turning from a discussion of the forums in which international negotiations in the field of arms control take place, it appears to be useful to discuss the various factors that go into those negotiations. There are several points that have to be dealt with and analyzed in the discussion of international negotiations, particularly in such security-related fields as arms control and disarmament.

The first is the assumption often made by theorists that nations participating in arms-control negotiations, or any other type of negotiations for that matter, are single, rational, decision-making units. This is simply not the case. But this does not mean that it is not a useful point of departure for analysis. After all, we have done quite well with mathematical analysis that started with the concept of a point, a line, and a plane, even though none of those three entities exist in the real world. But mathematical physics, and science generally, would not have gotten as far as it has had we not advanced beyond these relatively simplistic concepts. The need for going on from the original simplistic concepts is even greater in the field of international negotiations, indeed in any negotiations. With the possible exception of two bachelors negotiating the sale of a used car, with neither having access to information concerning the auction price of used cars in the region, it is difficult to think of a negotiation between two single self-contained decision-making units. For example, if either of the negotiators had been married, there would be concern as to what the spouse would think about the price or the car. If one of the negotiators was a salesman, there would be concern as to whether his supervisor would confirm the offer or, conversely, as to whether the salesman was not making a low offer, with the expectation that his supervisor would require him to raise it and that the buyer would have put in such an expenditure of time that he would go along with the increase rather than start over with someone else.

This illustration is itself simplistic as applied to the field of international negotiations on security matters; but it is used to introduce the idea of group decision making in negotiations – a process that becomes increasingly significant with the number of countries participating and the importance of the negotiations to the security of the countries involved. The process of group decision making must be considered at a variety of levels.

The first is group decision making at the national level. Here I can speak from personal experience only of the United States, but I have observed the process in other countries with varying degrees of perception. With our allies, for example, we have quite a good perception of their decision-making process; we have discussed it with them, and they with us, very frankly. With respect to other countries, particularly the USSR and the People's Republic of China, our knowledge is obviously much less. But if one observes the tenth of the iceberg that is above the water, one can make some educated extrapolations as to the motion of the nine-tenths of the iceberg that is below the water. This observation is particularly applicable to the USSR because we have been in direct negotiations with them and, thus, observed the visible motion of the iceberg for a much longer period of time than is the case with the People's Republic of China.

Directing attention to the group decision-making process in the United States, we find that under the Constitution of the United States there are two entities that have to make decisions concerning international negotiations: the president, usually acting through the secretary of state, and the Congress – in the ratification process, usually the Senate by a two-thirds vote but sometimes by a vote of simple majority in both the Senate and the House of Representatives. These are the entities that have the ultimate authority as far as the United States is concerned, but a good deal of preliminary work has to be done before questions are ripe for decision. In the United States, this includes consideration at various levels. This group will include representatives of: the United States Arms Control and Disarmament Agency (ACDA) (an agency created by an Act of Congress in 1961 to advise the president and the secretary of state on these matters), the secretary of state, the secretary of defense, the Joint Chiefs of Staff, the adviser to the president on national security affairs, the relevant intelligence agencies, and when appropriate, the various services.

Meetings are held, usually on the deputy level, at the initiative of the ACDA, and the first drafts of proposals under consideration usually have been prepared by the ACDA, although they may have been staffed with other agencies in advance. The issues are then sent to the senior officials in the organizations named, with final resolution of the issues to be made by the president. The names of the various groups participating in this process tend to change with various administrations, but the process is roughly the same. There have been two major variables, however. One is the relationship between the director of the ACDA and the special adviser to the president on national security affairs. This, of course, is largely a function of the personalities of the two officials and their relationships with the president. The second, and related variation, involves a decision whether to use the route of a staff paper presented to the president, either cleared or with an indication of differences, or to use the same staff structure to present to the office of the president the various considerations involved in a proposed course of action. This second method avoids a difficulty of the first method in that it delays a confrontation between the president and officials whom he might find difficult to overrule, until a final moment of decision.

In other words, it avoids a situation in which a member of the group decision-making process, such as the Joint Chiefs of Staff, can object to a proposal in its preliminary stage and can obviously not deny to the Congress, at a later stage, that they made this objection. The second method avoids a situation similar to that described in the "Rubaiyat" in which the moving finger having written, none of its writings may be canceled by piety, wit, or tears, or, for that matter, presidential directive.

The problem with the second method of group decision making is that it tends to channel an excessive amount of group decision making through the White House staff, requiring a buildup in that staff and a corresponding reduction in the influence of the other parts of the executive branch of the government.

Presidents Johnson and Carter used the approach of the cleared staff paper almost exclusively. President Nixon and Ford, doubtless due to the influence of Henry Kissinger, used the second method almost exclusively. President Kennedy was selective, on an ad hoc basis, between the two. It is too early to tell the approach of President Reagan.

One generalization may be useful no matter which variant, or combination, of the group decision-making process is used. It is that usually the lower the level of representation of the participants in the group decision-making process, the more rigid will be their adherence to the point of view that their organization represents. Only as the process gets higher in the bureaucracy, which is another way of saying closer to the president, do you find an increasing melding of interest, with the recognition that the position finally reached must be one that the entire administration is prepared to stand behind.

At the same time that the United States is going through the group decision-making process, it is necessary to consider another vital force in this process, the Congress: the Senate, if what is contemplated is the negotiation of a treaty; the House of Representatives, if what is contemplated is an agreement to be approved by both houses; both houses, in any case, because the executive branch will be involved in any event—no matter which route is taken.

The handling of consultations presents two problems. The first, which is often cited as a reason for delaying, or not having, advance consultation with the Congress, is the danger of leaks. When a variety of options are being considered in a negotiating situation, leaks are a danger. They are like letting an opponent in a poker game get a look at your hand before the betting. And there is no doubt that there is always a trade-off between the security necessary to prevent leaks and the exchange of information necessary to provide proper coordination. This trade-off is always present in coordination within the executive branch and in coordination with allies, as will be discussed later. In the experience of the author, however, the danger of leaks resulting from consultation with the Congress is, by far, the lowest of the three.

The second problem is a more subtle one of communications and varying perspectives. It is a truism in Washington that, with the exception of senators or congresspeople with the remarkable qualities of former Senator Mansfield, it is very difficult to get an objective political prediction from a member of Congress. This is because a prediction is itself a political act; it has the tendency to attract support to the cause predicted. The corollary of this syndrome is that, in asking for an evaluation of support on Capitol Hill for a particular measure of arms control, the answer may not be a true reflection as to whether support would be forthcoming, but rather an indication of whether the individual senator or congressperson would prefer not to be put to the test. An indication of this is found in the fact that a not inconsiderable number of the eighty senators who voted in favor of the limited test ban treaty, advised against it, in informal consultations, on the ground that it would not pass the Senate.

Neither of the two problems that have been mentioned are insurmountable. Congressional consultation, in advance, is a must.

The problem of group decision making extends to decisions within alliance relationships, when the allies are participating in the negotiations or, even if not, if their security interests would be affected by the results of the negotiation. Here the problem of decision making is rendered somewhat more complex by the fact that many more countries are involved but somewhat simpler because there is not the expectation that the discussion of the problems will be as detailed, particularly in view of the time pressures that usually exist between the interallied discussion and the beginning of actual negotiations.

This fact, however, does raise two interrelated problems. The first is the inevitable question by some members of the alliance: Are you really consulting us as part of the decision-making process, or are you merely advising us about something you have already decided to do? After all, they will point out, we have our own group decision-making process in our own capitals. This can make the process somewhat complicated, the United States will point out. It took us some weeks or months to arrive at this position, and we cannot be expected to change it in the short time we have remaining. There usually is assent, albeit sometimes grudgingly, to this position.

This, together with independent national allegiances that exist even in alliances, may be responsible for the source of leaks in allied consultation. If the government of an official in an alliance is not committed — is, in fact, opposed — to a position that is about to be put forward, the immediate incentives to leak the position are strong, and the immediate disincentive, personal reprisal through loss of job, is quite weak. This problem, of course, could be resolved if there is developed a general recognition that leaks will weaken an alliance consultation and, thereby, the alliance itself, which is every bit as important, if not more important, to the other allies as it is to the United States.

So far, the discussion of the international negotiating process, dealing with internal decision making, has not dealt with the fact that international negotiations do not end with the presentation by the various sides of the result of their respective decision-making processes. This is only the beginning.

What follows is a process taking months, more often years, in which the various sides explore their differences and attempt to see if a mutually satisfactory accommodation can be reached. Usually this exploration, or negotiation, is not conducted by the same people who are involved in the decision-making process in the capitals involved. After all, you cannot have key cabinet members, military leaders, or presidential advisers spending months or years around the negotiating table on a particular negotiation. As a result, one has to accept the fact that the people at the negotiating table will not be the same as the decision makers, although there may be some overlap.

An argument might be made that a "summit" meeting of heads of state is an exception to this rule, but experience has shown that, even in the case of a summit, a successful outcome requires extensive preparation by officials, other than the heads of state, themselves. Even in the case of the most crucial and dramatic negotiation in this generation, the settlement of the Cuban missile crisis, by direct communication between the heads of state, communications between officials in Washington — in particular the then Attorney General Robert Kennedy and the Soviet ambassador to the United States — were critical to success.

Looking at this from the point of view of the United States, this introduces the distinction between "Washington" and "the delegation," to use the somewhat pejorative terms that these two groups often apply to each other. Underlying these caustic references, there is usually an undertone that Washington regards the delegation as anxious to obtain an agreement at all costs and the delegation regards Washington as bureaucratically hidebound and insensitive to the true national interests involved in the negotiations. It has already been pointed out that the references to "Washington" as a unit involve such an oversimplification as to be inaccurate. The references to "the delegation" as a unit come somewhat closer to the mark. This is true despite the fact that in the case of most delegations, a substantive number, often a majority, of the members, when they return to "real life" in the United States, will not be working for the head of the delegation and hence do not owe their future career prospects to the delegation head. The reason for this cohesion, in the face of this seemingly built-in conflict, is found in a basic part of delegation life in which the delegation members are in constant communication, socially as well as officially. More often than not, it results in the delegation becoming quite united in its approach to the negotiations. On the occasions when this does not happen, the differences are usually sharp and bitter. There is very seldom a middle ground, although at the Washington end, a middle ground is almost invariably found.

The dynamics of the relationship between "Washington" and "the delegation" is an aspect of the process of international negotiations that has not been dealt with in depth by the scholars who have written on the subject of international negotiations. The next few pages of this chapter will attempt to do so; for the purpose of exposition, it will be put in terms of the rights and obligations of Washington and the delegation.

Turning first to the rights and obligations of the delegation, it is not difficult to stake out their outer limits. The first limit, of course, relates to the delegation's obligations to report. This can be overdone. One of the most effective obfuscations of the reporting process can be excessive detail. If everything is, so to speak, summed up in twenty thousand words, one can be assured that none of the salient points, which should be the object of reporting, will receive the attention they deserve by the decision makers. The other outer limit is the failure to report critical discussion at all. This can be very tempting when statements are made such as: "I don't know what Moscow and/or Washington thinks about this and I would appreciate your not reporting it because this is purely a personal suggestion." This technique is often used by negotiators representing all nations, but it should never be taken at face value. No responsible negotiator can expect that a negotiator representing another country will not report to his own government whatever he thinks the decision makers in that government should know, notwithstanding any whispers and murmurs that may take place between delegations that are purely personal suggestions and not to be reported. It is not duplicity; it is part of the accepted rules of the process of international negotiations.

Between the obligation to report enough but not too much, there is a particular obligation on the part of the chief negotiator that can only be described in general terms. This consists of his obligation to advise Washington as to his appraisal of the probable consequences of a course of action that he is recommending or has been instructed to take. It is, of course, the obligation of the negotiator to include in his reports his judgment on the effect of any proposed action on the negotiations and on the national security of the United States. This aspect of reporting should, obviously, be carried out with discretion. Continued cries from a negotiator of "ruin, havoc and decay unless my recommendations are accepted" or "if I have to carry out these instructions" will give the negotiator a reputation in "Washington" as a screamer and will result in his serious recommendations being discounted. The Greek fable of the boy who cried wolf too often is quite relevant here. This problem is often made more difficult by the natural tendency, referred to above, of "Washington" to regard "the delegation" as being excessively anxious to obtain an agreement.

There are a few other points that should be mentioned with respect to the functioning of a delegation. The first is the concept of "back-channel communications" by which members of "the delegation" report directly to their home office. Such communications are not only inevitable but, if used with discretion, they are valuable. There is nothing wrong with the representative of the Joint Chiefs of Staff, for example, having direct communications with his superiors in the military, and it would be foolish and counterproductive for a delegation head to insist that he must approve any such communication beforehand. A wise delegation head will rely on the esprit de corps on the part of his delegation, trusting that its members will not try to undercut him but will, in effect, advise their Washington superiors on the true state of negotiations. If they have difficulty with the way things are going, they will advise the delegation head who may then advise the appropriate authorities in Washington so that the necessary decision can be made.

Another problem with respect to delegation management is the extent to which communications are to be permitted by other than heads of delegations or, in fact, are to be encouraged. A very useful means of explanation can be statements by deputy heads of delegations or other members of the delegation to their opposite numbers along the following lines: "I don't know whether my delegation or my government would agree with this but I would like your reaction as to whether there is a worthwhile path for us to pursue." These statements should never be made without the approval of the delegation head and should, of course, be reported. They should normally be done by someone on the delegation who is recognized by the other side as having close relationship with the head of the delegation. This leads to the issue of statements to the media, either for attribution or otherwise. These statements are now a form of international communications and are a part of international negotiations. For that reason, there should be no statements to the press, in any form, with which the head of the delegation does not agree and for which he is not prepared to take responsibility.

The rights and duties of "Washington" with respect to "the delegation" are in most instances the opposite side of the coin of the rights and duties of the delegation that have been described, and it would be redundant to analyze them in the same detail. It is useful to point out, however, that the decision makers in Washington have a duty to give prompt instructions on substantive matters to the delegation. In addition, Washington should leave tactical decisions to the delegation with a sympathetic understanding of the delegation's approach to the status of the particular negotiation. The degree of this understanding, of course, bears a direct relation to the extent to which the decision makers in Washington regard the delegation, particularly its head, as a "screamer," a "realist," or perhaps, even — and this is relatively rare — an "understater."

No discussion of international negotiations in the field of national security would be complete without discussion of two concepts: the concept of bargaining chips (negotiating from strength) and the concept of looking at the worst case (you cannot be too careful when dealing with your nation's security). The trouble with these two concepts (and they have been discussed so often that they are now clichés) is that there is an element of truth in both of them. They are self-destructive concepts if they are applied mechanically; they are not if they are considered intelligently as part of the total decision-making process.

Dealing first with the bargaining-chip concept: in the context of arms-control negotiations, its more enthusiastic advocates would urge that if you intend to negotiate an arms-control agreement you must be prepared, in fact start, to engage in the very activities that you would like to make the subject of a ban. At least, they would argue, you have to give your opposite number the impression that this is what you are prepared to do or even are actually doing.

As indicated earlier, there is an element of validity in these arguments. All negotiations involve a quid pro quo; arms-control negotiations involve an institutionalized form of mutual restraints on armaments or on the reduction of armaments. If a party to a negotiation is convinced that the opposite number will not engage in the activity that is the subject of the negotiations whether those negotiations succeed or fail, it has no incentive to proceed to an agreement under which it would accept those restrictions on itself. Put in stark terms, if the United States had had a constitutional amendment prohibiting it from conducting any nuclear explosions, there would have been no incentive for the Soviet Union to agree to the limited test ban treaty, under which they could not conduct nuclear explosions in the atmosphere, in outer space, or underwater.

In considering this argument, however, consideration must also be given to the effect of a bargaining-chip decision on other parties to the negotiation. They, too, are not single decision-making units. Other countries, including the USSR, have their doves and their hawks; and although their decision-making processes may not be identical to that of the US, they exist. The factor that must be considered is the effect that a bargaining-chip announcement by the United States will have on this decision-making process. If stated strongly by the United States, it will give the hawks in the other country the argument that the United States is not really serious about the negotiations, so why should they be prepared to undertake any restriction on themselves.

In an analysis such as this, involving the intangibles of political decision making, one has to look at experience. On one side, it may well be that the Congressional action authorizing the Safeguard Anti-Ballistic Missile (ABM) system for the United States may well have been helpful in obtaining the SALT I ABM Treaty. There are other examples in which the balance was tipped in the other direction. The first involved the earliest arms-control negotiation, the Baruch Plan (1946). If the concept of the bargaining chips, negotiating from a position of strength, could ever have been automatically applied, this was the case. The United States had a monopoly on nuclear weapons that it was to maintain for three more years. Yet this did not put pressure on the USSR to eliminate nuclear weapons by internationalizing all nuclear activity. Instead, it persuaded the Soviets that the United States intended to perpetuate this monopoly; and their reaction was not to negotiate on the Baruch Plan but to press on with their plans for developing nuclear weapons.

Another time the principle of bargaining chips was tried and failed, the shoe was on the other foot. After the Soviets had launched Sputnik and were engaged in rocket-rattling diplomacy, it might have been argued that this would put pressure on the United States to negotiate a restriction on strategic nuclear-delivery systems. To the contrary, the reaction of the United States was to engage in a buildup of Minuteman ICBMs. This buildup was probably greater than that necessary to overcome any missile gap. This led, in turn, to further Soviet buildups and, ultimately, to the precarious position in which the two countries, and the rest of the world, now find themselves.

These are two illustrations in which the bargaining-chip concept has not worked. One also can consider at least two examples in which restraint in not playing the bargaining chip produced results. The first was the limited test ban treaty. Responding to an offer made by Chairman Khrushchev to negotiate a limited test ban treaty, President Kennedy announced that the United States would no longer conduct tests in the atmosphere so long as other states did not do so. Within less than two months there was agreement on the limited test ban treaty. It is highly unlikely that this result would have been obtained had President Kennedy announced the intention of the United States to engage in a massive series of nuclear tests in the atmosphere.

The second is found in the history of the negotiation of the Treaty on the Non-Proliferation of Nuclear Weapons. The negotiation of this treaty took a long time: from 1964 to 1968. The greatest part of this delay was caused by the concern of the Soviet Union that the United States, under the guise of the multilateral nuclear force or under some other guise, intended to transfer nuclear weapons to the Federal Republic of Germany. During these negotiations, the United States Senate began consideration of the Pastore Resolution, S. Res. 179, 89th Congress. This resolution commended the efforts of President Johnson to negotiate a treaty to prevent the spread of nuclear weapons. During its deliberation, it was made quite clear that neither the executive branch nor the Congress had any intention of permitting the transfer of control over nuclear weapons to the Federal Republic of Germany. The way was then cleared for the negotiation of the NPT.

The conclusion that can be drawn from these illustrations is that although it is not unhelpful to a nation's negotiating position to have "bargaining chips," it is not helpful to flaunt them or play them prematurely. It is most helpful if they are handled with the full recognition of their effect on the decision-making process of the opposite numbers in the negotiation.

In connection with the decision-making process, it is necessary to consider the "worst-case" approach to any possible risks in the proposed course of action in a negotiation as a reason for not going ahead. It is always possible to point out risks in any arms-control negotiation or, for that matter, any other negotiation or even any course of action, be it governmental or private.

To use a military analogy from the United States Civil War, the classic example of the worst-case approach is found in the activities of General McClellan in the Peninsula Campaign. He always looked at the worst case, consistently overestimated Confederate strength, losing opportunity after opportunity during seven days of intensive combat and ending up on the banks of the James River huddled under the protective fire of the Union navy instead of ending up with seige guns in front of Richmond where he could well have been. The worst-case analysis of any proposed course of action is, of course, only sensible if balanced against an equal appraisal of the risks of not taking the action. Once this is done, the worst-case approach no longer deserves its title. It becomes what it should be, a sensible analysis of the pros and cons of action versus nonaction as that decision affects national security.

The final dilemma in international negotiations is that it is inadvisable, in fact counterproductive, for any country to announce itself as a "winner." The self-proclamation of a negotiator as a winner is probably unwise in any form of negotiation because if there is to be a continuing relationship, a self-proclaimed "victory" will cause difficulties the next time around. This problem is made more acute in the field of international negotiations because any meaningful international agreement will only continue to be effective if the parties continue to see it as being, on balance, in their respective interests.

This dilemma presents a real problem to the international negotiator and may, perhaps, explain why the turnover in negotiators is quite high. A negotiator who will be blamed for his "defeats" but cannot claim credit for his "victories" will appear to be rather on the deficit side in the balance. Perhaps this concept of balance presents a solution to a negotiator faced with this dilemma. A defensible, and usually accurate, position would be: We did not get everything out of this negotiation that we started out to get; neither did other parties to the negotiation; there was give and take on all sides but, on balance, we believe the agreement arrived at serves the interests of our country.

In conclusion, notwithstanding all the difficulties and dilemmas involved in the process of international negotiation, it cannot be denied that it is preferable to fighting.

Editor's Comments on Disarmament Negotiations

These two chapters on disarmament negotiations complement each other. The first chapter gives an overview of the broad principles involved in disarmament negotiations, while the second is concerned with the in-depth formulation of negotiating positions and the process of presenting them to the other side and pursuing them.

The first chapter brings out the following significant points regarding multilateral disarmament negotiations:

1. Disarmament negotiations are essential, but the fact that they are closely intertwined with the fundamental issue of security makes them extremely delicate and highly dependent on a strong will to reach agreement. For various reasons, this necessary strong will to agree has been largely absent in the whole post–World War II period. The author illustrates this point by surveying the negotiations, or rather the lack of negotiations, for a comprehensive test ban treaty and the separate negotiations for a ban on the production, stockpiling, and use of chemical weapons.
2. The principle of equal security is a key factor, but it is one that is extremely difficult to define.
3. A common goal must be established, but in practice, this, too, is an extremely difficult matter when it comes to the substance of issues.
4. While paying lip service to UN resolutions on multilateral negotiations, the superpowers disregard these commitments and strongly favor direct adversarial negotiations.
5. Consensus is essential in this field, and this means, in the first instance, agreement among the superpowers.
6. The author hopes that new factors, such as the "new wave of disarmament" in Europe and elsewhere, will be taken into account by the negotiators.

The second chapter brings out the following interesting points related to the process of disarmament negotiations:

1. The first necessity is to identify the parties to arms negotiations. The superpowers are essential, but they must consult with their allies and, to some extent, with the nonaligned. They cannot really go it alone.
2. Each party is a composite, not a single-minded, rational indivisible entity. It consists of a number of facets: the ministry of foreign affairs or department of state, the president's office or the prime minister's office, the defense department, the military chiefs, the intelligence agencies and public opinion.
3. In the making of policy, the higher the level of representation of the above facets in the discussion to hammer out a position, the more successful the effort.
4. A constant problem in the formulation of a negotiating position is the avoidance of leaks that can seriously damage a negotiation.
5. Once a party's negotiating position is established, it is given to a negotiator who is often not part of the decision-making process in arriving at the negotiating position. Interaction between negotiator and the government is necessary.
6. Tactical decisions should be left to the negotiator.
7. Negotiating from strength is a cliché in the field of negotiation that seldom works in practice, for example, the Baruch Plan of 1946 and on the other side, the Soviet breakthrough in delivery systems as evidenced by the first Sputnik in 1956. The limited test ban treaty of 1963 was aided by Kennedy's decision to refrain from a show of strength by rejecting the idea of a new round of United States atmospheric tests.
8. The worst-case approach by a party can defeat a negotiation. A sensible analysis of the pros and cons is what is called for.
9. Never, never, should a country announce that it has won a negotiation. Such an announcement causes difficulties in the future relations of the countries concerned.

PART 6

NORTH-SOUTH NEGOTIATIONS

Chapter 9

A Methodological Summary

Johan Kaufmann†

INTRODUCTION: THE GENERAL FRAMEWORK OF MULTILATERAL NORTH-SOUTH NEGOTIATIONS

North-South negotiations can be defined as negotiations between the industrialized North and the less-developed countries of the South and aimed at achieving a better international economic order. A better international economic order is, by definition, a new international economic order. The New International Economic Order (NIEO) has been a subject of considerable controversy, caused, in part, by confusion about the question, "who negotiates where about what" and, perhaps to a larger extent, by disagreement about basic objectives and means to achieve those objectives.

This chapter will concentrate on multilateral North-South negotiations. Most North-South negotiations, however, have taken place in a framework in which a certain number of developed countries is negotiating with a number of developing countries. This configuration will constitute the main background of this chapter.

In 1923, Lloyd George stated: "The gibbers are beginning to say: Ah!

The author expresses his gratitude to Professor H. C. Bos, Erasmus University, Rotterdam; Mr. G. Ringnalda, Permanent Mission of the Netherlands to the United States, New York; and Professor H. W. Singer, Institute of Development Studies at the University of Sussex, Brighton, who have kindly offered criticisms and comments on an earlier draft. The end result is of course entirely the author's own responsibility.

†This chapter incorporates material from Johan Kaufmann, *Conference Diplomacy*, Leyden: Sijthoff; and Dobbs Ferry: Oceana, 1968, and Johan Kaufmann, *United Nations Decision Making*, Alphen and Rijn and Rockville, Maryland: Sijthoff & Noordhoff, 1980. The reader is referred to these works for a more extensive treatment of the subject.

Another Conference! Forty-five nations! A thousand experts! What folly! What extravagance! Yes, what extravagance — a thousand experts, financial, diplomatic, economic. They are cheaper than military experts. Their retinue is a smaller one."[1]

Large-scale conferences still abound. They result in "plans of action," which often turn out to be programs for inaction since the action plans themselves are filled with loopholes and are subject to national acceptance that may take place only after years, if at all. Negotiations in small formats, such as the CIEC (Paris 1975–1977) have often also resulted in a paucity of concrete decisions. What, therefore, is the way out, if there is one? What can the negotiator involved in North-South negotiations do to achieve his objectives, whether these are positive, in terms of results required, or negative, that is, to block certain initiatives from others?

Negotiations related to North-South problems can be broken down as to their objectives as follows:[2]

a) to serve as forum for general discussion of broad or specific issues;
b) to make non-binding recommendations to governments or international organizations.

These two objectives are found in all the large-scale meetings discussing North-South issues, such as the General Assembly, the UN Economic Social Council, the UNCTAD General Conference, and so forth.

c) to make decisions binding upon governments.

There are few North-South negotiations that directly result in decisions binding upon governments. Usually the maximum one can obtain is an international instrument that remains to be ratified and implemented. Of course, budget decisions in the organs of the United Nations and specialized agencies have the character of a binding decision. To the extent that such decisions allocate funds for the purpose of undertaking activities of importance to the development problem, they can be considered part of the North-South negotiations.

d) to make decisions giving guidance or instruction to the secretariat of an intergovernmental organization, or on the way in which a program financed by governments should be administered.

Examples of this category are provided by the decisions of governing organs of the various assistance programs in the United Nations family of organizations. The United Nations Development Programme (UNDP) governing council and the United Nations Children's Fund (UNICEF) executive board are examples. The guidance that these governing bodies give is relevant not only to the executive management of UNDP and UNICEF but also to donor and recipient governments whose policies are assumed to conform to that guidance.

e) to negotiate and draft a treaty or other formal international instrument.

This category, of course, constitutes the most important part of North-South negotiations because only a legally binding international instrument can be really effective (in practice, even a legally accepted instrument may turn out, for various reasons, to be a dead letter). The code of conduct for transnational corporations, now being negotiated in the United Nations, and the UNCTAD Code on the Transfer of Technology are examples. The Law of the Sea Treaty, if, as, and when completed, will contain many provisions significant for North-South relations. International commodity agreements are also an example, to the extent that they affect North-South trade.

The principal actors in North-South negotiations are undoubtedly governments, either acting individually or in some group. The two other principal actors are the presiding officers and the secretariat. Subsidiary actors in certain situations play an important role: nongovernmental organizations; intergovernmental organizations; private business, especially private business in some organized grouping; and trade unions. Expert advisers, either from within an organization or specially brought in, play a role of varying significance. On occasion, a report written by a group of advisers may influence the decision-making process. Thus, the report of a group of "eminent persons" on the impact of multinational corporations on development and on international relations (1974) preceded the establishment of the UN Commission on Transnational Corporations.

Governments are no doubt the principal actors in North-South negotiations, but it must not be forgotten that the private sector (business, trade unions, individual entrepreneurs, and workers) is, in many countries, the main force in the process of development. Governments can only provide a general structure and background on which economic growth occurs. Some of the disappointment in the development process is no doubt due to the fact that general conditions set by governments, in part as a result of North-South negotiations, have not provided the right climate for economic growth. Sometimes, political events have undone what was accomplished as the result of North-South negotiations. On other occasions, the behavior of governments both of the North and of the South was different from what would seem to emanate from accepted international recommendations (e.g., the decision to transfer 0.7% in Official Development Assistance [ODA] to developing countries).

THE ROLE OF GOVERNMENTS

A government participating in North-South negotiations is represented by a delegation. It is therefore important to devote some attention to the composition and functioning of delegations.

A distinction must be made between a "mission" to the United Nations and a "delegation" to a particular meeting. A permanent mission is headed by a permanent representative, generally with the rank and status of an ambassador, and has a varying complement of alternate or deputy permanent representatives; ministers; counsellors; first, second, and third secretaries with supporting staffs. A "delegation" is established and accredited (usually by a formal note to the secretary-general) for a particular meeting or series of meetings.

The instructions under which a delegation operates are of crucial importance. There are considerable differences in the amount and nature of instructions that delegations receive. Some are given lengthy and detailed instructions that severely limit their freedom of maneuver. Some governments instruct their delegations in terms of the position of other governments, that is, "Vote more or less like. . . . " "If . . . votes 'no' you can abstain." Some governments provide no instructions at all, leaving matters to the discretion of the delegation.

Ideal instructions would be specific as to objectives and the degree of activity required but would leave considerable freedom of action to the delegation if events took an unexpected turn. The precise drafting of the language of a resolution cannot usually be done on the basis of instructions prepared in advance. Increasingly, instructions are the result of consultation or coordination within certain groupings, for example, the European Community, the Group of 77, or the Nonaligned Movement.

On decisions of great importance there is often a "strategic postponement" to give delegations time to obtain instructions from home. The distance to the national capital and the efficiency of the confidential communications facilities available also influence the type of instructions possible for each delegation.

In many cases, North-South negotiations are strongly influenced by the behavior of groups, usually the Group of 77 representing the developing countries and a not always identically composed group of developed countries, called Group B in some instances, especially in UNCTAD. The Group of 77 has, increasingly, to take into account various subgroups, in particular the least developed countries, who are often separately referred to in resolutions. Politically the Group of 77 usually presents — often after long internal discussion and negotiation — a common front, although economically, the interests of its members are varied. The developed countries are politically more divided, often not presenting publicly a common front, although from an economic point of view their interests are more homogeneous.

The North-South negotiator should be aware of the different functions of groups. They can be distinguished in the following way:

a) to exchange information on all or part of the agenda of a conference, either in advance or during the conference;
b) to develop common general positions on important agenda items, without definite voting commitment.

In this case, there is not only an exchange of information but also an effort to arrive at approximately identical positions for all delegations participating in group meetings. The OECD members, expanded by certain non-members, endeavor as the so-called Group B to coordinate their positions on various issues and agenda items in UNCTAD meetings.

Early in 1975, the Netherlands and Norway took the initiative to convene a group of countries assumed to be "like-minded" on development issues, that is, Denmark, Sweden, the United Kingdom, and the two initiating countries. Meeting at the level of high officials, the purpose was to arrive at common positions and, if possible, initiatives in the United Nations in general and ECOSOC in particular. The group met, also at the level of ministers responsible for development cooperation, at irregular intervals and with a composition changing at almost every meeting. The group remained essentially consultative and did not aspire to formalize itself. It was occasionally successful in developing certain common concepts prior to important international conferences. At the fourth conference of UNCTAD (Nairobi 1976) the like-minded countries took the initiative regarding a statement on the question of the so-called "integrated commodities program." They continue to meet once or twice a year, with varying attendance.

c) to develop common positions on certain agenda items or initiatives with agreement on how to vote.

Efforts to find not only common positions, but also agreements on how to vote, can and do occur in almost every group. They occur systematically in groups of nations bound together by a treaty requiring common points of view on certain questions as is the case for the member countries of the European Community, or in less formal groups such as the Group of 77. More and more in UN meetings, one can encounter examples of geographical, political, or ad hoc groups deciding to vote in a certain way on draft proposals, on amendments, or on an expected procedural move. Explicit coordination of voting behavior is increasing, while in the past, tacit or at most an improvised understanding arrived at just before voting led to voting alignments. Frequently, there is an explanation of the vote by one member of a group on behalf of that whole group. The "common position" involves putting pressure on those who might disagree (see [f]).

d) to agree on candidates to be put forward by the group or on a common vote for candidates outside the group.

This is one of the functions in which the development of a common point of view has meaning only if there is also agreement on how to vote. This may be for a single agreed slate of candidates of the grouping itself as well as for some combination out of a number of competing candidates of other groups. In connection with such election agreements there may be a joint plan of campaign for or against other candidates.

e) To agree on a common spokesperson and on the contents of the statement to be delivered.

A group of sponsors of a draft resolution usually agrees on a common spokesperson to introduce its text in the meeting. Furthermore, any of the groups that we have discussed above may, in a particular situation, decide on a spokesperson. The Group of 77 and the European Community normally have their statements delivered by the delegation of the country that is the current chairperson.

f) To undertake joint action for or against a proposal.

Although linked to functions (b) and (c) such a "lobbying" function can be separate. A common position and an agreement on voting do not necessarily entail joint lobbying. Conversely, a joint lobbying campaign obviously requires an agreed position on the proposal or issue behind it.

Any delegation involved in North-South negotiations has to determine how strongly it wishes to associate itself with group solidarity. The individual delegation must consider carefully whether, within the group to which it belongs, it wishes to put forward some proposal, initiative, or suggestion in order to gain group endorsement. If there is a "group within the group" to which the delegation belongs, it will try to get prior support for its ideas from such a subgroup. If a delegation wants to "go it alone," without group endorsement, it must have mapped out a strategy to gain support from other groups or from some ad hoc combination of delegations.

A special tactical situation exists when a country wishes to dissociate itself from an emerging group position. There will, on occasion, be heavy pressure (which may assume the form of blackmail) to have a "dissident" conform to "group solidarity."

Effects of the Group System on North-South Negotiations

There has been much discussion on the effects of the group negotiating system on North-South relations. On the positive side, there has certainly been a gain in conference efficiency, especially if negotiating procedures between groups become an established routine and communications between groups are made easier by the existence of such procedures. Moreover, in so far as statements by group spokesmen replace a large number of individual speeches, time is saved. On the negative side, it has become apparent that the willingness to accept compromises is often replaced by group inflexibility, which makes the negotiation of compromise agreements more difficult. This is likely to occur when a "demand-offer" type of conflict arises: A group of countries presents maximum demands to another group that tends to respond with minimum offers.

More recent experience shows that a contact group, consisting of a small number of persons delegated from both sides, can undertake a great deal of activity leading toward constructive compromises. Provided such a group is created early enough during a conference and has the confidence of those not themselves members of it, it can take away a great deal of the inbuilt rigidities of the group system (see also p. 49 of *Conference Diplomacy*).

SECRETARIATS

North-South negotiations have been helped a great deal by international secretariats; occasionally they may have been handicapped by secretariats. The vast amount of documentation emanating from international secretariats must have been a mixed blessing. Increasingly, the abundance of material has provoked the effect of not being able to "see the forest for the trees." It can therefore be quite important that prior to crucial conferences there is a single central report from the secretariat, listing the principal issues, and coming forward with recommendations. Such a report, written by the first secretary-general of UNCTAD, Dr. R. Prebisch, preceded the establishment of UNCTAD at the 1964 Geneva Conference.

A distinction must be made between the head of the secretariat, often referred to as the "executive head," and the rest of the secretariat. In some cases, the executive head is active and the secretariat more passively inclined or vice versa.

There are specific factors directly affecting the role of the secretariat and, in particular, of its head. The principal factors are:

1. *The statutory role of the executive head and of the secretariat.*
   The constitution and other basic instruments of an organization indicate the powers or functions of the executive head, his rights to take initiatives and his duties vis-à-vis the organization and the membership. Alternatively, the constitution may be silent on the powers of the secretariat. In certain extreme cases, there is no constitution, and therefore, limitations on the role of the executive head will follow from any decisions of the governing bodies and from gradually developed habits.
2. *The personality of the executive head.*
   He may be a man of action, exploiting every possibility for new initiatives and for strengthening his own position and that of the secretariat, or he may be more inclined to be an "administrator," in the strict sense of the word.
3. *The degree of confidence that member states have in the executive head and his secretariat.*
   Such confidence is determined by a combination of influences: the character and objectives of the organization served by the executive head; the position taken on various issues by the governments; whether the executive head was appointed with the full cooperation of the governments from

which confidence is expected; and finally, whether there is a good personal relationship between the executive head and high-level officials of member governments.

It can be argued that the confluence of these three factors determines what might be called the "intensity" of secretariat activity, which can be defined as the combined quantity and quality of new secretariat activities; undertaken either on the initiative of the secretariat itself or of governments.

The heads of most of the international secretariats are called secretaries-general. Some of them act more like a secretary, others more like a general. In other words, some are emphasizing the administrative side of their function, faithfully executing assigned tasks; and others develop new initiatives and try to align governments to those initiatives. An executive head may find it advantageous to present himself as a radical fighter for new causes or, conversely, as the guardian of accepted truths. In certain situations, the secretariats can "fill up" the vacuum left by inaction on the part of governments. Thus, the initial activity of the United Nations in the field of multinational corporations was clearly influenced by research in the Department of Economic Affairs of the UN secretariat, then headed by Under-Secretary-General Philippe de Seynes. Of course the subject must be "ripe" for international action, lest a secretariat initiative fall into, rather than fill, a vacuum.

Constructive action by the head of an international secretariat may take place in the absence of action by governments or serve as a trigger to prod governments into doing what is necessary. The alert delegate will weigh the pros and cons of such action by a secretariat. If he does not like it, he will have to get a majority for an alternative action that he does want; he will only be successful if the action he has in mind has more appeal for this majority than the action contemplated by the secretariat. Such weighing of pros and cons can only take place if the proposed secretariat action is made known in advance.

Sometimes secretariat action will assume the character of an accomplished fact, a real "filling of a vacuum." At all times, secretariats may be pressed by delegations who believe their proposals will fare better if they can be assured of secretariat support. If the secretariat allies itself with a group of delegations for "political" reasons (e.g., to obtain support for a secretariat proposal), the risk is not only discord because of opposition of other delegations but also the premature adoption of recommendations that may not have been sufficiently researched as to their economic or other impact.

PRESIDING OFFICERS

In general, presiding officers do not exercise a decisive influence on the success or failure of North-South negotiations. Yet, in certain situations, their role can be quite important. The potentially useful role of a presiding officer (or of the "bureau" of meetings, that is, the chairperson and vice-chairperson, possibly assisted by a rapporteur) can be illustrated by two examples.

In the thirty-fifth session of the General Assembly (1980) the president, R. von Wechmar, undertook an impressive amount of activity to achieve agreement on conditions for the start of the new round of global negotiations.

In the Second (Economic and Financial) Committee of the General Assembly, a practice has developed according to which each of the two vice-chairpeople becomes the chairperson of an informal negotiating group dealing with the various draft resolutions. Experience has shown that these vice-chairpeople can thus be considerably more important than their formal task of occasionally substituting for the chairperson would indicate.

The ideal chairperson is able to keep delegates' statements within a reasonable length, to limit himself to an occasional observation in order to remind delegates of the subject before them, and to summarize occasionally but not too frequently lest he be accused of talking too much. A good chairperson will also give rapid and correct rulings on procedural questions. He will keep in touch with delegates before and after sessions, in informal meetings at which he may be present, and at various social events. If there are a number of committees or subcommittees functioning under his supervision, he will see to it that he keeps in touch with the committee chairpeople.

One of the most important functions, indeed duties, of a presiding officer is to leave sufficient time for informal negotiations. Thus, at the Seventh Special Session of the General Assembly (1975) on "Development and International Economic Cooperation," the chairman of the ad hoc committee (Mr. J. P. Pronk of the Netherlands) quickly realized that effective results had to come from negotiations in relatively small groups. The atmosphere and negotiations of that session have been characterized by the UN as follows:

> The Seventh Special Session of the United Nations General Assembly met, literally, at two levels. At the upper level, in the gold-domed grandeur of the Assembly Hall, delegates listened to the slow unfolding of the formal debate. The proceedings went strictly by tradition and rule, with Algerian Foreign Minister Abdelaziz Bouteflika presiding from the green marble podium as representatives of 108 countries outlined their views and proposals on development and economic co-operation. Meanwhile, in the basement directly under the Assembly floor, work proceeded at a different pace. In small conference rooms blue with cigarette smoke, delegates met in closed sessions to haggle and argue over the issues dividing them. Here there was little formality to begin with and, as negotiations wore through long days and ever later into the nights, all unnecessary frills disappeared. Jackets were slung over the backs of chairs, shirt sleeves were rolled up, ties loosened, and voices rasped increasingly with fatigue and, occasionally, irritation.
>
> The negotiations in the basement conference rooms of the Assembly were between "contact groups." In the main, they were between the 27-member contact group of the Group of 77 (developing countries) and the 12-member contact group of Western European and Other countries (WEO). This was as much because the socialist countries of Eastern Europe and China supported the posi-

tion of the developing countries as it was because they did not play a major part in those aspects of the international economy that the developing countries want changed.

Negotiations between the contact groups of the developing countries and the WEO countries were entirely in closed sessions. One set of negotiators met on the major problem areas of trade and transfer of resources; a second set worked on the four items of the agenda, industrialization, science and technology, food and agriculture, and restructuring of the United Nations. The position of the European Community on major sections of the basic working paper tabled by the Group of 77 had already been subject to some negotiations during the preparatory phase of the Special Session. The United States' position, articulated as it was for the first time on the opening day of the conference, and containing as it did so many proposals, presented a major task for the negotiators.

As the first week passed and then the second, differences narrowed but not enough to warrant a full consensus. The scheduled end of the session came and went but the negotiators continued. They continued over the weekend of 13 September, continued all day and night on Monday. Finally in the early dawn of Tuesday the bleary-eyed delegates reached agreement.

The resolution they agreed on consists of seven parts and covers all the major topics considered during the session. It was adopted without a vote in the closing plenary meeting on 16 September.[3]

SUBSIDIARY ACTORS: INTERGOVERNMENTAL ORGANIZATIONS, NONGOVERNMENTAL ORGANIZATIONS, AND THE PRIVATE SECTOR

Intergovernmental organizations can influence the North-South negotiating process, especially if their members come to a negotiating session with precoordinated points of view. How much flexibility such precoordination leaves will be important. Again, a minimum amount of flexibility will be indispensable, lest the negotiating session be shipwrecked on the cliffs of preexisting rigidity. Many intergovernmental organizations have official observer or similar status with various conferences.

Non-governmental organizations (NGOs) on occasion play an important role in the negotiating process. It must be recalled that Article 71 of the UN Charter gave the ECOSOC the right to make "suitable arrangements for consultation" with NGOs. Some 800 NGOs have consultative status with ECOSOC.

In many cases, papers submitted by NGOs, or speeches delivered by their representatives, receive only little attention. One must neither underestimate nor overestimate the role of many NGOs to pave the way for new governmental positions. Both within nations and internationally, negotiations on human rights, on the NIEO, and on the environment have certainly been influenced, to an extent which is difficult to measure with precision, by positions and activities of NGOs.

Sometimes representatives of business and/or the trade unions are directly involved in North-South negotiations. In the International Labour Organization (ILO), employers and workers are constitutionally on the same level as governments. Negotiations related to the establishment of a code for multinational corporations are attended by experts appointed by trade unions and business firms. In certain international commodity agreement negotiations, it is customary that representatives from the business sector involved attend the meetings although not always the closed negotiating sessions.

TACTICS IN NORTH-SOUTH NEGOTIATIONS

The tactics available to the North-South negotiator either to push or to oppose a proposal are not essentially different from those of multilateral diplomacy in general. In all cases, familiarity with the rules of procedure applicable to the meeting in question is essential. The knowledge of these rules and their practical applicability will enable the negotiator to propose, at a proper moment, the suspension or the adjournment of a meeting or to proceed to a vote immediately.

A delegation wishing to push a proposal can use any or all of the following methods:

1. It will try to advance all possible arguments (intellectual, historic, and other) in favor of its proposal.
2. It can try to exercise some sort of pressure on other countries, in particular, in fields not related to the United Nations settings, for example, aid or trade matters. It is obvious that this sort of pressure, in addition to its ethical undesirability, is not available to the vast majority of UN member states.
3. It can propose a "deal," a log-trading transaction within the UN setting, for example, support for some initiative or the candidacy of another delegation. This sort of leverage is available to many UN members.
4. It can and will organize an energetic campaign, in many cases weeks or months before the session in which the initiative is to be launched, in favor of its proposal (this, however, may also alert opponents at an early date).

On the other hand, a delegation opposing a proposal can avail itself of all four tactical moves mentioned above (in the case of [4] this would be a sort of "counter-campaign"), plus all the tricks permitted by the United Nations rules and practices of procedure, some of which are:

5. An opposing delegation can try to have an initiative referred to another body, whether inside or outside the UN. I have called this kind of tactic the "Ping-Pong game" because with skill it can be applied successively in a number of bodies.
6. An alternative draft resolution can be presented by opposing delegations prior to the tabling of the initiative itself. This is all the easier if the initiating delegation has given wide advance knowledge of its proposal, thus, hav-

ing forewarned its opponents. The alternative draft resolution will perhaps request a long-lasting inquiry by the secretary-general among member states, a well-known device to obtain a lengthy deferment. The inquiry would be the alternative to the action involved in the initiative.

7. The opposing delegation(s) can use procedural motions to adjourn a meeting or to adjourn the debate.
8. The opposing delegation(s) can engage in informal or formal consultations or negotiations and then enter into delaying tactics (e.g., "I have to get instructions from my government on this new text," etc.). If there is enough delay, there may, in the rush of finishing a session, not be enough time to put the proposal of the initiating delegation to a vote.

Some other tactical stances are:

1. "Black Peter"—I do not like this proposal, but I tell people I support it, expecting that country X, which is against it, will be left with the stigma of having been responsible for its rejection.
2. "Hide and seek"—my arguments are hidden beneath a mass of rhetoric and of largely irrelevant considerations. If you search carefully, you may dig up some of them, but it will not change things.
3. "Poker"—I hide my hand. I have a lot of trumps, but I do not show anything.
4. "Waiting for Godot"—we must wait till the time is ripe.

Another important tactical (some would say political) aspect is whether to aim at a consensus or to have any texts adopted by majority vote. It is tempting to argue that decisions adopted on a consensus basis will find fuller implementation than those adopted by majority vote; however, in many situations there is what can be called pseudo-consensus. An example is the Programme of Action for the establishment of a New International Economic Order adopted "without a vote" at the Sixth Special Session of the General Assembly (1974). Immediately after adoption, a number of important delegations put on record their reservations regarding several parts of the Programme of Action. The resolution of the Seventh Special Session (1975) can be considered a real consensus, but its implementation met with great difficulties because of a disagreement on concrete follow-up action. In some negotiating conferences there is a prior understanding that the consensus method will prevail. The consensus principle has been, for example, incorporated in the rules of procedure of the UN Conference on the Law of the Sea. Most North-South negotiating conferences are dealing with sensitive issues. It would therefore be logical if an understanding could be achieved as to which issues should be decided by consensus and which other, relatively secondary, points could be decided by a vote, perhaps by a qualified majority such as the prescription of a two-thirds majority. The present situation, in which real consensus and pseudo-consensus, from a formal point of view, are hardly distinguishable (except for recorded statements with reservations), is clearly unsatisfactory, since it increases hopes for implementation that remain unfulfilled. It is sometimes cynically said: If one is in favor of a proposal, one can vote yes or no or abstain; if one is against a proposal one can also vote yes or no or abstain. My suggestion to distinguish between issues to be decided by consensus and issues to be decided by a vote will only make sense if the concept "consensus" is brought back to its real meaning and if countries would be willing to have their views more realistically reflected in their votes. Ideally, this would mean that abstentions would become an exception (as in the early days of the United Nations).

Weighted or qualified voting systems as an alternative to the "one-country-one-vote" system prevailing in the United Nations and in most specialized agencies might be examined from the point of view of facilitating the achievement of agreed-upon solutions. For example, the effort to obtain additional development finance might be easier if voting rights would somehow be related to contributions. The success of the International Fund for Agricultural Development (IFAD) in obtaining funds is apparently related to an original voting system whereby countries are divided into three groups, according to their contribution. On the other hand, developing nations have objected to the large influence of certain powers in the IMF and the International Bank for Reconstruction and Development (IBRD), in which voting rights are based on capital shares. The present system (which has already been adapted to reflect the economic strength of oil-producing and other countries) is defended by the large Western economic powers. At some point, it would seem necessary to achieve an understanding that delicate issues in North-South relations are to be negotiated in such a way that the legitimate interests of all concerned are, in principle, duly safeguarded.

IMPROVING THE NEGOTIATING SYSTEM AND METHODS OF NORTH-SOUTH NEGOTIATIONS

1. *Greater clarity of objectives will facilitate determination of the negotiating framework*. The configuration of any particular negotiation should logically be dictated by its actual contents. Thus, successive rounds of negotiations under the General Agreement on Tariffs and Trade (GATT) auspices have found their logical format in the form of small negotiating groups, either by pairs of countries or by subject, the results of which were, in a later phase of the negotiating round, "multilateralized." The abolition of trade and tariff barriers on a mutually acceptable basis was the generally accepted objective of these negotiations.

If one contrasts these GATT negotiations with those related to the

NIEO, one is struck by the fact that the latter lacked clarity from the beginning. The developing countries presented a set of objectives in which the actual aims and the instruments to achieve these aims were not carefully distinguished. As one observer has noted:

> The objectives of the dialogue were not clearly perceived. At least two distinct schools of thought emerged. One bargained for short-term structural change. The first school would have been satisfied with more aid, more debt relief, more trade concessions, etc.; the second would regard such "progress" as an increase, not a reduction, in dependency. The second school sought a fundamental change in prevailing market rules and a loosening of ties between North and South, including a major uncoupling of trade and aid relationships. The confusion between various objectives made it difficult to pursue any consistent strategy of negotiations.[4]

The achievement of greater clarity of basic objectives is a primary condition for determining the optimal negotiating framework.

2. *The size of a negotiating meeting should be such that it inspires the confidence of those present and of those absent.* It is generally assumed that a small conference or meeting is, in principle, more likely to have success than a larger one. There is no doubt that a limited number of people can more easily talk to each other and negotiate than a very large number of people. A crucial difficulty is that unless the delegates to a small conference operate on the basis of a clearly formulated mandate of the larger groupings to which they belong, they are likely to be disavowed by countries not directly represented in the conference. This, together with the timing right after the first oil crisis, was probably the main reason for the failure of the Conference on International Economic Cooperation (CIEC). In the CIEC a twenty-seven nation group of developed and developing countries met from 1975 to 1977 outside the framework of the United Nations. While some valuable analytic work was undertaken, the only specific result was the transfer of a certain amount of money to the "most seriously affected countries." It was decided that negotiations would continue in the United Nations.

Since the CIEC, there has been strong pressure, in organs and conferences under the auspices of the United Nations, that all countries should be represented, at least nominally. There is a tendency to have more and more "committees of the whole." The increasing desire to make ECOSOC open-ended reflects this trend. It can be demonstrated that the larger the meeting or conference, the smaller negotiating groups tend to become. Thus, at the United Nations Industrial Development Organization (UNIDO) Conference (New Delhi, 1980), the conference president (the Indian minister for foreign affairs), in the last ten days of the sessions, met with a small number of "friends of the president," in which the Group of 77 and the Western industrialized countries were represented by two or, at most, three persons each; the Eastern European countries by a single person. The negotiating group during the Eleventh Special Session of the General Assembly (August-September 1980) was no larger than about eight persons — quite small, given the size of the meeting with over 150 countries represented. What is necessary is a constant keeping in touch of those participating in the small negotiating group with those "outside." The simultaneous physical proximity of the nonrepresented to the negotiating few is a requirement and, while not guaranteeing success, at least prevents failure as a result of a breakdown of communications.

A small conference should not be confused with a small meeting. A small meeting within the framework of a (large or small) conference can be the right format to overcome negotiating obstacles.

The general assumption is that a large conference cannot give results. Yet, the continuing series of sessions of the UN Conference on the Law of the Sea, spread over a long period, has shown that a large-sized conference can function, provided its work can be broken up by groups that are small and efficient enough to tackle particular issues. If the Law of the Sea Conference finally delivers an agreed treaty, it will also have been shown that the package deal approach continues to have merits.

3. *Given the large number of bodies available and still being created for North-South negotiations, the North-South negotiator must carefully select where and how he will wish to deal with an issue or problem.* At the time of the founding of the United Nations, the setup for economic negotiations, including North-South issues that were already identified in the Charter of the United Nations, was simple: A general ECOSOC was supposed to coordinate the work of the specialized agencies. It soon turned out that the specialized agencies were going to lead lives of their own and did not wish to be dictated to, concerning their methods of work and their objectives, by what they saw as an outside body like ECOSOC. A certain lack of coordination in many governments, in which ministries of health, agriculture, and so forth, considered themselves totally competent for the activities of groups such as the World Health Organization or the Food and Agriculture Organization (FAO), played havoc with the efforts by ministries of foreign affairs or finance to obtain general coordination through the ECOSOC.

One of the fundamental difficulties for the ECOSOC has been that while many programs and other detailed questions are discussed by the council, a number of other major problems have often been handled in other bodies. The central point for discussing important economic questions in other bodies has increasingly been the General Assembly in which, contrary to ECOSOC, all UN members participate on an equal footing.

Starting in 1964, the UN General Assembly began to organize world conferences on economic and social matters outside the framework of the

ECOSOC and then, subsequently, created new bodies whose mandates overlapped with those of the council. These new organs came under the General Assembly rather than the ECOSOC (although they usually report to the Assembly through the council) and, in some cases, had their own separate secretariats. These organs were also often backed by powerful groups of countries or specific interest groups focusing on a new problem, which took the limelight away from the council. The United Nations Conference on Trade and Development (UNCTAD), established in 1964, the United Nations Industrial Development Organization (UNIDO), established in 1966; the United Nations Environment Programme (UNEP), established in 1972; and the World Food Council (WFC), established in 1974, are typical examples.

In addition, several specialized agencies, such as the International Labour Organization (ILO) and the Food and Agricultural Organization (FAO) were, and continue to be, involved in major economic policy issues.

The ECOSOC has, moreover, been criticized for real or presumed inefficiency, its sessions lasting too long, and its agendas being too broad. A shortening of the summer session to three weeks should overcome some of this criticism.

The start of a new round of global negotiations is now under negotiation in the United Nations. The new round of global negotiations, according to General Assembly Resolution 34/138 (December 1979), should:

a) take place within the United Nations system with the participation, in accordance with the procedures of relevant bodies, of all states and within a specified time frame, without prejudice to the central role of the General Assembly;
b) include major issues in the field of raw materials, energy, trade, development, money, and finance;
c) contribute to the implementation of the international development strategy for the third United Nations development decade;
d) contribute to the solution of international economic problems, within the framework of the restructuring of international economic relations, and to steady global economic development, in particular, the development of developing countries, and, to this end, reflect the mutual benefit, the common interest, and the responsibilities of the parties concerned, taking into account the general economic capability of each country.

It is not surprising that in view of the complexity of the issues and the generality of the wording spelling out the objectives of the "new round," its start was delayed. Some issues of disagreement were:

1. the degree of autonomy that various organizations such as the World Bank, the IMF, and GATT would continue to have;
2. the exact significance of the "central role of the General Assembly" or of

any new body that would "monitor" (what is "monitor"?) progress in negotiations in various specialized bodies;

3. the scope and details of the agenda of the global negotiations.

With or without a new round of global negotiations, it is obvious that the North-South negotiatior should very carefully consider, in each case, in which group he wants to bring up a particular issue or initiative, or whether it might be useful to bring the issue up in several bodies at the same time. The latter practice might, to some extent, present the danger of the "Ping-Pong game."

This brings us to the fundamental point of the ultimate rationale of North-South negotiations. As long as the claims and proposals of less-developed countries or, for that matter, of developed nations are dealt with in a confrontational atmosphere, North-South negotiations have the characteristics of a zero-sum game in which one party's loss is the other party's gain. Yet, the ultimate objective should be to recognize that all will benefit from internationally agreed-upon measures leading to accelerated world growth, a "positive-sum" game, a real "planetary bargain."[5]

It would be a possibly large step forward if new proposals for "action" would first be studied by the secretariat(s) of the organization(s) concerned, assisted, when necessary, by groups of expert advisers regarding their implications for various groups of countries. In other words, feasibility studies combined with cost-benefit analysis should be normal procedure. To refer "difficultly-arrived-at" recommendations straight away to some intergovernmental body, whether newly created or existing, is asking for trouble since difficulties may be magnified and positions be made more rigid.

As the Brandt Commission has said:

> Wherever possible, negotiations should look for joint gains, rather than slowly wresting uncertain "concessions." The starting point has to be some perception of mutual interests in change. In North-South negotiations immediate or short-term reciprocal benefits cannot always be expected, and greater equity will sometimes require non-reciprocity. Mutual interests are often longer-term, and overall they need to be supplemented with considerations of forward-looking solidarity which go beyond strict "bargaining." All sides have an interest in a framework which is designed to enlarge their common ground and the dialogue must be structured to allow the participants to perceive their specific mutual interests clearly on each issue. The agenda should be balanced, or synchronized with other negotiations, to allow "trade-offs" and "packaging." At the same time, the mechanism of negotiation should be able to accommodate the principles of universality and joint responsibility . . .
>
> All countries should be represented at the plenary sessions of the negotiating forum, but on each separate issue (like commodities, or trade) each Group should nominate a limited number of countries most seriously interested in that issue to the negotiating group, the number varying with the scope of the issue, and maintaining an appropriate balance between developing and industrialized countries. These representatives would then naturally maintain close and continuous contact with other members of their Group. On issues such as money

and finance, which interest all countries in one or more of their aspects, participation could be by representatives of regions or sub-regions. Negotiations would thus take place in smaller, but self-chosen groups; but any agreements should be endorsed, after full discussion, by the plenary session.[6]

SOME CONCLUDING SUGGESTIONS AND OBSERVATIONS

Some negotiations end in failure because of linguistic or conceptual misunderstanding. There is very often disagreement on fundamental notions. I have therefore advocated the establishment of a United Nations ad hoc committee on concepts and definitions, composed of scholars and practitioners, which, with the addition of experts on specific questions, would help to clarify the meaning of certain notions, concepts, and ideas.[7]

Prior to the Stockholm Conference on the Human Environment (1972), a special committee worked on definitions of various concepts. This has no doubt facilitated the path-breaking results of the Stockholm Conference, perhaps the most successful of the UN conferences dealing with new global issues held under UN auspices.

Some international negotiating sessions fail not so much because of disagreement on the issues discussed but because of an erroneous sense of timing. This may be especially so if meetings start out with a long series of unilateral statements setting forth policy questions, usually called the "general debate" (although in reality, far removed from a debate).

Thus, successive UNCTAD general conferences have suffered from the difficulty that much time and effort were absorbed by general debates, so that too little time and human resources were available for negotiating sessions.

At this point, a word about "summit meetings" along the lines of the Heads of Governments Meeting (October 1981, Cancun, Mexico), with the attendance of a small number of developed and developing countries.

As a negotiating forum, such meetings are unlikely to be useful since most countries are not willing to leave important decisions to a meeting of small numbers of governments to whom they have given no negotiating mandate. As a means to draw worldwide attention to certain crucial North-South issues, summit meetings are potentially useful, although it is questionable what the real impact is. Also, summit meetings may be useful to the extent that certain heads of state or governments would undergo more direct exposure to North-South problems than might otherwise be the case. From that point of view, some advantage might be gained by holding summit meetings related to North-South problems in a really poor country, with the squalid conditions in which a large part of mankind lives directly visible to the participants.

It is also questionable whether the summit-meeting technique, tending to have a very wide agenda (or perhaps no agenda) and a small number of participants, is not directly the opposite of what experience seems to indicate as a more sensible approach: a detailed, small series of issues of separate conferences or meetings before a large number of participants who then establish informal or formal small negotiating groups.

The informed North-South negotiator will want to be sure who his friends and who his enemies are and to make a tactical plan as to how to achieve the results he desires. The particular influence of each actor on the multilateral negotiating process is different in each case. In Table 9.1 an effort toward some sort of systematization has been made to illustrate the potential influence of actors in the multilateral negotiating process; h = high; h/m = high to medium; m = medium; m/l = medium to low; l = low. The assigned influence coefficients are obviously highly tentative. Each actor should assess his and other actors' influence in each particular situation. Under "groups of governments," I have in mind for categories (1) and (2) the Group of 77 or Group B; for category (2), the nonaligned movement, and so forth. "Doctrine-oriented" NGOs are supposed to include, for example, human rights movements and politically inspired international groupings. "Business-oriented" NGOs is a broad category covering, for example, employers' associations such as the International Chamber of Commerce, international trade unions, producers' associations, and so forth.

Finally, a word on the confidence factor: the confidence factor has been almost totally neglected by practitioners and scientific observers of international negotiations. Yet, in the first and last instance, this may be the factor deciding between success and failure. Unless negotiating partners have a minimum of confidence in their reciprocal motives, success is difficult to achieve. Similarly, an international secretariat may be scientifically competent; if he or she does not have the confidence of one particular important grouping, perhaps because that grouping believes that the secretariat is biased, the negotiations will be unfavorably affected.

The establishment of a "think tank" for the United Nations, perhaps by drawing on the integrated efforts of the United Nations University (UNU), including a newly created UNU Global Economics Policy Research Institution and the UNITAR, might contribute to a deeper and politically more acceptable insight in the significance of various proposed measures.

In conclusion, an optimal framework for North-South negotiations, leading to a "new multilateralism"[8] would require:

1. confidence among all negotiating partners;
2. a deep insight into obstacles to achieving consensus, and both the political and the technical will to overcome these obstacles;
3. a realization of the time framework for the negotiations;
4. more and better feasibility studies and cost-benefit analysis on proposed actions and measures;

Table 9.1. ACTORS.

TYPE OF MEETING AND SUBJECT	GOVERNMENTS			SECRETARIATS	NGOS	
	INDIVIDUAL GOVERNMENTS	GROUPS OF GOVERNMENTS	PRESIDING OFFICERS		"DOCTRINE ORIENTED"	"BUSINESS ORIENTED"
1. Deliberate recommendatory meeting with broad agenda (General Assembly, ECOSOC, UNCTAD)	h	h/m	m	n	m/l	m/l
2. Same as (1) but with narrow agenda (political and other noneconomic items, e.g., human rights)	h	h/m	m	n	h/m	l/m
3. Same as (2) but with narrow agenda (economic items):						
trade/raw materials	m	m	l/m	l	l	m
energy	m	h	l		l	m
transnational corporations	m	m	l		l	h/m
international monetary order	h	m/l	l		l	m/l
transfer of financial resoures	h	m	l	l	l	m

Note: h = high; h/m = high to medium; m = medium; m/l = medium to low; l = low.

5. the correct assessment of one's own influence (individually or as a member of a group) and that of other negotiating partners; and

6. a streamlining of negotiating bodies involved in North-South negotiations.

NOTES

1. J. Saxon Mills, *The Genoa Conference* (London: Hutchinson and Co., 1922), 18.

2. This methodology follows largely that put forward in Johan Kaufmann, *Conference Diplomacy* (Leyden: Sijthoff; and Dobbs Ferry: Oceana, 1968), 25-28.

3. United Nations, "The Seventh Session of the General Assembly, September 1-16, 1975," *Round-up and Resolutions* (New York: United Nations, 1975).

4. Mahbub ul Haq, "Negotiating the Future," *Foreign Affairs*, 59: 400-401 (Winter 1980-81).

5. See Harlan Cleveland, "The Mutation of World Institutions," in A. J. Dolman, editor, *Global Planning and Resource Management* (Elmsford, N.Y.: Pergamon Press, 1980).

6. See the Brandt Report, *North-South; A Program for Survival*: the report of the Independent Commission on International Development Issues under the chair position of Willy Brandt (Cambridge: Massachusetts Institute of Technology Press, 1980), 263.

7. See Johan Kaufmann, *United Nations Decision Making*, 214-15; also A. J. Dolman, "The United Nations as a World Development Authority," in *Global Planning and Resource Management*, 103-16.

8. Term used by Miriam Camps in an unpublished paper for the Trilateral Commission to whom it had been suggested by William Diebold (Council on Foreign Relations). "New multilateralism" would mean getting away from the "confrontational stance" characterizing North-South relations and revamping the international organizations involved, combined with the creation of new global international trade organizations, which would absorb the present GATT and UNCTAD.

Chapter 10

The Main Forces at Work

Muchkund Dubey

THE NEGOTIATION CYCLE

North-South negotiations, like any other multilateral negotiation, constitute a multiphase and multifaceted process. The process can be said to start with the quest of ideas that become the basis of negotiations. The ideas get converted into issues that are joined by individual and groups of countries. The formulation of individual country, subregional, regional, and wider group positions on the issues is a very important phase of the negotiating process. Important trade-offs among the countries of the South and North are involved during this phase. Then comes the crucial stage of trade-offs and compromises between the North and South resulting in the adoption of resolutions, declarations, and decisions either by consensus or by majority voting. Finally, there remains the task of getting the ideas translated into concrete actions, maintaining their continuity, and insuring progress in their evolution in order to insure the progression of international economic relations to higher and higher levels of excellence.

The nearly complete cycle of the negotiating process described in the above paragraph is a somewhat rationalized and idealized version of what happens in actual practice. We have resorted to such a rationalization mainly for the purpose of facilitating comprehension and orderly discussion. The negotiating process seldom unfolds itself in as neatly divided phases as in the cycle described above. Quite often, one phase of the negotiation merges into the next. National and group interests sometimes constitute the mainspring of the evolution of ideas. The countries of the North inexorably exert pressures and use all the leverages at their command to influence the formulation of the country, subregional, regional, and wider group positions of the South. Likewise, the countries of the South seek to influence the process of the formulation of the group position of the North. Or, otherwise, in order to arrive at a realistic and negotiable group position, each group duly has to take into account the interests of the other groups in the formulation of its own group position. While introducing the first draft of the International Development Strategy for the Second United Nations Development Decade in the Second Committee at the twenty-fifth commemorative session of the General Assembly and addressing the other groups of countries represented in the committee, the then chairman of the Group of 77 (the author of this chapter) said, "When in the early hours of this morning I was finalizing the text of this draft, you were more overwhelmingly present before me than ever during the last two-year period of negotiations on this document." Intra- and inter-group negotiations are involved at each phase of the cycle. These negotiations do not always involve confrontation or the physical presence of the negotiating parties. They are so inextricably tied in the web of international relations that each party is constantly under the influence of the others while engaged in the process of formulating its individual country or group position.

Every negotiating process does not have as well-defined and comprehensive a cycle as the one outlined above. Some negotiating processes are much shorter and quite mechanical. But, then, many of these shorter processes can be linked to the larger cycle of North-South negotiations centered on certain key ideas that might be going on at the same time. Similarly, each country or delegate need not be involved with each phase of the cycle. The extent of the involvement with the cycle of a particular country depends upon its perceived national interest in the idea constituting the focus of the negotiation; its perception of its stake in the wider regional and global objectives sought to be achieved through the negotiation; and the general alertness, intelligence, and effectiveness of its delegate.

The final phase of the cycle, that is, getting the ideas translated into concrete action, maintaining their continuity, and insuring progress in their evolution, is the most difficult and complex part of the negotiating process. Most of the resolutions/declarations incorporating the end result of an important negotiating process, provide for a built-in review mechanism to assess progress in implementation. But, more frequently, in order to insure implementation, it becomes necessary to initiate a whole series of new negotiating processes. Each of these processes may constitute a separate cycle of negotiation. Insuring the continuity of ideas and progress in their evolution calls for an extraordinary degree of alertness, sensitivity, and tenacity on the part of the delegates. A delegate must be intellectually and professionally equipped to handle this difficult and most challenging task. But even those who are so equipped find their tasks rendered very difficult and quite often hopeless because of the inability of most governments to perceive their national interests in the preservation of, and further progress in, the basic ideas and fundamental objectives of international development cooperation.

SOURCES OF IDEAS

Ideas that are subsequently converted into issues for negotiation emanate from a variety of sources such as academic quarters, individual governments, secretariats of UN organizations, study groups, committees, and commissions set up by intergovernmental decisions or at the initiative of the UN secretariats. Ideas emanating from academic quarters are generally of a basic nature, whereas those advanced by governments, UN secretariats, UN study groups/commissions, and so forth, have a greater operational content. Basic ideas from which many negotiating issues have been derived are, indeed, very few. Some of these ideas are: trade as an engine of growth; extension of the planning approach and model for guiding international development cooperation; international accountability; departure from the most-favored nation principle, and so forth. The Haberter Committee (1958) was one of the earliest group of experts to come out with ideas and proposals that became the basis of much of the subsequent negotiations with GATT. Professor Ragnar Nurske was mainly responsible for propounding the concept of trade as an engine of growth. Professor Jan Tinbergen and Raul Prebisch have been the pioneers in advancing ideas for the extension of the national development planning method and model to guide international economic cooperation. The concept of international development strategy was mainly derived from a book on international development planning written by Prof. Tinbergen in the mid-1960s, whereas Dr. Prebisch was the first person to use the term "international development strategy." Important ideas of international accountability were conceived, elaborated, and advanced by individual governments with the assistance of UN secretariats. For example, India played a very important role in the evolution of, and negotiations on, such concepts of international accountability as targets for aid flows and action programs for the removal of barriers to the exports of developing countries.

The performance of UN study groups, committees, and commissions in advancing ideas has been of a mixed nature. Some of them have come out with strikingly original or significant ideas such as the "link" and "commodity reserve currency." Some of them have merely refurbished and presented in a systematic, elaborate, and coherent framework, ideas that had been floating about for some time. A striking example in this category is the country programming approach recommended by the UNDP Commission headed by Sir Robert Jackson. A large number of study groups and committees/commissions degenerate into presenting a mere summary of the state of the art and providing justifications for the pet prejudices and vested interests of particular secretariats or groups of countries. There are examples of committees and commissions having been set up without first consulting or seeking the approval of governments. Quite often, the commissioners heading the commissions and chairpeople of the study groups and committees are so selected as to influence the outcome of the deliberations of the committees/commissions in particular directions. For the same purpose, there is also a great deal of behind-the-scenes maneuvering to influence the composition of the committees and commissions. Thus, the notion of the objectivity of experts functioning in their personal capacity as members of UN study groups, committees, and so forth, is, more often than not, illusory. Prejudice is introduced at various stages and levels of their functioning. It is not uncommon for independent experts to come fully briefed by their governments and to function at their behest. Many expert groups have been aborted and have produced mere statements of differing positions of governments rather than ideas based on objective considerations because of the ever-present propensity of governments to influence the opinions of their experts.

A really effective delegate must be alert to all such developments. He should make a conscious effort to be aware of the motivations behind, and the vested interests involved in, the setting up of various UN study groups, committees, and commissions from which ideas are expected to emerge. He must know what is happening in these bodies and seek to influence their deliberations in the interest of objectivity. Beyond that, he must keep in touch with other sources of ideas, that is, work done in academic quarters and by UN secretariats and by governments of important countries.

CONVERTING IDEAS INTO ISSUES

Once the ideas come to light, the task of the negotiator is to convert them into issues for intergovernmental negotiations. An important part of the negotiations lies in agitating the ideas so that they are converted into issues. Pioneers of ideas are frequently surprised — at times pleasantly so but, more often, with a sense of anguish and frustration — to see the shape their ideas assume when they are converted into issues and, even more so, when they gain intergovernmental acceptability in the form of obligations or commitments. Ideas are generally in the form of norms. The task of the negotiators is to impart to them as wide an acceptability as possible in the form of moral obligations or contractual commitments. Negotiation bridges the gap between ideas as norms and ideas in the form of obligation or commitments.

SELECTION OF IDEAS

Great care must be exercised in selecting ideas to be converted into negotiating issues. All the ideas that clamor for being turned into issues for multilateral negotiations do not deserve to be elevated to this status. Many of them do not serve any wider regional or general interests, even though they may serve the peripheral national interest of one or a few countries. If proper discretion and judgment is not applied and peripheral ideas or issues are taken up for negotiation, then there is the danger of the entire negotiating process being discredited. This will raise doubts about the seriousness of purpose of the negotiators and deflect attention from more important, wider North-South issues to minor matters involving the interests of a particular secretariat or one or a few countries. Quite often, a whole edifice of ideas is erected in order to justify the creation of additional posts or the upgrading of existing posts in a secretariat. Moreover, many of the ideas strongly championed by individual delegations turn out to be a mere camouflage for getting their nationals appointed to high positions. As in the national context, so in the context of a multi-national negotiation, there is often a person behind the idea, wanting to serve his own, or his country's, narrow selfish interest. It has frequently been seen that toward the concluding stages of the negotiations, the basic idea and the country positions on them are readily sacrificed at the altar of acquiring high posts for particular individuals. Quite often, the delegates know what the entire game is about, yet they readily play this game for political reasons. Recently, there has been an increasing tendency for the entire negotiating process in a conference being geared to the creation of new institutions designed to accommodate the persons involved in the preparation and the conduct of the conference. The most important points in the recent series of global conferences centered on specific points such as desertification, water management, and environment and have seen the creation of new institutions and funding. As a result, the generalists have come to dominate these conferences on specialized subjects, while specialists have been pushed to the back seat. It is true that institutions, either new or existing ones duly strengthened, are necessary to monitor progress in the implementation of the decisions of a conference, carry forward the idea behind the conference, and mobilize support for it on a continuing basis. But the entire negotiating process becomes distorted when it is patent right from the beginning that the ultimate purpose of the negotiation is going to be to accommodate the interests of certain individuals and the empire-building ambitions of some branch of a secretariat.

SELLING THE IDEA

Sometimes, a long educating process must precede actual negotiations among developing countries. Many delegations do not easily grasp the significance of the idea to be converted into a negotiating issue. Nor do they know about the approach to be adopted for this purpose. When the idea of an international development strategy was first mooted in 1968, many delegations had thought that it would just be a general resolution of the kind that launched the First United Nations Development Decade. It was left to a few delegates to conceive the entire idea of an international development strategy in the form of a projection at the international level of the basic national development planning model. These delegates then worked out the details of the model, explained to their colleagues from other developing countries the great significance of this model for making progress in negotiations and as a comprehensive mechanism for international accountability, and defined the main negotiating issues, both for developing countries themselves and between developed and developing countries. The educating process started well before the commencement of the negotiations among developing countries and continued simultaneously with these negotiations and those between developed and developing countries.

Similarly, before commencing the negotiations on the international development strategy for the 1980s, it became necessary to launch a long educating process to resolve the conflict that a powerful group of developing countries perceived between a new international development strategy and the NIEO. This conflict lasted till almost the end of the negotiating process, and so did the educating process.

PREVENTING DEFLECTION FROM THE MAIN IDEA

Another important challenge that the negotiators face is to be able to discard ideas, the purpose of which is to get the negotiations deflected from the main idea and the issue, and to divert them into byways. At the time of the negotiation on the International Development Strategy for the Second United Nations Development Decade, the secretariat at first suggested that the strategy should be a mere set of norms that the governments could subscribe to by adopting a general resolution. This would have meant that the strategy document, as such, would have required no negotiations; only the general resolution adopting the strategy would have been negotiated. This would have reduced the strategy to a set of pious declarations without embodying any commitment on behalf of governments. At a later stage of the negotiations on the strategy, another attempt was made — this time by the prestigious Committee on Development Planning — to divert the exercise into a byway by suggesting that the strategy should consist of a general declaration followed by individual declarations of governments. Obviously, only the general declaration part of the strategy would have been negotiated and subscribed to by all governments. Individual declarations would have reflected the mere intentions of governments, and not their commitment, to adopt certain policy measures to implement the goals and objectives of the strategy. Different countries would have declared their intention to adopt different sets of policy measures. This would have hardly resulted in any progress from the prevailing position and would have given the international community no standard yardstick to measure progress. The negotiators of the south had to wage a Herculean battle to stick to the model of the strategy originally conceived by them and to make it a totally negotiated document embodying the commitment of governments.

CONTINUITY OF IDEAS

It is important to maintain the continuity of ideas that are taken as a basis of North-South negotiations. This, in fact, is the only way to make progress in the evolution of ideas and to insure the progression of international economic relations to higher and still higher levels of excellence. For this purpose, the negotiators must know the present state of the art. Otherwise, they will be rediscovering the wheel and going to-and-fro all the time.

Unfortunately, during the last ten years or so, continuity in many of the ideas has been disrupted. In many areas, negotiations have led to the erosion of the gains already achieved in the past and the adoption of retrogressive measures. "Ad hocism" has replaced progressive development of ideas. For example, increases in financial assistance available for activities in certain areas have been agreed upon, while there has simultaneously been a continuing decline in the proportion of the Gross National Product (GNP) made available as official development assistance. A series of bilateral quotas at revised levels, with regard to a number of products in which developing countries have a competitive advantage, have been negotiated, while, at the same time, there has been a general increase in the protectionist barriers against these commodities. A series of ad hoc qualitatively similar measures have been adopted in different areas to create a semblance of progress, while there has at the same time been a retreat from the general position reached long ago. Speaking at the second regular session of the ECOSOC in 1979 in his capacity as the chairman of the preparatory committee for the New International Development Strategy, the author of this article stated: "The present process of the North-South dialogue has become too general and too repetitive without being cumulative."

Sometimes, due to a deterioration in the international economic and political environment, it becomes necessary to withdraw from the positions reached in the past. This has been particularly true since the onset of the decade of the 1970s when most of the developed market economies have been in a grip of recession and when there has been a worldwide inflation accompanied by socially unacceptable levels of unemployment. During this period, the world economy also entered a phase of selective scarcity of key natural resources, brought about mainly by excessive consumption of these resources in developed countries. Concern with the environment has led to a conscious effort to change prevailing life-styles even at the cost of material prosperity.

In this unfavorable climate for international development cooperation, many of the gains achieved earlier in the progressive development of ideas have been eroded. The presently agreed-upon position on the target for the flow of official development assistance represents a retreat from the position reached in the International Development Strategy for the Second United Nations Development Decade. Many of the advances made in the 1960s for removal of barriers to the exports of developing countries have been drastically eroded. The system of coordinated and unified programming of all technical cooperation activities of the UN system instituted in the early 1970s is now virtually in shambles. The intrusion into multilateral programs of bilateral prejudices and influences has been carried to a point at which it poses a threat not only to the very identity of the multilateral programs but also to the ideals and objectives of the United Nations.

Tactical withdrawals from positions reached earlier become inevitable in certain circumstances. First, it may be desirable to stage a tactical retreat from positions reached earlier, on issues that were regarded as very important at that time but that are no longer so, in order to make progress on issues that have now become the burning concern of the international community. For example, in recent negotiations, major NIEO issues have rightly been given priority over such issues as commodity-pricing policies or ad hoc tariff reductions, which prominently figured in earlier negotiations. Second, when the climate for negotiations is unfavorable, it is tactically important to preserve an idea, even in a diluted form, instead of allowing it to be totally discarded. For example, in the prevailing unfavorable situation with regard to the flow of official development assistance, it is important to preserve the concept of commitment of the developed market-economy countries to a specified target for the official development aid (ODA) flow, even though it may not be possible to adhere to the deadlines previously agreed upon for achieving this target. Whereas tactical retreats from previously agreed-upon positions may be desirable, important ideas on which consensus has been reached in the past should not be allowed to be diluted or given up for short-term ad hoc gains of an opportunistic nature.

FORMULATIONS OF COUNTRY POSITIONS AND THE ROLE OF INDIVIDUAL DELEGATES

Once an idea assumes the form of a negotiating issue, it becomes necessary for individual governments to formulate their positions on various aspects of the issue. The educating process that goes on in multilateral groups is an important aid to the formulation of such positions. A country formulates its position, basically, in the light of its perception of national, regional, and wider group interests involved in the negotiating issue. Very few countries are immediately able to see the regional or general interests to be articulated and safeguarded in the negotiating process. The vast majority of them come unprepared to the negotiating table, quite willing to be guided by, and to cooperate with, those who happen to know better.

Even with regard to national interests, very few countries come to a negotiating conference with clearly defined and well-formulated national positions. Many of these countries do not have at their disposal the necessary expertise to analyze and grasp the significance of an idea that has matured into a negotiating issue; to assess how it affects their national, regional, and wider group interests; and to formulate a clear-cut position reflecting those interests. However, delegates of most of these countries have a broad notion of how their national interests are affected during the course of the negotiations. Even then, many of these delegates do not think it necessary to play an active role in the negotiating process. They generally leave it to the delegates of other similarly placed countries to take care of their interests. They intervene only when they feel that if they continue to remain on the sidelines, their national interests will go by default.

When an issue is politically sensitive and a country does not want to adopt an open and categorical position on it, the country gives its delegate a defensive brief. The delegate is asked to resist the temptation of playing a leadership and a too active role and to get his national positions reflected through other delegates who do not suffer from the same constraints. When the issue is politically so sensitive that even canvassing for support with other delegates is likely to have an adverse effect on bilateral relations, then the delegate is asked to keep quiet and to wait for others to do his job, and if others do not oblige, then to reconcile himself to a measure of erosion in the known position of his country on the negotiating issue. In the negotiations under the aegis of UNCTAD on the convention on the transit trade of landlocked countries, the Indian delegate very often found himself precisely in this unenviable position. He was asked not to intervene and to wait for the other transit countries to intervene and make the points that he would normally have been called upon to make. At some stages in the negotiating process, this kind of brief to most of the leading transit country delegates created the impossible situation in which none of them would intervene in the expectation that others would do so, and in the process, the general interests of the transit countries, as a whole, were allowed to be compromised.

Countries that go to a negotiating conference with a well-formulated position are the ones that assume the leadership role in such conferences. There is generally a direct correlation between the degree of national or regional interests involved and the extent of preparedness and the clarity and elaborateness of the country's position evolved for the negotiations. A leadership role generally derives from the perception of national or regional interests. It was, therefore, natural that India was one of the leaders in the negotiations on the liberalization of trade in manufactures, preferences, and aid flows; and that Malaysia and Australia assumed the leadership role in the negotiations on commodities and Upper Volta and the Sudan and, recently, Bangladesh, on special measures in favor of the least developed among developing countries.

On issues like principles governing international economic cooperation and international development strategy, in which the national interest involved is not so apparent, a leadership role is assumed by those countries and delegates who have done their homework and have perceived more clearly than others the general, as well as their enlightened long-term national, interest in the negotiating issue.

An interesting situation arises when delegates who have no immediate national interest involved are able to see the general interest and their enlightened long-term national interests more clearly than the delegates directly concerned are able to see their immediate national interests. In such a situation, the former category of delegates can play an important role by providing leadership. Since, for them, no immediate national interests are involved, they have no reason to be timid in championing the general cause. They are also in a stronger bargaining position than the countries whose immediate interests are involved. In appropriate circumstances, they can thus safeguard the national interests of the latter countries better than the delegates of those countries can. They can also insure, to the extent possible, that no conditions or guidelines are imposed on the countries with a weak bargaining position that can subsequently be used as a precedent for being applied generally, thus, affecting adversely their own national interests and those of similarly placed countries. This author played such a role at the time of the negotiations in an agreement between the then government of Cambodia and donor countries for the funding and implementation of a project in the Cambodian territory under the Mekong Project. India had been invited to participate in the negotiation as a minor donor country. However, this kind of situation does not arise too frequently. A delegate must eschew the temptation of being active when there is no risk of his country's long-term interest being adversely affected through the general application of the conditions or criteria being negotiated and, particularly, when the division between the negotiating parties is sharp and has pronounced political overtones. An activist role in such a situation can, at best, prove to be a nuisance and, at worst, may be misunderstood by the parties concerned as an obstruction. In the negotiations in the first UNCTAD on the problems of the transit trade of landlocked countries, the delegates of some of the European transit countries that were not at all involved in the issue tried to play an active role and were soon branded, by the chairman of the working group on this subject, as obstructionists and were asked to keep out of the controversy.

A good Samaritan role, by way of assisting in drafting, is generally appreciated and contributes to the success of the negotiation; but the delegate playing the good Samaritan should not become too obtrusive and should not, in any event, abuse this role to have substantive changes of a partisan nature introduced. The resulting loss of credibility is too heavy a price for any delegate to pay just for the sake of being seen as playing an active role in the conference.

FORMULATION OF REGIONAL POSITIONS

The processes involved, and the considerations to be taken into account, in formulating regional positions are not very different from those that go into the formulation of the positions of the Group of 77. As these will be discussed later, the present section is confined to the discussion of some general aspects of the problem of formulating regional positions.

A regional position is not the sum total of the positions of the individual countries of the region. It must reflect the distinctive regional experience, aspirations, and needs. But every document that emerges from a regional forum does not simply reflect distinctive regional positions. Many elements of such documents are common to those incorporated in documents emanating from other regional or global forums. Distinctive regional positions prevail with regard to a very few issues; and these positions alone constitute distinctive regional contributions to the development of ideas of general interest to all developing countries. For example, in the UNCTAD forum, distinctive contributions of Asia have been in the field of shipping, state trading, and planning; Latin American contributions have been in the sphere of regional and subregional integration and commodities; and the African countries have placed a great deal of emphasis on human resource development and development of institutional and physical infrastructure.

Regional positions, like country and wider group positions, evolve with changes in the world economy and the economies of the region. By the early 1970s, regional and subregional integration no longer remained the battle cry for the Latin American countries as it was during the first UNCTAD. This was because the Latin American countries could not make the various schemes of regional and subregional integration work effectively. In the most populous and generally energy-deficient regions of Asia, there has naturally been a shift of attention toward problems of poverty, food, and energy.

FORMULATION OF THE POSITION
OF THE GROUP OF 77

The classical method followed to reconcile the differences in the positions of individual, and groups of, developing countries and, thereby, to evolve the common position of the developing countries as a whole has been to fashion, and agree upon, a package of measures, some of which are of interest to all developing countries, while some are of interest to only a few of these countries. An essential precondition for the acceptance of the package is that it must incorporate some measure to take care of the interest of each and every developing country. At the same time, the package should be realistic and feasible enough to serve as a basis of negotiation with developed countries.

This presupposes that each member of the Group of 77 must accept and welcome the inclusion, in the package, of measures that are not of any direct or indirect interest to it but that have a vital bearing on the outcome of the development effort of the other members of the group. Members of the group should not only just put up with measures in the package that may not be of any interest to them but should also espouse them in the interest of group solidarity and actively work to have them included in the package. For example, India must show an understanding of what may appear as the obsession of many African countries with technical assistance and human resources infrastructure development. The fact that India is no longer at the receiving end of these measures of international development cooperation should, instead of engendering indifference, enable India to appreciate how important progress in these fields is for accelerating development. Similarly, India, by virtue of its pursuit of a pragmatic policy toward multinational companies, right from the beginning of its development effort, did not have much of a problem with them. But given their bitter experience of dealing with these companies India must understand the obsession of the Latin American countries, concerning the question of the nationalization of foreign companies. Likewise, India, with its diversified export structure, was in a better position to dispense with existing preferences and to agree to get these merged into a generalized system of preferences from which it had more to gain than other developing countries. But India was expected to show an understanding of the insistence of many of the Caribbean and African countries on preserving the existing preferences or on demanding compensation for allowing them to be merged with a generalized system of preferences. With their monoculture economies and one or a few commodities accounting for the bulk of their national incomes and export earnings, these countries had practically everything to lose if they had given up the existing preferences without demanding compensation.

On the other hand, the least-developed countries and other countries suffering from particular disabilities should realize that some of the problems faced by the relatively more developed among the developing countries, such as India, are not as irrelevant to them as it may appear superficially. These least-developed countries are themselves going to face these problems at subsequent stages in their development. Sooner or later, all these countries will have to industrialize, to diversify their economies, and, generally, to make their economies self-reliant and vibrant. If the measures that they are likely to need at later stages of their development are adopted now in response to the demands of countries like India, and if at least some of the rules of the game are thus changed in favor of the developing countries as a whole and the framework of international economic relations is restructured, it will make the task of development so much easier for these countries. When they launch upon the next phases of their development, they will no longer be required to cross some of those hurdles that more-developed countries are at present struggling to overcome.

Thus, a part — and a very significant one for that matter — of the problem of evolving a common package for the developing countries is one of sympathy with, and understanding of, the problems of others and seeing in others' immediate interests one's own long-term enlightened interests. But the more formidable part of the problem stems from the fact that the thrashing out of the package involves not only the incorporation of different measures of interest to different groups of developing countries but also measures regarding which there is a clear conflict of interest among different groups of developing countries. This conflict must be resolved before the package becomes generally acceptable. We have discussed why some of the countries enjoying existing preferences were unable to countenance any erosion of them without receiving compensatory benefits. Therefore, they were opposed to a general system of preferences into which these special existing preferences were supposed to merge. Herein lay the cause of conflict that had to be resolved before the package could become acceptable. A conflict situation invariably arises with regard to measures for increasing the flow of assistance to particular areas or for particular activities. Since the overall flow of resources is limited and subject to a declining trend in real terms, resources available for activities in one area are at the cost of those in other areas. Therefore, the group of countries interested in the latter category of activities find their interest in conflict with those interested in the former category of activities. Some of the least-developed countries have put so much at stake in claiming a larger share of the existing level of available ODA resources that as a bargaining counter for this with developed countries, they are prepared to adopt a lukewarm attitude toward, if not withdraw their support from, the demand for an increase in the overall availability of resources. Countries at the relatively early stages of development have sometimes been lured by selective commodity-by-commodity preferences and by proposals for introducing a system of graduation in the extension of preferences, simply because of their perception that, in the short run, they stand to gain from such approaches even though it may be at the cost of the general interest of the developing countries.

The best chance for resolving such conflicts lies in the ability of the countries concerned, or the groups of countries concerned, to adjust at least some of their own long-term interests to the pressing interests of others and to eschew those of their demands that conflict with the general interest of the developing countries and, hence, their own best advantage. Thus, even if it may not be in their immediate interest, the least developed among the developing countries and other countries suffering from special disabilities must go enthusiastically along with other developing countries in having the rules of the game changed; in building institutions that they will themselves desperately need in the not-too-distant future; and in putting in place, on a permanent basis, systems, frameworks, and facilities that will be indispensable at the subsequent stages of their economic development. The more advanced among the developing countries, on the other hand, should grant unilateral tariff preferences to the least developed among them in the expectation of implicit reciprocity. They should agree to the inclusion, in the common package, of measures that are designed to harness fully the productive capacity of the least developed among the developing countries. Prosperity is as much indivisible in the developing world as it is in the world as a whole. In the ultimate analysis, the more advanced among the developing countries can prosper best only by agreeing to measures designed to promote the prosperity of the least developed among them.

An important principle for resolving conflict situations should be always to stop short of taking the differences of interest to a breaking point because in order to put the package together, in the ultimate analysis, the principal parties involved in the conflict will have to make some sacrifice for the sake of the general cause of the developing countries, which is bound to suffer if the package collapses.

Sometimes, it is best to postpone decisions on issues involving a conflict of interest. Subsequent events demonstrate that these issues had appeared larger than life-size because of their topicality and the passion of the moment but dwindled into insignificance with the passage of time. For example, at the first UNCTAD, the Latin American countries had made a big issue out of the question of getting endorsement for their schemes of regional and subregional integration at the cost of the idea of more flexible and ad hoc forms of cooperation or interregional cooperation among developing countries. At the time of the second UNCTAD, this issue lost much of its momentum as it became evident that schemes of regional and subregional integration in Latin America were proving to be, at best, a highly qualified success, if not a failure. On the other hand, the tactics adopted at the second UNCTAD to postpone the issue of identifying the least developed among developing countries apparently misfired. The issue became so pressing that it was vigorously agitated in other forums in which a set of not entirely scientific criteria were agreed upon and applied for identifying those countries. Thus, UNCTAD lost a very important initiative in its sphere of activity, which it only was able to regain a few years later.

Sometimes, there has to be a strategic bargain between major groups of developing countries in order to evolve an agreed-upon package as a basis of negotiation with developed countries. This happened at the Havana Summit Conference of the Nonaligned Countries in 1979 when the oil-importing developing countries agreed to lend their full support to the proposal of some of the major OPEC countries for a new global round of negotiations, in lieu of the latter countries agreeing to enter into a serious South-South dialogue as a preparation for, and side by side with, the global round of negotiations.

The OPEC countries sponsoring the proposal for a global round of negotiations had the following purposes in view:

1. They wanted to deflect in other directions the pressure being put on them by both non-oil-exporting developed and developing countries, designed to mitigate the harmful effects on their economies of the second steep rise in the oil prices in 1979.
2. They wanted to demonstrate that the world economy was afflicted by a number of malaises and that, seen in this perspective, the oil price increase was not such a major problem.
3. In order to stagger the use of their oil resources, they were interested in a discussion on measures for intensifying energy resources and development and preservation of energy resources.
4. They were interested in safeguarding the massive assets they had acquired out of the recycling of their surplus oil reserves in developed market economies, against inflation in these countries, and against other risks, including those of a political nature.
5. They were interested in devising institutions, and exercising their due control over these and existing institutions, for facilitating the flow of their surplus resources to both developed and developing countries on satisfactory terms and conditions.
6. Finally, to elicit the support of non-oil-exporting developing countries for their proposal, they held out the temptation of using their oil weapon for obliging developed countries to accept some of the major demands of the developing countries in connection with the establishment of NIEO.

In the beginning, many oil-importing developing countries were skeptical about the proposal for global negotiations because:

1. Their interest lay precisely in not allowing attention to be diverted from their demands on the OPEC countries to take measures, by way of offering concessional prices for oil, guaranteeing an oil supply in periods of shortage, and so forth, in order to minimize the adverse impact of the oil price increases on their economies.
2. They comprehended that the new global round of negotiations would interrupt the ongoing negotiations in various UN forums. This had already started adversely affecting the ongoing negotiations on a new international development strategy.
3. They were not quite sure that the OPEC countries would, in the ultimate analysis, really use their oil weapon for the sake of developing countries as a whole.

The above conflict situation was resolved by the strategic bargaining linking the proposal for a global round of negotiations with South-South dialogue. The outcome was the adoption of a separate resolution on a global round of negotiations committing all the nonaligned countries to work for the developed countries agreeing to participate in these negotiations and, in general, for the success of the negotiations; and a set of guidelines for consolidating solidarity among the nonaligned countries, an important element of which was an implicit commitment by OPEC countries to supply oil to oil-importing, nonaligned countries on a priority and on a government-to-government basis in periods of shortage.

NORTH-SOUTH BARGAINING

Selection of Issues for Negotiation

All negotiations involve trade-offs between losses and gains. It often is suggested that only those issues should be selected for North-South bargaining that make a positive-sum game, that is, when there is a net positive gain to be shared by both parties. Ipso facto, issues in which the negotiations involve a zero-sum game, that is, when a gain for one party is a loss for the other, should not be taken up in North-South negotiations. Examples have been given of issues that can make the negotiations a positive-sum game and of those that make them a zero-sum game. The former category of issues are supposed to include price stabilization measures, trade liberalization, and multilateral balance-of-payments financing, including the safety and the preservation of the value of assets kept abroad. Aid issues, price enhancement measures, indexation, debt cancellation, and so forth, are supposed to fall under the category of a zero-sum game.

It is, of course, convenient to look at issues in the perspective of whether they make for positive-sum or zero-sum game negotiations. However, this is an oversimplified way of selecting issues for North-South bargaining. There is nothing intrinsic about an issue that makes the negotiations on it a positive-sum or a zero-sum game; it is the perception by the parties to the negotiations of interests involved in the issue that determines whether the negotiations on it are going to be a positive-sum or a zero-sum game. And perception of interests depends upon a variety of factors such as the objectives to be pursued through the negotiations, the economic and political circumstances in which the negotiating countries are placed, and the other party's capacity to inflict losses.

There could be three-tier objectives and perceptions of interest involved in North-South negotiations. First, there are the broader long-term objectives of peace, stability, harmony among nations, international social justice, and human solidarity to be achieved by such negotiations. These objectives provide a rationale for making the development of developing countries the common concern of the entire international community and for measures for eradication of poverty and equitable global redistribution of incomes and resources. Factors might emerge in the world economy or international economic relations that make some of these long-term objectives a matter of immediate international concern. For example, development of developing countries is now taken more seriously as the concern of all countries than was the case in the immediate postwar years. Similarly, interdependence among the economies of the North and South has become an imperative necessity after the appearance of selective scarcity of key natural resources and the new perception that has been gained of global environmental problems. It would be too simple or cynical to assume that these objectives do not provide any but a moral basis for bargaining because the parties to the negotiation do not perceive their short- and medium-term interest in them.

Then there are what may be regarded as medium-term objectives such as the realization of genuine interdependence, unilateral removal of barriers in the expectation of implicit reciprocity, fighting inflation in developed countries through increased imports from developing countries, and a more rational utilization of the global resources by adopting appropriate international measures for harnessing the productive resources of the developing countries. The third tier of objectives are those that involve immediate loss or gain such as preventing a loss in employment, the disruption of industries and balance-of-payments problems resulting from an increase in imports from developing countries, and avoiding budgetary problems created by increased financial flows to these countries.

The matter is further complicated by the fact that in negotiations on the same issue, some developed countries perceive a positive-sum game and others a zero-sum game. This depends upon how the individual or groups of developed countries discount their general longer-term, medium- to long-term, and short-term objectives. The rate of discount will depend upon the country's geographical position, the size and structure of its economies, the degree of economic autonomy it achieves, its economic and political vulnerability to significant changes in the world economy or international relations, and its geopolitical strategies and objectives. It is very well known that because of the above factors, many of the negotiating games that the United States regards as zero sum are regarded as positive sum by the Nordic countries and the Netherlands. Due to the same reason, even among the so-called hardliners among the countries of the North, there are important nuances in the perception of interest and important shifts in negotiating positions of one or another among those countries taking place from time to time thereby changing the entire complexion of the game. The recent decision of the UK government not to insist on proportionality with the United States in its contribution to the International Development Association (IDA) changed the very complexion of the issue of preventing the stretching out of the period of the sixth IDA replacement.

Perceptions of gain fluctuate with a moving time perspective. A zero-sum situation might be converted into a positive-sum one once it is perceived that short-term costs are more than compensated for by long-term benefits. Moreover, a game becomes positive-sum not only when the more powerful partners perceive that they will be better off in terms of the net benefit that the negotiations will yield but also when they can be made to perceive that in the absence of a compromise, they will be worse off. Herein comes the role of the bargaining power of the less powerful partners and what they can do to enhance it. It should also be borne in mind that pressure exerted in one area need not have its effect in that area alone; its spin-offs in other areas must also be counted in assessing whether the game is going to be a positive-sum or zero-sum one. For example, it is commonly believed that the struggle that the developing countries waged for the establishment of a Capital Development Fund within the UN led to the creation of not only the special fund within the UN but also the IDA within the World Bank. Similarly, the pressure that the developing countries mounted with UNCTAD to have a supplementary financing facility created was, in no small measure, responsible for the improvement of the IMF Compensatory Financing Facility and the establishment of the Extended Fund Facility.

Finally, we should not underestimate the capacity — which has been demonstrated time and again — of the developing countries to perceive their long-term interests clearly and to give precedence to them over their short-term interests. Developing countries, as a group, regard a change in the power relations to be more important than marginal concessions on the volume, the terms, and the conditions of aid or in terms of the removal of trade barriers. They also realize that in the area of money and finance, basic structural changes in the system are required and that they will not get anywhere by being timid or raising marginal issues.

GUIDELINES FOR NORTH-SOUTH NEGOTIATIONS

Decision by Consensus or by a Majority Vote

When the proposals of the South (such as aid flows, contributions to special funds, and setting up of institutions requiring large funding) cannot be implemented without the North's active support and when their acceptance by the North involves a direct sacrifice on their part, the South must not try to force the issue. In other words, the developing countries must agree to enough concessions to make it worthwhile for the developed countries to accord their willing consent. It is impracticable to legislate sacrifices to be made by the North by a majority vote without their consent. Of course, the South should use all its bargaining clout to keep the North under pressure till the end, but the decision ultimately must be by consensus.

But on issues involving broader long-term objectives, that is, when a principle or an idea on which there can be only step-by-step progress is to be preserved and taken forward, a degree of confrontation between the North and the South may become unavoidable and even desirable. It is necessary to go on agitating about these ideas and keep them alive by majority votes. For example, it is unrealistic to expect that, at the present stage of international economic relations, the developed countries would accept such ideas as an international taxation system, a drastic restructuring of the world financial and monetary systems, the control of the developing countries over institutions such as the IMF and the World Bank, or drastic changes in the rules governing international trade. At the same time, these are key issues related to the establishment of a NIEO, and, therefore, the developing countries cannot afford to give them up. They must be voted upon in order to be kept alive.

Using the Bargaining Position of the South

It is not only the perception by the North of gains from cooperation but, also, its perception of loss from noncooperation that stimulates negotiation. And nothing is more conducive to inculcating a perception of loss by the North than the bargaining power of the South. The South should, therefore, select those issues for negotiation on which it is perceived by the North to have a strong bargaining position.

Selecting Issues on Which the South has a Strong Bargaining Position

Commodities were regarded as the right subject for negotiation at UNCTAD IV because the South had, at that time, demonstrated its commodity power through OPEC's price enhancement action. The North accepted this issue, particularly the idea of a common fund, for negotiation as a concession in deference to the newly acquired negotiating strength of the South, but the negotiation was inconclusive.

The problem with a price enhancement measure is that it may involve a zero-sum game not only for the developed countries' consumers of the commodity in question but also for the developing countries' consumers. Therefore, in order to have effectively used their newly acquired strong bargaining position in the field of commodities, the developing countries should not have put themselves in the straitjacket of selecting only one negotiating issue (i.e., commodities), but they should have made it a package including measures that would have compensated those developing countries that stood to lose by price actions in the commodity field and, at the same time, would not have provided such an easy escape route for the North, which the negotiations confined to commodities did. The package for negotiations in and after UNCTAD-IV, therefore, should have included measures in the field of money and finance, manufacturing, trade liberalizations, industrialization, and the transfer of technology. The adoption of such a comprehensive approach accounted for the success of the first three UNCTAD conferences. Concentration on a single issue in UNCTAD-IV turned out to be a mistake in retrospect, a mistake that not only failed to produce the desired result but was also mainly responsible for deflecting UNCTAD from the course chartered at the time of its establishment in 1964, that of being the supreme surveyor of all trade and development matters. UNCTAD is still struggling to regain the role of its halcyon days.

Enhancing the Bargaining Power of the South

In general, the bargaining power of the South derives from its unity and cohesion, which are essentially based on a subjective perception of identity or convergence of interests. Developing countries have a shared understanding of the dynamics of the present international order, and they agree among themselves on both the necessity of, and method for, removing disparity in the wealth and income between them and the developed countries. But this is as far as it goes. In order to enhance the bargaining strength of the developing countries, a subjective sense of unity must be backed by a material basis for solidarity.

Evolving a satisfactory package of measures, constituting the common negotiating position of the Group of 77, provides a good material basis for the solidarity of the group. We have already discussed what is the best way of putting together such a package.

South-South cooperation is the most important means for providing a material basis for the solidarity of the Group of 77. In this context, an early implementation of such proposals as the Common Fund of the developing countries themselves, a council of producers' alliances, a nonaligned solidarity fund, and the Project Development Fund of the nonaligned and other developing countries acquire special importance.

South-South negotiations have sometimes demonstrated effects that can influence the North-South dialogue in a positive direction. For example, the impression that the developing countries create through these negotiations, about their ability to discharge their obligations to each other, can be a factor influencing the manner in which the developed countries will discharge their obligation to developing countries.

FORMAT OF NORTH-SOUTH NEGOTIATIONS

The effective functioning of the group mechanism is a practical necessity for negotiations in a large multilateral forum. In any negotiation among a large number of countries, coalitions of countries with similarity of interest inevitably tend to get constituted. The question is whether groups should operate on an ad hoc basis for different negotiations or on the basis of well-established and firmly institutionalized entities representing broadly common interests. Practical necessity will point to an inevitability of the latter type of arrangement. If groups crystalize and start functioning only after the negotiations, negotiation will become a highly chaotic, cumbersome, and time-consuming process. Functioning through institutionalized groups helps to make a continuing exercise of a more orderly and systematic nature.

Well-established groups have existed in the UN since its formulation. Even under the charter, elections to UN bodies have been provided for on the basis of acceptable geographical representation from different regional groups. Western and Socialist groups started functioning soon after the establishment of the UN. As regards the developing countries, there was, in the beginning, the Afro-Asian group that was concerned, mainly, with political issues, but, occasionally, it also adopted specific positions on economic issues. The Afro-Asian group was soon substituted by the nonaligned group. The Group of 75 was established in 1963 in the context of the preparation for the first UNCTAD and it was transformed into the Group of 77 by the time the conference was concluded. Since then it has remained as the Group of 77 because of the great symbolic value it has acquired, even though more than 115 developing countries are now represented in the group. It was also during the first UNCTAD that the group mechanism was formally recognized in a UN resolution and was thus firmly institutionalized.

While developed countries tend to say that the functioning of the group mechanism, particularly that of the Group of 77, has introduced rigidities in North-South negotiations, they themselves are very well organized into groups of their own. In the UN forums, they function as Group B countries as defined in one of the decisions of the first UNCTAD (Annex. A.V:I of the Final Act). Moreover, they regularly and systematically coordinate their policies and harmonize their positions through the institutions of the OECD and the EEC. They have at their disposal very efficient and prestigious secretariats, the world's top experts, and sizable resources. The Group of 77, on the other hand, has not even been able to establish a secretariat of its own, has hardly any organized group of experts working for it, and chronically suffers from paucity of resources to carry out research work to support its negotiating activities. Thanks to their organizational resources and regular habits of coordination, the developed countries generally are better prepared to negotiate conferences than is the Group of 77. They are able to project a consistent position when the same issue comes up for discussion in different forums, and they do not miss a single opportunity to advance their objectives. The developing countries, in contrast, work at cross-purposes in many negotiating forums, and they are known to have allowed important objectives to go by default out of sheer inertia, or for want of persistence.

However, on broader long-term objectives of a more fundamental nature, the developing countries have repeatedly demonstrated their ability and their will to remain united and alert. This unity is based on a kind of class consciousness among them. They all perceive themselves in what Prebisch called the "periphery of the world economy" and at the receiving end of the present international economic order. They feel very strongly that they are the poor, undeveloped, and underprivileged segment of the world; that they do not have full control over their resources; that they are left outside the main decision-making process regarding the management of the world economy; that they cannot very much influence the world financial and monetary systems that are such a key determinant of their position in the world economy; and that they are at the bottom of the ladder of technological progress. Apart from this subjective perception of their unity, they have now learned that they must provide a solid objective basis, by undertaking negotiations of their own, for promoting and strengthening their collective self-reliance.

It is futile to predict the disappearance of the Group of 77. It will remain a reality as long as the outcome of negotiations on the world economic system continues to depend mainly on the bargaining power of the negotiating partners. The group will continue to exist for quite some time to come not only because the functioning of group mechanism is a practical necessity for any negotiation but because it just does not make any sense for the developing countries to give up the only bargaining power they have, and that is their unity, their standing together as a group.

An important indictment of the Group of 77 has been that the group is so large and unwieldly that it is highly time-consuming and, at times, even impracticable to carry on negotiations on behalf of the group as a whole. It is therefore suggested that for insuring the effectiveness and speed of negotiations, the participants in them should be only principal interest groups or countries directly involved in the issue under negotiation.

In actual practice, even when negotiations are conducted on behalf of the Group of 77, the real participants are those whose interests are directly involved and those who represent principal interest groups. Hard bargaining and serious negotiations always take place in smaller groups. This is in spite of the recent tendency to make all important negotiating committees, committees of the whole, and all ad hoc/working/drafting groups open-ended. This development reflects the recent trend of increasing democratization of all UN organizations and bodies and of the keen desire of even the smallest country to seize every opportunity to assert its sovereignty, one of the most visible forms of which is representation in UN bodies.

However, once the committee of the whole or the open-ended working group is set up and starts meeting, a sizable proportion of the countries represented in it does not turn up. This is mainly because they do not have at their disposal the personnel or expertise to participate in these negotiating committees or groups. The proportion of dropouts in the open-ended groups is even higher because, there, real expertise and almost full-time attendance is required. Thus, the negotiations automatically are confined to the delegates representing the principal interests involved in the issue under the negotiations.

However, the outcome of the negotiations in smaller groups must be democratically discussed and endorsed. These are, of course, time-consuming procedures. But they are far less time-consuming than what would be the case if there were no preestablished groups continuously negotiating among themselves and with the other groups. Besides, the time devoted to the maintenance of the democratic form is very worthwhile because it enables a lot of time to be saved in the actual negotiation that takes place in smaller groups.

Editor's Comments on North-South Negotiations

These chapters deal with negotiations on the sharing of the world cake. They are of interest to all countries and to everyone. The result is that the groups of states actually involved in negotiations are at their maximum potential size. This creates special problems in negotiation, calling for the development of special techniques. Based on their great experience in the field, the authors of these chapters offer their views on the developments that have taken place and that have been utilized in negotiations on North-South issues. Again, the two chapters are, in many ways, complementary.

The first chapter makes the following very interesting contributions to the understanding of the processes of negotiation:

1. Large groups of states such as the "77" and "Group B" tend to promote a "strength in unity" attitude with consequent rigidities. Rigidities lead to deadlocks in negotiations. The negotiators have found a way around this situation by developing the contact group technique. Each large group sets up some of its members as a small contact group and the contact groups meet quietly in an atmosphere of informality. This kind of negotiating activity can lead to constructive compromises as it did, for example, in August–September 1975, at the Seventh Special Session of the General Assembly on Development and International Cooperation. This technique is comparable with the informal behind-the-scenes meetings of the Security Council members.
2. Secretariats can stimulate delegates by producing new ideas, analyses, and data. Per contra, secretariats can play a very low keyed role. In these matters, much depends on the attitude of the head of the secretariat: the secretary-general or the director-general.
3. On important issues, consensus is essential, but it must be genuine. If it is followed by statements of reservations — especially by important delegations — it remains a dead letter.
4. Whatever the decision-making procedure — voting or consensus — the interests of all the major groups must be safeguarded.
5. The objectives in the negotiation must be clearly defined. They seldom are.

177

6. Perceptions of mutual interest in the results aimed at are essential for success in negotiations in the economic field. (See Fisher, Chapter 8 on disarmament negotiations. This is generally true of all negotiations.)

7. The negotiating parties must have a working confidence in each other.

The second chapter highlights the following points in regard to negotiating procedures and techniques:

1. The genesis of proposals for negotiation lies in ideas thought up by scholars, research institutes and secretariats or suggested to governments by their own experience in the economic sphere.

2. A government, or a group of governments in communication with each other, converts an idea into an issue or proposal for negotiation.

3. Negotiations seek to bridge the gap between ideas as norms and ideas as commitments and obligations.

4. Those ideas can be converted into negotiating issues that serve the interests of a large number of states, not of just one or two. Similarly, an idea that primarily serves the personal interests of its promoter might be launched, but it is unlikely to succeed in negotiation.

5. Even when an idea that serves the interests of a very large number of states, or all states, is converted into an issue for negotiation, an intensive process of education is frequently required to make all states fully aware of the potential value of the issue.

6. Issues that remain valid — some lose validity with the passage of time — should continue to be pursued even when circumstances are unfavorable, such as an economic recession.

7. Not all issues are equally important to all countries. A country tends to be active in the negotiation of those aspects of an economic issue that affect its well-being.

8. The larger the group of countries that negotiates (e.g., the Group of 77), the more its joint stand will contain positions of special concern to subgroups within the large group almost exclusively. But such sectional positions have to be supported by the whole group.

9. When immediate objectives are involved (e.g., the redressing of balance-of-payments problems), negotiations tend to become zero-sum situations. When long-term objectives predominate (e.g., agreement to work for a more equitable world order), then the negotiating situation tends to be perceived as a positive-sum one.

10. When immediate concessions are sought by either side, consensus is necessary. But when matters of principle are involved, such as restructuring the world's monetary and financial systems, confrontation keeps

the issue alive and may be desirable, says the author. In these circumstances, votes should be pressed.

11. Each side tends to select those issues in which it perceives itself to be
strong. But this attitude can polarize negotiations and is often self-
defeating.

PART 7

INTERNATIONAL LAW AND NEGOTIATION

Chapter 11

International Law, Mediation, and Negotiation

Manfred Lachs

The theme of my reflections is the relationship between international law and negotiations. The relationship is dominated by the fact that international law creates a framework for state activities in international relations, and within this system of relationships, which knows various situations and developments, negotiations play a special role. In fact, the word for this role is multi-colored, and it has gone through various and interesting stages in the course of history. From the very day when two states came into being, problems arose that called for them to establish certain relations. Thus, relationships were a necessary consequence of their existence. This goal could be achieved only by negotiations. The original and basic institution charged with the function of negotiations was diplomacy; thus, it was the oldest and the most fundamental of all functions related to international law. The dictionary describes these functions as follows: "The management of international relations by negotiations, the methods by which these relations are adjusted and managed by ambassadors and envoys; the business or art of the diplomatist."[1]

Thus, diplomacy has constituted, and still constitutes, a special chapter of international law and, also, of negotiations. It is an instrument of foreign policy and there is an interdependence between the political activities of the state and its diplomacy: an interdependence that could be described as a relationship between strategy and tactics.[2]

In fact, diplomacy has been shaped by the historical transformation of the state, reflecting its changing status in international relations. There was the diplomacy of the days of Dante, Boccaccio, and Machiavelli; the traveling missions of Ivan the Terrible; and messengers sent out by the Kings of Poland, who at first employed foreigners only and later came to the conclusion that missions at foreign courts could be entrusted only to Polish nobility.

As to the tools of diplomacy, they were also described in various ways and in different forms at different stages of history. Suffice it to recall that Talley-rand-Périgord, in his last speech delivered at the French Academy in 1838, disclaimed that diplomacy was an art of duplicity and untruth. On another occasion, he is alleged to have said: "To lie is a good thing, but one should not abuse it."

Turning to a more serious analysis of the situation, negotiations aim at the establishment of conditions of permanent relations among states (by treaty or otherwise), serve their maintenance, and solve problems that arise through-out the existence of those relations. They serve as basic instruments for settle-ment of disputes. Today, when states have so many mutual contacts and rela-tions are spread over so many fields, negotiations have a special function to perform; They enter many fields and cover almost all the spheres of the ac-tivities concerning the state as such and, also, its physical and juridical persons.

The element of negotiation is today much more in the foreground than ever before. The wealth of problems that states face in their economic, polit-ical, scientific, and other relations imposes upon them the obligation, I would say the necessity, to negotiate in a wide sense. Thus, the instruments of ne-gotiation have multiplied, and negotiations have acquired a new and impor-tant dimension.

Approaching the subject of negotiation in its wider dimensions, we are bound to define its place within international law and its relations to it. First, there is the object of the function itself. The greater rapprochement of states and the growth of daily contacts between them has created not only a closer relationship between them but has brought into the open a host of problems that require regulation. In order to create the basis of such regulation, negotia-tions are necessary to establish conditions for mutual relations of a perma-nent character through treaties or by the establishment of international organ-izations, in a wider sense of the word, or any other instruments that would resolve specific problems among states in their relationships, at least for a certain period of time. The second object of negotiations is the settlement of disputes. That is the resolution of confrontation and different views, dif-ferent approaches, of states on a specific issue or on a series of issues. The function of the negotiator in both cases is of essential importance as he is called upon to produce agreement, and this agreement is linked with law be-cause it must correspond to the requirements of international law.

Turning to the process of negotiation itself, two points should be recalled: (1) the relationship of the parties, and (2) the relationship of their mutual in-terests. As to the relationship of the parties, there is a basic premise that dis-tinguishes negotiations from dictates, or the imposition of the will by one party upon the other or others. The very essence of negotiation is agreement, agreement freely arrived at. History offers a whole host of illustrations in which, under the guise of negotiation, decisions were reached that were the result of pressure exercised by one party upon the other. Some examples are the treaty on Japan's protectorate over Korea (1905), the treaties between Japan and China concluded prior to World War I, and a large number of colonial relationships that dominated the international scene for centuries. To this list, other treaties of recent origin may be added such as the Munich Agreement of 1938. Have these methods disappeared? Pressure in a more subtle way has remained one of the instruments used by states in their mutual relations. It might be in the guise of economic, political, or even military measures. In most cases, it is almost unnoticeable. The outcome may be an instrument that has all the form and shape of a document corresponding to the freely expressed will of the parties, but, in fact, it is the result of one yielding to the other, not due to conviction or persuasion. It is well known that the charter has proclaimed "the sovereign equality of States," that every state has one vote in international relations. The weight of the vote and the substantive value of equality remain valid. It is only through a common effort of the international community and through the intervention of all involved that this equality can become a reality in all its manifestations. It should — and here the intervention of law is very essential — guarantee the possibility of free expression of will at all stages of negotiations and bar parties from exercising an influence that is undue and that may be tantamount to pressure. The recognition of equality is a constructive element in reaching agreement. In the long run, it is in the interest of both the strong and the weak that this equality be protected. For it is in it that the guarantee of the value of the instrument, its observance, its durability rests. In the process of negotiations, as in the instrument itself, military, political, and economic coercion though resolved should not be used. In fact, they are barred by contemporary international law in regard to treaties.[3] This equally applies to all stages of the relationship between states leading to the conclusion of a treaty. Even more important is the effect of an error, of fraud, or the corruption of a representative of a state in the process of negotiations. The coercion of a representative of a state, the threat or use of force, may be invoked as invalidating consent, deprive it of legal effect, or make it void.

The second important element in the process of negotiations is that concerning the interests of the parties in the conclusion of an instrument or the resolution of a dispute. As to the first, the parties may have unequal interests: one may be more concerned with the conclusion of an instrument, be it a treaty or an agreement, while the other considers it useful but not essential; a treaty may also come into existence when negotiations are embarked upon because of the difference of the interests of the parties. A simple illustration is given by negotiations in which one party is the buyer and the other party is the seller of goods. It is only in view of this relationship that a treaty or an agreement would come into existence. In other situations, treaties come into operation due to identical interests of the parties, vis-à-vis other states, or their common effort to achieve a common goal. This objective of the treaty must be reflected in the process of negotiations, and the negotiations themselves will therefore be a mirror of the concerns, interests, and status of the parties participating in them. At each stage of the negotiation, the legal aspect is present, even if invisible. It is present because the parties discuss; agree or disagree; try to draft a formula that is to become part of a wider consensus that contains legal aspects; and, as I indicated earlier, the mere relationship between them in this process has a legal aspect. This leads me to the substance of negotiations, that is, the consideration of all the circumstances and the setting in which negotiations take place.

The background of the parties is the world of facts: geography, history, social and economic relations, political considerations. All of them constitute a point of departure and continue to be companions of the parties negotiating throughout the process of the negotiations. In many domains, the position of the parties may be more or less on the same level; equality leaves no room for doubt. In others, their relationship may be uneven, though from a declaratory point of view, it remains equal. At any rate, we have to bear in mind that this relationship in the process of negotiations is a developing phenomenon with various stages succeeding one another. The background is the reality of the world of today even if reduced to the reality of the status of those states that take part in the negotiation. In brief, negotiations constitute a dialogue between contemporaries — even if they concern matters of the past or intend to project their interests into the future. To be successful, this dialogue cannot be one between yesterday and today, or of yesterday and tomorrow, but must take into account, and it does take into account, consciously or unconsciously, the realities of the moment at which it takes place. Part of these realities is law. Here we find another of the basic premises of an objective character in the process of negotiations. Apart from bringing a dynamic into the relationship between the parties, the realities also add a background that is relevant, that is the world of today: the development of relations between other states and the general situation in a particular field or the general political and legal situation. Thus, there are various settings in which negotiations take place. Recently, a frequent type of negotiations has concerned the granting of independence to former colonial and other dependent peoples.[4] The reality was, of course, the relationship between the metropolitan power and the representatives of the liberation movements. Here the question of the equality of the parties was certainly one of crucial importance for it was necessary to assure those who were striving for the establishment of their independence that they would be given all the facilities to present their views and that the outcome would not be only a formal but a real mission of independence. This required a special setting that was secured by the United Nations: a series of resolutions determining not only the principles but also conditions and a timetable. In many cases the process has taken place outside the United Nations, and in several cases, it still continues. These negotiations then rely on the relationship between the colonial power and the liberation movements supported by those states that have been liberated only recently. Here again a de facto multilateral setting appears, though the problem in itself is a bilateral one. The legal aspects of it are of a particular interest for the colonial power, or the state that controls the territories also has allies that may be invisible in the registration itself but may support its case.

Thus, through negotiations, a series of principles acquired a certain legal status and became a guide for the future development of the law. Among them are some specific aspects of self-determination. Though, as is well known, the relevant decisions of the United Nations are mere resolutions, it has been held that they constitute a further important stage in the law-making and law-application process.

A further interesting factor in this sphere of the relationship between newly established states and former metropolitan powers or other developed states is the question of sovereignty over natural resources. Here, again, the new law has been the result of negotiations and settlement of disputes that have arisen in this area. It has been confirmed by UN resolutions: the principle of sovereignty of a state over its natural resources.[5] Another important issue in which negotiations have played a very important role (mentioned only in passing) is compensation for nationalized property.[6]

I have referred to only two domains that are in the forefront of problems dividing old and new states in the world of today. They, like many others, may be resolved by negotiations leading (as indicated) to the development of a new law. The phenomenon of negotiations is of no lesser importance in the shaping of the relationships between states of different systems. For a long time, special attention has been devoted to this aspect of international relations, and it was claimed that the ideological gap or differences of philosophical outlook make negotiations impossible and, hence, agreements unattainable. It was even claimed that the maximum one might hope for was an armistice. This, of course, is an untenable position for history reports no period in which all states were of an identical or even similar system. From their very birth, international relations were developing between different philosophical or religious beliefs, and this pluralism of systems has been a permanent factor on the international scene throughout history. Thus, the very roots of international relations lie in the recognition of these differences. Moreover, it is interesting to note that to negotiate and reach agreement, one must assume that there are differences of an important nature between the parties, and they very frequently arise between states belonging to the same system. Here again, law gives an indication of these differences by recognizing the "coexistence of States of different systems" and the coexistence of interests legally protected of various states.

In classifying negotiation further, all sorts of settings may be visualized:

negotiations between neighboring states and those removed from one another; states with conflicting interests on their territories or beyond their territories; states seeking the resolution of conflicts concerning them alone but also differences that concern other states. Thus, negotiations may be required in many areas and on many levels. They touch almost all problems of international relations and, in doing so, touch on questions of law; they are bound to remain within the bounds of law or, without violating it, help its further development.

So far, I have been dealing with what I would call the physical aspects of negotiations as a background prior to approaching the very essence of the process itself. Before completing this chapter on my reflections, one more aspect should be taken into account, that is, the number of the parties. Traditionally and historically, the oldest negotiations were of a bilateral character: Two states were usually engaged in settling their disputes or differences, working together for the elaboration of a treaty. With the growth in the number of states and the links that have been established in many areas, diplomacy has acquired a new multilateral pattern. This has obviously had its impact on the process of negotiation as a method for settling multilateral relations and the impact of law on them. Here again, different forms are possible. Negotiations may have a coalition character: representatives of two groups of states belonging to two different alliances or organizations of a regional or political character face one another, speaking on behalf of their respective allies. Formally negotiations remain bilateral, but in substance, they usually reflect more than two points of view and interests of more than two states. The legal basis of each of the parties seems to be clearly defined, but, not infrequently, one or two of the allies do not support the common position. Ever more frequently, negotiations themselves become multilateral, that is, a number of states sit at the negotiating table. They reflect a multitude of conflicting interests that are not organized nor set in an institutional form. Though they may be members of no more than two organizations, their interests within the framework of these organizations differ, and each of them sits at the negotiation table as an independent entity. As to the legal aspects of this type of relationship, the consent of all of them is necessary to reach an agreement unless it is a partial agreement with some of the parties refusing to adhere to it and remaining at odds on issues on which they refuse to subscribe to the views of the others. We have, for instance, as an illustration the North-South dialogue in which groups of states (each of which has certain common interests binding it together) confront one another as groups of states, but they do not necessarily represent identical interest, and views within each group may differ. Thus, you have the interesting illustration of a situation in which, for some, agreements may be reached in a limited sphere concerning only some issues. Speaking in legal terms, full success of the North-South dialogue would amount to the establishment of a new international economic order, something based on a multilateral treaty including all the members of the United Nations. It is, however, possible and likely that, in the interim, agreement may be reached between groups of states such as those in need and those more amenable to the claims of the poorer countries and more ready to bear their share to improve their situation.

Finally, we have the possibility of negotiations that directly concern five or six states but may affect humanity as a whole. What I obviously have in mind are negotiations between the big powers, the relationship between which is of basic importance and paramount influence on the relationship of all states, for peace and peaceful relations in global dimensions. The number may be reduced even to two in the question of nuclear weapons and the limitation of nuclear arsenals; here the two big powers are involved in negotiation that may be decisive for others. Thus, other states not taking part in the negotiations have a vital interest in an agreement being reached between the two. Here you have an illustration of two actors engaged in negotiations representing, in law, their own interests but, in fact, representing the interests of humanity as a whole. Strictly speaking, there are three stages involved. There are two powers negotiating the limitation on the manufacturing and the stationing of nuclear weapons; there are the alliances to which they are connected; and there are other states that are not members of the alliances — the neutral or nonaligned states that constitute the great majority of mankind. There are two actors only, but their decisions and their agreement or disagreement have a legal impact on the alliances and beyond them. In view of the interrelationship between members of the alliances, the armaments controlled by the big powers are not only placed on their own territories but also on the territories of other states. Therefore, should one of the two disagree on certain disarmament measures and, due to this disagreement, refuse to accept the limitation of armaments, the armament race will not stop. The legal basis for it is that the alliances constitute legal entities and, by their stipulations, provide common measures for defense. Thus, law intervenes by prompting decisions of a collective character to bring about the limitation of armaments.

On the other hand, should an agreement be reached as to the reduction of armaments, this would affect not only the two powers that dispose of the largest military potential in the world but all their allies, again by the operation of the treaties that are in force; this would also reduce their armaments, and, thus, a chain reaction would be produced. Indirectly, this may also affect the situation in the nonaligned countries, some of which are increasing their armaments not only in view of their relationship with their neighboring countries but also in view of the increase of armaments within the framework of the two big alliances dominating the world picture — their impact creeping into areas beyond their membership. Disarmament agreements are lawmaking treaties in a domain vital to humanity. Due to the specific structure of the international community, decisions taken by a very few may in this domain affect all. Thus, it is so important that the great majority of states, particularly the nonaligned states and peoples, exercise some influence in the shaping of the will — hence, the decision making — of these few. History shows that this is not an easy process; however, in the long run, it may produce practical results. It may also have a legal effect on the will and decisions of the alliance.

Finally, there is the framework within which the negotiations take place. They may proceed within an ad hoc setting for the solution of an ad hoc problem. They may have a continuous character and, therefore, build in a system of a legal nature, which is permanent: a typical illustration of the latter is an international organization or an organization that has been established for the solution of certain problems. In this respect, the United Nations is a very interesting illustration. It is a body within which negotiations permanently take place. From a legal point of view, debates in the United Nations have the character of negotiations. Its constitution provides for various subjects to be dealt with by various organs within various time limits and on a specific basis. The intention of the drafters of the charter was not to make it a forum of confrontation and decision making by fluctuating majorities but an instrument of coordination and cooperation through negotiations. Discussion in the Security Council is a form of negotiation. Draft resolutions submitted are proposals, and resolutions are often legal instruments binding upon the parties in accordance with Articles 24 and 25 of the charter. Unfortunately, these debates have degenerated into confrontations; in most cases, instead of negotiations, one faces a series of inflexible statements; the principle of unanimity intended to lead to agreements has become known as the veto (Art. 27, para. 3). In the course of time, the General Assembly, one of the principal organs of the United Nations intended "to consider the general principles of cooperation," has become a forum for raising grievances, conflicts, and confrontations existing in the world of today. Yet it should have become an instrument of a forum for negotiation and, thus, for lawmaking. Fortunately enough, in some respects, it has retained this character. Committees of the General Assembly are fora in which not only ad hoc problems are solved but also treaties are worked out, and these are obviously the product of negotiations. Both have a legal character and may have far-reaching legal consequences. Treaties such as those concerning the status of women and children, the protection of human rights, and the elaboration of details in many spheres of international cooperation are the result of negotiations held within the United Nations. It may be worth recalling that one of the first treaties elaborated by the United Nations was the Convention on the Prevention and Punishment of the Crime of Genocide in 1948. The two Covenants on Human Rights, which had their origin in the famous Universal Declaration of Human Rights of 10 December 1948, were also elaborated within the United Nations. Here the process is one of perhaps a specific nature; it takes a two-stage approach. The first stage is a resolution of the General Assembly. By the provisions of the charter and the clear will of the founders of the organization, decisions of the General Assembly, with some exceptions only, are mere recommendations; they are therefore not binding on states and do not create law, but they contribute to the creation of law. However, there are some resolutions, again as the result of negotiation, that do create law and the link between the resolution and the lawmaking process is very close. But usually, a General Assembly resolution is the first stage toward the lawmaking process. The second stage is the conclusion of an instrument of a treaty character (as was, for instance, the case with human rights just mentioned).

Similar is the situation in other international organizations such as the International Labour Organization (which has a very special provision on the subject), the World Health Organization, and the family of specialized agencies and other organizations outside their ambit.

All this shows how rich is the agenda of negotiations and how widely spread the network that, through negotiations, leads to lawmaking: the creation of binding rules in relations between states. We face a great variety of formal aspects of negotiations. They may appear minor but are frequently of major importance because the setting may in some circumstances be decisive for the result and the final success of the operation itself. It may be decisive in reaching an agreement or in dragging on the differences; so that an agreement becomes ever more remote, or the parties to it do not come closer to each other. I would conclude this part of my reflections by stating that negotiations, as a whole, are the basic instrument in interstate relations and that the rules of international law rely on negotiations: they are born through negotiations and are shaped by them.

However, the freedom of states to negotiate is not unlimited. States that have negotiated a treaty cannot abolish it without the participation of all those who were parties to it. Moreover, international law has developed a new notion that prohibits the conclusion of an instrument that, at the time of its negotiation, "conflicts with the peremptory norms of general international law" (Art. 53 of the Convention on the Law of Treaties, Vienna, 1969). (As is well-known, "a peremptory norm of general international law is a norm accepted and recognized by the international community of states as a whole as a norm from which no derogation is permitted and which can be modified only by a subsequent norm of general international law having the same character" [loc. cit.].) Existing law has not defined or specifically indicated which of its rules could be regarded as "peremptory," yet one could assume that some are obviously in this category. I would suggest that in regard to genocide, being a crime against humanity, its prevention is a peremptory rule of law. The same is true in regard to slavery or to war crimes; but, as to these, the right of negotiations of the parties is clearly very limited or even excluded. No state could negotiate with another state the establishment of a bilateral system of slavery even without any other state taking part in it. They could not legalize slavery in view of the fact that it has been outlawed by the international community. Nor could one admit the right of two states to commit an act of aggression against a third state; or to divide part or whole of its territory. It is here that the freedom of action of states is limited. They cannot negotiate and enter into agreement to institute practices or establish relations on principles that are contrary to generally binding principles of law. Nor can they negotiate, as earlier indicated, treaties that are contrary to other existing treaties; for instance, the Charter of the United Nations. However, at the same time, this limitation of the sphere of negotiations, or what one may call the freedom of negotiation, stresses the wide area of possibilities existing in this domain. For, as I indicated earlier, negotiations serve two purposes: (1) the establishment of peaceful relations between states and (2) the resolution of disputes existing between them. In regard to both areas, the freedom of action of states is limited only by the existence of certain peremptory rules of law. They cannot resolve a dispute by reaching an agreement that would impose obligations, or imply the right to conduct hostilities, against a third state or deprive its people of freedom or independence.

In the sphere of the settlement of disputes, negotiations have a paramount role to perform and are, again, closely linked with law. Each dispute touches upon issues of law for there is hardly any that would not have some legal aspects: the application, maintenance, or termination of, or compliance with, a legal relationship. Disputes arising out of these call for resolutions. Thus, directly or indirectly, negotiations of disputes lead to the modification of the existing relationships or the establishment of a new legal relationship. The resolution of any conflict enriches law every time by adding a new chapter to the existing body of rules and their interpretation. It helps the solution of a problem, perhaps of more than one, in existence and may assist the solution of those that may arise in the future. However, one should be aware of the risk that a particular outcome of negotiations may create more problems or make the resolution of other disputes more difficult. The growing interdependence of events and states calls for careful consideration of all implications of a decision before it is taken. It may be overexacting to require states, while solving their conflicts, to bear in mind potential or existing disputes between other states or to consider their value as precedents. However, even if they limit themselves to reflections on their own interests, they are bound to visualize themselves in a reverse situation and, thus, be mindful of the risks involved.

Here, then, lies the close relationship between negotiations and international law. The continuously expanding body of international law covers almost all areas of international relations, and, therefore, each negotiation in its legal implications cannot be viewed in isolation. All possible means should be used to arrive at a mutual and adaptable solution. The orthodox methods of negotiation need not be followed. For example, the dispute may be divided into several parts, and the solution of each of them enshrined in a separate instrument. Though it is difficult to visualize all possible situations in which the parties may find themselves in the future, a series of further comments may be worth adding in this respect. One concerns the time factor, which has both political and legal aspects. One of the parties may be interested in a speedy solution, the other in delaying the decision. Thus, a meeting of minds on the date by which a decision is to be reached is of primary importance. Here a balance must be struck between the advantages flowing from short negotiations and those of a protracted character. Sometimes, blinded by success in the battlefield or through diplomatic action, statesmen delay decisions hoping for an even greater advantage. Yet this need not necessarily follow — it may produce the opposite effect. A precarious advantage gained may dictate an immediate termination of a conflict with the consequences flowing from it, rather than its continuation into an uncertain future.

The time factor has also another aspect. It may be a purely legal dispute yet of a political character; or, as a result of protracted negotiations, a legal dispute may become politicized, arousing public opinion and the resentment of an important part of the population. More developments may threaten the government in power, provoke questions in parliament, and transform the whole issue into one of heated public debate in which the political element begins to dominate. Thus, the relationship between the political and legal may not only be the result of the substance of the dispute itself but of the conditions in which it arises and the time at which it matures and the negotiations begin. Here, therefore, care should be taken to negotiate at the moment that is not inconvenient to either of the parties because, in many circumstances, though they are independent states, they may not be free agents — being dependent on many factors (e.g., public opinion) that they cannot easily control.

Finally, negotiations in today's world, because of the great interdependence of states and events, should not be used to press the other party to the wall. Some leeway must be left. Relations between total winners and total losers at the negotiation table are rarely successful, or, if successful, do not augur a lasting result. After all, two or more states, whether neighbors are not, are bound to maintain mutual, lasting peaceful relations. Obviously, the victim of an unprovoked attack, of an economic or other pressure, is bound to seek compensation for damage suffered and guarantees against similar events occurring in the future. But the penalty should not be so high as to provoke ill feeling that may leave a painful heritage and prevent the development of future friendly relations. Even more so, a similar situation arises when disputes are of a less acute character. If one of the parties has really suffered a disadvantage, it should not overreact and try to use the situation to impose upon the other party a burden that will be too painful to carry for a long period of time. Here, again, law is helpful by offering all sorts of devices that parties may use in assuring their interests and regulating their relationship. Once agreement is reached and in order to avoid future disputes or difficulties, a permanent organ may be created to watch the implementation of the agreement. Should smaller difficulties arise and should the parties disagree on the interpretation of the agreement, a special body may be created and called upon to assist them in the solution of difficulties that may arise in the future. This may be a conciliation or mediation commission, or a similar organ, that would settle differences without affecting the validity of the agreement or creating a situation of confrontation between the parties.

But negotiations, as such, may in some circumstances become impossible because of the tense situation between the parties and the impossibility of bringing them to the negotiating table. In such a situation, perhaps, the intervention of a third party, the good offices of a personality playing a specific role, may be of great importance. This legal device (provided by Art. 33 of the Charter of the United Nations) should be used as soon as possible in order to avoid the deterioration of the relationship between the parties. Such an action may speed the rapprochement between the parties and, thus, the possibility of direct negotiations. This third-party factor may be limited to bringing two states to the negotiation table and to presiding at the first meeting, leaving them alone for subsequent meetings.

Finally, in order to avoid endless negotiations as a result of disagreements on substance, it may be advisable to fix a time limit after which states may resort to third-party intervention on a permanent basis. This, while advisable, is not always possible. There is one domain in which the intervention of a single third party would not be acceptable, that is, the vital domain of disarmament; there, no assistance of a third state is likely to be helpful. What could be of assistance is the pressure of world opinion and of a considerable number of states, not beneficiaries but possible victims of the arms race. In these and similar negotiations, a two- or three-stage approach may be advisable. Failure or deadlock at a lower level may encourage a meeting at a higher one and, finally, at the summit. It is well known that the reverse approach is also advocated: Summit meetings are suggested only if agreement is reached at a lower level, to avoid what some claim may become a confrontation between the leaders. The function of the summit is seen as sealing an agreement reached at a lower level. However, I feel that both approaches are acceptable. Past summit meetings have in many cases been successful; (the Congresses of Vienna, Paris, and Berlin produced lasting results). The practice, as is well known, was continued during World War I (in 1916) and after World War II. Some of them were successful, others less so. The Munich meeting that preceded World War II was certainly a calamity. On the other hand, some held during the last few decades have produced certain results: their outcomes were treaties of major importance. There is of course no ready-made recipe for the stages and instruments of negotiations. The general principle that should be applied in this respect is certainly the principle of the means serving the end. All methods should be used in order to achieve a result that is desired by the parties concerned; ingenuity and inventiveness should remain permanent companions of policy planners.

In this brief survey, I have tried to show how wide a range negotiations cover in the world of the international relations of today. I have tried to stress the close relationship between negotiations and international law. Relying on law, negotiations are intended to maintain the rule of law and possibly create new rules of law. No separation between law and negotiations is possible. Of course, negotiation may be predominantly of a political nature and dominated by political considerations, but, even so, legal elements will always be present. The basic principles are that peaceful relations among states must be maintained and protected and that the great achievements of international law, as reflected in the Charter of the United Nations and the many instruments that followed it, should not only be maintained but further enhanced. This is the way to respect the principles of peaceful settlement of disputes, of self-determination, and the abolition of confrontation whatever its source may be.

In all these domains there are legal premises that should be followed, developed, and enriched. It is through negotiation that this can be done, and the goodwill of states must manifest itself at the negotiating table so that disaster may be avoided and better relations among states of East and West and North and South be assured.

NOTES

1. *Shorter Oxford Dictionary*, 3rd ed., vol. 1 (Oxford: Oxford University Press, 1950), 514; cf., in particular, the earlier important work by Sir Ernest Satow, *Guide to Diplomatic Practice*, 2nd ed., (London: Longmans, Green & Co., 1922), 1, in which diplomatic activity is defined and practical indications are given as to its conduct.

2. Sir Victor Wellesley, *Diplomacy in Fetters*, (London, Hutchinson & Co., 1943), 30.

3. "Declaration on the Prohibition of Military, Political or Economic Coercion in the Conclusion of Treaties," adopted by the UN Conference on the Law of Treaties, Vienna, May 22, 1969.

4. "Declaration on the Granting of Independence to Colonial Countries and Peoples," GA Res. 1514 (XX), Dec. 14, 1960, and its evaluation in the advisory opinion of the International Court of Justice on Namibia, *I. C. J. Reports 1971*, 31, para. 52.

5. "Declaration of Permanent Sovereignty over Natural Resources," GA Res. 1803 (XVII), Dec. 14, 1962.

6. "Declaration on the Establishment of a New International Economic Order," GA Res. 3201 (S-VI), May 1, 1974; "Charter of Economic Rights and Duties of States," GA Res. 3281 (XXIX), Dec. 12, 1974.

Editor's Comments on International Law and Negotiation

This section shows how international law creates a framework for relations among states, including negotiations between them. International law is therefore fundamental to the process of negotiation.

Agreements among states reached through negotiation must correspond to the requirements of international law.

Agreements and treaties that are the result of pressures are not true agreements freely arrived at. Coercion by any party in negotiating agreements is barred by international law.

There is today, more than ever before, a widely spread network through which negotiation stimulates the process of lawmaking.

The UN was set up as an ongoing legal system, that is, a system created by international law, to be an instrument for international coordination and cooperation through negotiations.

Though there is often confrontation in UN General Assembly debates, constructive work is done, too, for example, the adoption of resolutions that have led to the elaboration of treaties such as the Human Rights Covenants.

Negotiation as a whole is the basic instrument of international relations, and it is on negotiations that the rules of international law rely; they are born through negotiations and are shaped by them. At the same time, negotiations rely on international law and are intended to maintain and strengthen the rule of law.

But there are limits on the freedom of states to negotiate. They are precluded from negotiating to achieve results contrary to existing treaties such as the Charter of the UN. A treaty can be altered only with the participation and the consent, in the negotiations, of all the states that are parties to it.

This final section of this book makes explicit a fundamental premise that has been implicit in the rest of the text, namely, the close relationship and mutual dependence between negotiation and mediation, in all their phases, and international law.

List of Acronyms

ABM	Anti-Ballistic Missile
ACDA	Arms Control and Disarmament Agency
BCW	Bacteriological Chemical Weapons
BW	Bacteriological Weapons
CBW	Chemical and Bacteriological Weapons
CCD	Conference of the Committee on Disarmament
CD	Committee on Disarmament
CFTC	Commonwealth Fund for Technical Cooperation
CIEC	Conference on International Economic Cooperation
CSFP	Commonwealth Scholarship and Fellowship Fund
CSG	Commonwealth Secretary-General
CTBT	Comprehensive Nuclear Weapons Test Ban Treaty
CW	Chemical Weapons
ECOSOC	Economic and Social Council
EEC	European Economic Community
ENDC	Eighteen-Nation Disarmament Committee
ENMOD	Environmental Modification Techniques
FAO	Food and Agriculture Organization of the United Nations
GATT	General Agreement on Tariffs and Trade
GNP	Gross National Product
HGM	Heads of Governments Meetings
IBRD	International Bank for Reconstruction and Development
ICBM	Intercontinental Ballistic Missile
IDA	International Development Association
IFAD	International Fund for Agricultural Development
ILO	International Labour Organization
IMF	International Monetary Fund
MAC	Mixed Armistice Commission
NATO	North Atlantic Treaty Organization
NGO	Non-Governmental Organization
NIEO	New International Economic Order
NPT	Non-Proliferation Treaty

OAS	Organization of American States
OAU	Organization of African Unity
ODA	Official Development Aid (or) Assistance
OECD	Organization for Economic Cooperation and Development
OPEC	Organization of Petroleum Exporting Countries
PLO	Palestine Liberation Organization
PCC	Palestine Conciliation Commission
SSOD-I	First Special Session on Disarmament, May 23–July 11, 1978
SSOD-II	Second Session on Disarmament, June 7–July 9, 1982
SALT	Strategic Arms Limitation Talks
UAR	United Arab Republic
UNCTAD	United Nations Conference on Trade and Development
UNDOF	United Nations Disengagement Observer Force
UNDP	United Nations Development Programme
UNEF	United Nations Emergency Force
UNEP	United Nations Environment Programme
UNESCO	UN Educational, Scientific, and Cultural Organization
UNICEF	United Nations Children's Fund
UNIDO	United Nations Industrial Development Organization
UNIFIL	United Nations Interim Force in Lebanon
UNITAR	United Nations Institute for Training and Research
UNSCOP	United Nations Special Committee on Palestine
UNTSO	United Nations Truce Supervision Organization in Palestine
UNU	United Nations University
WEO	Western European and Other (countries)
WHO	World Health Organization
WFC	World Food Council

Index